CONTEMPORARY CONCERT MUSIC BY WOMEN

Compiled and Edited by
JUDITH LANG ZAIMONT and KAREN FAMERA

CONTEMPORARY CONCERT MUSIC BY WOMEN

A Directory
of the Composers and Their Works

A Project of the International League of Women Composers, Inc.

GREENWOOD PRESS
WESTPORT, CONNECTICUT • LONDON, ENGLAND

Library of Congress Cataloging in Publication Data

Zaimont, Judith Lang.
  Contemporary concert music by women.

  Discography: p.
  Includes index.
   1. Music—Bio-bibliography. 2. Women composers—
Directories. I. Famera, Karen McNerney.
II. International League of Women Composers.
III. Title.
ML105.Z34   780'.92'2   80-39572
ISBN 0-313-22921-X (lib. bdg.)

Library of Congress Catalog Card Number: 80-39572
ISBN: 0-313-22921-X

First published in 1981

Greenwood Press
A division of Congressional Information Service, Inc.
88 Post Road West, Westport, Connecticut 06881

Printed in the United States of America

10 9 8 7 6 5 4 3 2 1

CONTENTS

FOREWORD

The International League of Women Composers takes great pride in presenting *Contemporary Concert Music by Women: A Directory of the Composers and Their Works*. This pioneer volume reflects the League's continuing effort to increase public awareness of the large and neglected repertory of music by women. Intended to be equally useful to performers and those engaged in research, it provides biographical material and programmatic information, as well as lists of works and information about their availability. While it is not an exhaustive compilation of the output of today's women composers, it succeeds very well in demonstrating the great range and variety of their music.

No book now available presents an extensive survey of women composers and their works though there has been wide interest in the topic. Each year the League receives innumerable requests for information about women composers from scholars doing research at all levels and an even larger number of requests from performers who wish to program music by women but cannot easily find it. *Contemporary Concert Music by Women* will help bring together those interested in the music of women with the people who create it.

The dearth of information about women composers attests to their relative position in the field. They are, in fact, numerous, and they are writing excellent music; yet, it rarely reaches the public. The International League of Women Composers developed out of the need for women to act as advocates in their own behalf. Founded in 1975, the League's primary goal was to redress the obvious imbalance between men and women composers in the areas of orchestral performance, commissions, and recordings. Its establishment during International Women's Year seemed particularly appropriate. It was then even more difficult than it is now to locate women's music for study or performance, and the League very quickly became the leading source for information about contemporary women composers.

Disseminating information about women composers is only one small part of the League's activity. A newsletter, published four or more times each year, informs members of opportunities for performance, publication, and career advancement. An annual Search for New Music for women student composers between the ages of eighteen and twenty-eight assists younger composers at a time when they might feel most insecure about public acceptance of their work. An ongoing radio series of one-hour programs makes League music available through the broadcast media. The League also sponsors a program of lectures and lecture-demonstrations by member composers, designed for schools and colleges who offer their students career guidance. Concerts of women's music, beginning in 1975 at the Summergarden of the Museum of Modern Art in New York and continuing with a regular series of free chamber music concerts in Honolulu, have introduced the public to music that they would not otherwise have had the opportunity to hear. In March, 1980, a Conference on Twentieth Century String Quartets by Women Composers was presented in New York by the League, in cooperation with the First National Congress on Women in Music, that featured concerts by the Manhattan String Quartet and the Crescent String Quartet, panel discussions, a portable score and tape library, and a variety of programs intended to introduce musicians and interested amateurs to string quartets by women.

The League has 150 members in eight countries; in 1978 it was renamed the International League of Women Composers. It is a nonprofit, tax-exempt corporation whose activities are entirely realized through the voluntary efforts of its members, all established professional musicians. The League is in frequent contact with European women musicians' groups who wish to coordinate their activities with those of their American colleagues. The first cooperative project between American and European women musicians took place in Germany in the autumn of 1980 when *Frau und Musik* sponsored a festival of women's music with substantial representation from the League. League members have also served as representatives to International Music Council meetings in Czechoslovakia and Australia.

The League also cooperates with domestic arts organizations and is a member of the National Music Council and the Coalition of Women's Arts Organizations. Arsis Press of Washington, D.C., which publishes only concert music by women, and Leonarda Productions, Inc., which specializes in the recording of historical women composers and all contemporary composers, are affiliated organizations.

It is difficult to present a comprehensive summary of the League's activities or to do justice to the vast communications network it has created in its first six years. The League is especially gratified that Greenwood Press recognizes the degree of its impact on the musical life of our country and understands that women will not again be almost totally excluded from the mainstream of new music. Obtaining biographical material about women composers and ready access to their work have remained serious problems, however, which this directory should remedy. Periodic supplements and subsequent editions will keep the information as up-to-date as possible.

Contemporary Concert Music by Women was realized through the tireless efforts of Judith Lang Zaimont and Karen Famera, League members who served as project coordinators. Their dedication and enthusiasm brought a unique idea to splendid reality.

Nancy Van de Vate, Chairperson
International League of Women Composers, Inc.

PREFACE

In the spring of 1979, members of the International League of Women Composers met to consider an important issue: while several excellent reference volumes had appeared recently on the general topic of women in music—including works that profiled a handful of individual composers—no work had yet been issued that focused on the music itself, listing entire outputs of a great number of composers in a format designed to be of use equally to scholar and performer. Thus was born the idea for the present directory, *Contemporary Concert Music by Women.* The directory is intended to serve as a primary reference volume on contemporary women composers of serious music and their works. Every composer is individually profiled in the biographical section, and to best serve the performer, the master list of all their compositions has been collated and arranged by genre.

Materials for the book were collected during 1979 and 1980, following announcement of the project in the League's newsletter. Each composer was asked to submit information on herself and her music, including:

- an up-to-date list of compositions, with each piece labelled as to its length, level of difficulty, and the source from which to obtain performance materials
- a separate list of her music on disc
- a biography, written in her own words
- a photograph and a sample score page, to round out the biography

Other women music professionals affiliated with the League were also invited to participate: scholars, librarians, writers, performers, record producers, and others. Each of these is represented by a biography and photo.

In its final form the directory contains:

- biographies of composers and other music professionals, representing the United States, Italy, Belgium, Germany, and Australia
- master list of compositions, subdivided into the following ten genres: solo vocal music, chamber vocal music, solo instrumental music, chamber instrumental music, electronic music, orchestral music, band music, choral music, stage works, and music for young people
- publisher/archive/composer address list
- discography, including record company address list
- composer index

Supplements to the book will be issued at regular intervals for both the master list of music and the biographies of composers and other music professionals.

Judith Lang Zaimont
Karen Famera

COMPOSERS' BIOGRAPHIES

JUDITH SHATIN ALLEN

(BMI)

Judith Shatin Allen, born in Boston in 1949, joined the faculty at the University of Virginia in 1979. She holds an A.B. from Douglass College, a Master of Music from the Juilliard School, and M.F.A. and Ph.D. degrees from Princeton University, where her principal teachers were Milton Babbitt and J. K. Randall. She furthered her studies through two composition fellowships at Tanglewood and participation in the Aspen Music Festival. She has received grants for her work from the New Jersey State Council on the Arts, "Meet the Composer," the American Music Center, and the Memorial Foundation for Jewish Culture. Her *Quatrain,* for violin, viola, clarinet, and bass clarinet, received the East and West Artists' Composition Award in 1978. Her music is available through the American Composers' Alliance in New York.

Recent works, reflecting Ms. Allen's concern with the articulation of structural ideas by the music's surface, and her sense of the necessity of the listener's ability to locate himself specifically and specially in the evolving moments of each piece, include *Arche* for viola and orchestra, *Lost Angels* for trumpet, bassoon, and piano, and *Wind Song* for wind quintet. She has composed numerous other works for chamber ensemble, orchestra, and chorus. In addition to her other activities, Ms. Allen has been a member of the Board of Directors of the League of Composers/International Society for Contemporary Music, to which she was elected for two terms, beginning in 1974.

BETH ANDERSON

(BMI)

Beth Anderson works in a variety of artistic, musical, and poetic modes. She is currently focusing her attention on the performance of text-sound, that is, the use of text as the sounding medium. In these works, the musical material consists of words and word fragments; as the elements are altered, fragmented, and recombined rhythmically, musical meanings supplement the verbal meaning normally attached to the words.

The texts and sometimes the melodies of the pieces are 'deciphered' in various ways to create a musical setting of pitches and rhythms. The information derived from the words or original melodies is treated modally; the modes and coding methodology modulate during the course of the work.

A native of Kentucky, Beth Anderson studied composition with Bob Ashley, Terry Riley, and John Cage. Her oratorio *Joan* was commissioned by the California Arts Commission and was performed in 1974 at the Cabrillo Music Festival. Other composition credits include the opera, *Queen Cristina,* pieces for solo instruments and tape, sound environments, and various sorts of performance art.

A coeditor of *Ear Magazine* since 1973, she has published scores, articles, poems, text-sound works, and reviews in *Heute Kunst, Flash Art, Women's Work, Big Deal,* and recently published and edited a series of nine issues of community criticism dealing with the New York new music scene called *Reports from the Front.* She has also had pieces anthologized on "Black Box #15" (1978) and on the album "10+2=12 American Text-sound Pieces," a 1750 Arch Street release.

Anderson was recently awarded a grant from the National Endowment for the Arts and continues to teach at the College of New Rochelle.

4

JAY ANDERSON

Jay Anderson was born in New England in 1920. Soon afterward she began commuting between Europe and the misty shore of Maine, thus acquiring the culture of two worlds. Being innately reclusive, she sought refuge in her own world by inventing "tunes" to produce whatever mood she wanted. She began composing at age six. Thereafter, whenever she found herself in either alien or unhappy surroundings, she painted mental murals in music. Finally at thirteen, having given a number of small recitals, (she was living in Southern California) she was given simple solfège and piano lessons so she could write down her inspirations. At eighteen, she entered the Longy School of Music in Cambridge, Massachusetts, receiving two scholarships. At that time, Europe was at war, and many excellent instructors had fled to the United States. Among those teachers at Longy School was the famed Nadia Boulanger. Jay received her certificate in solfège, with studies in composition, harmony, and counterpoint.

Upon graduation from music school, she joined the WACs for three years serving under General MacArthur in the South Pacific. After her discharge, she resumed composing for the next twenty years, writing mostly songs and pieces for SSA, about one hundred altogether. Many of these were performed in the Midwest where she and her husband and three daughters lived. During that time, she was also a resource teacher of "creative writing" and "Cultures East and West," presenting Japanese music and her own American folk songs. During a trip to Japan, she extended her resource teaching to several Japanese schools.

After her husband's retirement, they moved to Hawaii. Today she still feels that music or sound of any kind creates an atmosphere. She enjoys the particular atmosphere which gives joy or sunlight or tranquility to the soul. She works in Honolulu at the Hilton Hawaiian Village Hotel and likes to return to the quiet of her home in Kailua. Often she takes up her guitar in the evening and, just as she used to do as a child, she sings and paints mental murals in music.

CAROL BARNETT

Carol Barnett received her B.A. in 1972 and her M.A. in 1976 from the University of Minnesota where she studied composition with Paul Fetler and Dominick Argento. At present, she is living in Minneapolis, Minnesota, and working as a free-lance musician—as a copyist, composer, and pianist. She is a member of the Minnesota Composers Forum and has received several commissions in the Minneapolis area, including a grant from the Composers Commissioning Program of the Jerome Foundation for a collaboration with the Minnesota Dance Theatre.

JOYCE BARTHELSON

(ASCAP)

Joyce Holloway Barthelson (Mrs. B. M. Steigman) was born in Yakima, Washington, in the early nineteen hundreds. She received her early education in Oakland, California and studied for two years at the University of California in Berkeley. She pursued her musical career as vocal accompanist and pianist at NBC in San Francisco and as a member of the well-known Arion Trio.

Moving to New York City with the advent of TV she became assistant conductor of the New York Women's Symphony under Dr. Antonia Brico, before joining the faculty of Western Maryland College as composer-in-residence. Her two years at Western Maryland were interspersed with concert tours presenting music by American composers at universities and at women's clubs throughout the country—from Columbia in New York, to Stanford in California.

In 1944, Joyce Barthelson joined Mrs. Virginia Hoff in founding the Hoff-Barthelson Music School in Scarsdale, N.Y. During Miss Barthelson's years in Scarsdale, her conducting experience was put to use with choral groups throughout Westchester County, from Yonkers to White Plains and Hartsdale.

In 1967, the conductor-teacher-composer won first prize of $1,000, in an ASCAP-NFMC competition for a short opera, *Chanticleer,* based on Chaucer. This had been preceded by the performance of other short works by the composer and in 1979, she resigned from the Hoff-Barthelson Music School to concentrate on opera composition activities—librettos and music.

Though all of Joyce Barthelson's operas are comedies, each incorporates melodic material and dramatic action with a festive close. Her musical idiom is romantic melody for arias and ensemble numbers, with dissonant and consonant connecting material.

BETTY BEATH

Betty Beath is an Australian composer who has produced much work in the fields of art song and music drama. Her works for children have been performed extensively by amateur and professional theatre and opera companies. In recent years she has become increasingly involved in transcultural composition, drawing from the music of eastern Asia.

In 1975, Betty and her husband, David Cox, who is a writer and illustrator, were granted a fellowship by the Australian government to carry out research in Indonesia and in 1976 received a grant to allow further research in Bali. In 1979, invited to deliver a lecture at the Arts Centre, Jakarta, they spent three months in Java and Bali. From this experience they have produced as a team many lectures, broadcasts, a children's book, and a music drama for children. Betty also composed *Indonesian Triptych,* settings for the poetry of the Indonesian writer, Goenawan Mohamad. These songs have been broadcast on national radio and sung in recitals. At a world conference of musicologists in Honolulu in 1977, the American musicologist, Dr. Dale Craig used *Indonesian Triptych* and also *In the Carnarvon Ranges,* a song on an Australian aboriginal theme, to illustrate Australian transcultural composition.

Her latest work, also transcultural, is a group of songs, *Poems from the Chinese,* settings of Kenneth Rexroth's translations of classical Chinese poetry. At the present time, Betty and her husband are compiling a book on Indonesia, entitled *Spice and Magic,* which has to do with people and the arts, with the emphasis on people.

Betty was born in the Queensland town of Bundaberg. She began piano studies at the age of three and was twice a finalist, at the ages of fifteen and sixteen, in the Australian Broadcasting Commission's concerto competitions. At seventeen she won a Queensland University scholarship and later graduated in piano and voice at the Queensland Conservatorium of Music. Betty's interest in Australia's near northern neighbors stems from her first marriage to a patrol officer in New Guinea, during which she lived on an isolated island, Abau, and took part in jungle patrols. She now lives in Brisbane where, as well as composition, she is involved in education and performance. Her works are published by J. Albert & Son Pty. Ltd., Sydney and Playlab Press, Brisbane.

ELIZABETH RUTH BEESON

Elizabeth Beeson began her composing career at the age of sixteen. Her first song, *Faraway Love,* was written during this time and has just recently been accepted for inclusion in a new album entitled "Now Sounds of Today" which will soon be released by Columbine Record Company, Hollywood, California. At the age of seventeen, four of her piano works were broadcast twice over Houston FM radio. One of the works featured was *The Days in New England,* which in the same year won honors in an original composition contest sponsored by the Houston Music Teachers Association. Elizabeth minored in composition in graduate school at the University of Houston. Later, her *A Tribute,* written for her father, was premiered over KTRK-TV in Houston and performed live at First Methodist Church in downtown Houston. The following year, *Anita,* an original art song, was premiered in Houston's Museum of Fine Arts.

Elizabeth has written works for choir, small instrumental ensemble, piano, solo vocalists, and violin with piano accompaniment. At present, she holds a Master of Music degree in piano and is organist at Fairbanks Methodist Church in Houston, Texas. She is also a member of the National Piano Guild, Sigma Alpha Iota National Women's Music Fraternity, American College of Musicians, Pi Mu National Music Society, International League of Women Composers, and the Tuesday Musical Club of Houston, Texas.

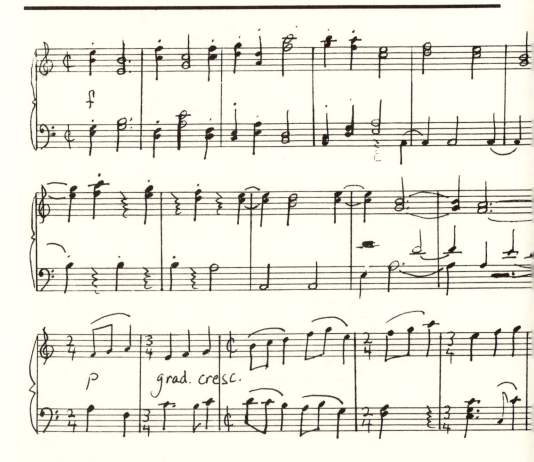

HARRIETT BOLZ

(ASCAP)

Harriett Bolz is a composer, pianist, writer, and lecturer on contemporary music. A native of Cleveland, she received her B.A. degree in music from Case Western Reserve University, having studied previously at the Cleveland Institute of Music. She earned her M.A. degree with a composition major at Ohio State University. Following undergraduate work she studied composition privately with Leo Sowerby, and more recently with Paul Creston.

She is a member of ASCAP; Phi Beta National Professional Fraternity of Music and Speech; League of Women Composers; National Association of Composers; American Women Composers; American Music Center; she is a life member, National Federation of Music Clubs; member of the State Board and Chairman for Adult Composers of the Ohio Federation of Music Clubs; and member of the Board of the Women's Music Club of Columbus, Ohio, member of the National League of American Pen Women.

Mrs. Bolz has received many national awards. She was chosen Outstanding Artist of the Year in Columbus, Ohio by the *Citizen-Journal,* a Scripps-Howard newspaper in 1962. In 1965 she won first prize from the National Federation of Music Clubs for *Floret—A Mood Caprice for Piano;* and in 1968 a first prize from Phi Beta Fraternity. Since 1970, she has received ten awards from the National League of American Pen Women, including the 1976 Special Bicentennial Award for *Such Be the Thought;* the Triennial Rose Award for Career Achievement from Phi Beta Fraternity; and in 1978, a grant from the New York State Arts Council to appear on WNYC radio in New York City.

She is listed in *Who's Who of American Women; World Who's Who of Women; Dictionary of International Biography; International Who's Who in Music and Musicians' Directory;* and the *Encyclopaedia of Modern Music* published in Germany.

Her compositions are published by Sam Fox Publishing Company; Choral Art Publications; Beckenhorst Press; Harold Branch Publishing, Inc.; and Arsis Press.

Performances of her works have been heard in major cities throughout the country, including performances at Lincoln Center in New York City, in Chicago, Minneapolis, Miami Beach, Salt Lake City, Detroit, Indianapolis, and Washington, D.C.

CLARA LYLE BOONE (Lyle de Bohun)
(BMI)

in the mir - ror of a rain - drop I can

see __ your face _____ re - flect - ed in min - ia-

ture from my mem - o - ry.

Lyle de Bohun is a native of Kentucky, a descendant of Samuel Boone, eldest brother of Daniel Boone. She presently lives in Washington, D.C. where she owns and operates Arsis Press for the publication of music by serious women composers. She uses the original French spelling of her name because "it so neatly conceals my sex."

In addition to her songs, choral and chamber music, she has written *Annunciation of Spring* and *Motive and Chorale* for orchestra. She is a former composition student of the late Darius Milhaud.

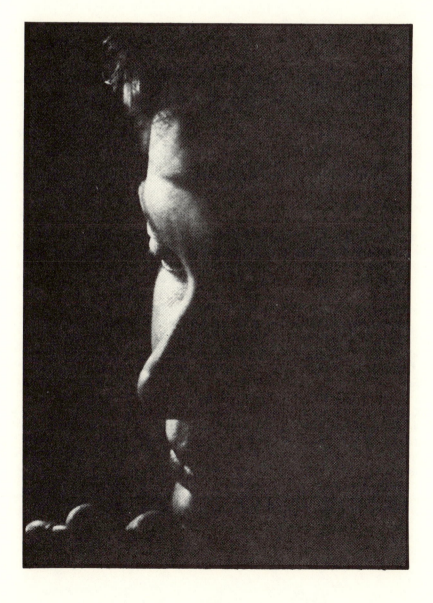

Moderato

Alto

(La la . . . . .) *simile*

Bass

ROSAMOND DROOKER BRENNER

Rosamond Drooker Brenner's earliest musical training consisted of private piano lessons, starting at age five. At first, her parents were not sure that she would like music, so they started out with a wooden keyboard only. Then they bought the piano.

While piano lessons continued throughout elementary school, she became acquainted with chamber and orchestral music during her high school years. Her class song was published in the school paper and performed at graduation, and she was cowinner of the music prize.

She studied music theory, composition, and history at Radcliffe College where she played viola in the orchestra and sang in the Radcliffe Choral Society. She also studied organ privately with Melville Smith at the Longy School of Music. A graduation present helped move her to Fontainebleau, France, where she studied organ with Rolande Falcinelli and vocal ensemble with Nadia Boulanger. Graduate work brought her back to Radcliffe Graduate School for the Master of Arts in Teaching degree in secondary school music.

A two-year Fulbright grant led to a stay in Vienna, Austria, with organ study with Anton Heiller, and harpsichord study with Gustav Leonhardt. After a year's work toward the Ph.D. at Brandeis University, Waltham, Mass., Mrs. Brenner married and went for a honeymoon in Geneva, Switzerland, where she stayed to study organ with Pierre Segond at the Geneva Conservatory of Music and to attain the Certificate. Returning home she continued graduate school and earned a Ph.D. in 1968, nine years and two children later. Mrs. Brenner was a teaching fellow at Brandeis and then a faculty member of the Boston Conservatory of Music and mother of a third child before moving to the Midwest. In Glen Ellyn, she has been involved in composition, particularly to the Baha'i Writings, church music, and teaching, both at college and conservatory, and privately.

RADIE BRITAIN

(ASCAP)

Radie Britain was born on a ranch near Amarillo, Texas. After having graduated with honors from the American Conservatory in Chicago she made her debut as a composer in Munich, Germany, while studying with Albert Noelte. Leopold Godowsky, Heniot Levy, R. Deane Shure, Joseph Pembaur, and Alice Ripper contributed to her piano training. A gold medal in organ led her to further study with Pietro Yon, and Marcel Dupre in Paris.

After returning to the United States, she spent two seasons at the MacDowell Colony in Peterboro, New Hampshire, where *Southern Symphony* and *Light* were created. Since then her compositions have been programmed by America's leading symphonic organizations as well as symphonies in Europe, Egypt, and Moscow.

Lament was performed in the White House. In 1945 she became the first woman composer to receive the Juilliard Publication Award for *Heroic Poem.* Over fifty compositions of hers have received international and national awards.

She is a member of ASCAP; National League of American Pen Women; life member of the Musicians Union, Local 47; Los Angeles Music Teachers Association; National Association for American Composers and Conductors, Washington, D.C. and Los Angeles chapters; life member of Texas Composers; and director of National Society of Arts and Letters of Santa Barbara, California. She is an honorary member of Sigma Alpha Iota, Schubert Club of Los Angeles, Texas Federation of Music Clubs, Texas Teachers Association, Philharmonic Club of Amarillo, Texas, and the Etude Club of Los Angeles.

The Honorary Doctor of Music was given to Miss Britain by the Musical Arts Conservatory of Amarillo, Texas, and the Award of Merit by the National League of American Pen Women, Washington, D.C. She has received commissions from the Marygrove College of Detroit, Michigan, and Saint Mary's College of Omaha, Nebraska.

Her pupils have been the recipients of many awards from her Chicago and Hollywood studios. Her husband, Ted Morton, is one of the pioneers of aviation.

23

RUTH BRUSH

(ASCAP)

Ruth J. Brush was born in Fairfax, Oklahoma, and received her Bachelor of Music degree from the Conservatory of Music, Kansas City, Missouri. She worked as studio accompanist and soloist at Radio Station WHB in Kansas City for several years, and served as head of the piano department at Frank Phillips College in Borger, Texas for three years.

Mrs. Brush is a member of State and National Music Teachers Associations; Musical Research Society, Bartlesville; Sigma Alpha Iota; ASCAP; she is listed in *Who's Who of American Women; World Who's Who of Women; Personalities of the South; International Who's Who in Music;* and other listings. She received first place in American Women Performance Awards from the National Federation of Music Clubs and has received awards from the Texas Composers Guild, the Texas Manuscript Society, and from Composers' Press. She served as chairman of Junior Composers for six years for the National Federation of Music Clubs. At present she serves as a reviewer of new music for the National Music Teachers Association. She is an honorary life member of Bartlesville Chapter Accredited Music Teachers. She has received an award from Allied Arts and Humanities, and an award as Oklahoma Woman Composer from the Oklahoma Federation of Music Clubs.

Her violin composition *Romance sans Paroles* was performed by Mary Findley, concert violinist, in Washington, D.C., on Oklahoma Day of the Bicentennial; it has also been performed in Tulsa, Oklahoma and in Bartlesville in concert. Other works have been performed in New York City by Aldonna Kepalaite, pianist; Gena Marette, soprano; and others. Orchestral works have been played by orchestras in Oklahoma and Texas. Programs of her compositions have been presented by music clubs, study clubs, civic organizations, and on television. Mrs. Brush was named 1980 Oklahoma Musician of the Year by the Oklahoma Federation of Music Clubs.

Slowly

Piano I

Piano II

25

A recipient of several honors and commissions, Cecconi-Bates feels she was "discovered" by poets and painters, not the least of whom was Norman Rockwell.

Born in Syracuse, New York, on August 9, 1933, daughter of Peter T. Cecconi and Emily (Romano) Cecconi, she graduated as valedictorian from both junior high and senior high. She continued her education at Syracuse University, where she gained her B.A. degree with honors in 1956 and her M.A. in musicology in 1960. She has also studied composition under Robert Palmer at Cornell University.

On February 27, 1960, she married Robert N. Bates, Sr., in Syracuse, and as a result has three stepchildren, Robert, Jr., Daniel, and Nancy.

Her cantata for chorus, soloists, and orchestra, dedicated to Martin Luther King, Jr., was premiered at the Syracuse School District Music Festival in April 1974. *Willie was Different* for speaker and seven instruments, from a book by Molly and Norman Rockwell, was performed at a dinner honoring the artist in 1976.

Cecconi-Bates has travelled extensively and has heard her works performed in England and in Italy. Since 1977, she has had many programs of her works performed under various auspices throughout the United States. Most recently, the Chicago Symphonic Wind Ensemble premiered her *Pasticcio* on April 20, 1980.

Her works have received honorable mentions in several competitions and since 1977 Cecconi-Bates has been composer-in-residence for the summer Vermont Music and Arts Festival in Lyndonville, Vermont. In 1964, she held a professorship at Maria Regina College and since 1968 she has been a teacher in the Syracuse schools.

Cecconi-Bates holds memberships in the following organizations: International League of Women Composers, Music Educator's National Conference, New York State School Music Association, Sigma Alpha Iota, Society for New Music, Oswego County Council on the Arts, Centro Italiano, and Pro Art. Her biographical note appears in: *International Who's Who in Music, Notable Americans, Dictionary of International Biography, Women of Distinction,* the American Biographical Institute's *Book of Honor, International Register of Profiles,* and *World Who's Who of Women.*

I: sun greeting

NANCY LAIRD CHANCE

(ASCAP)

Nancy Laird Chance was graduated in 1949, magna cum laude, from the Foxcroft School, and attended Bryn Mawr College from 1949 to 1950, Columbia University from 1959 to 1967, and C.W. Post College from 1971 to 1975. She studied piano with William R. Smith and Lilias MacKinnon, and theory and composition with Vladimir Ussachevsky and Otto Luening. From 1973 to 1978 she lived in Nairobi, Kenya, where she continued her composing and taught piano and theory. She is now living in New York.

Important performances of her works include: a concert at the Museum of Modern Art in 1975, which presented *Daysongs* and *Rilke Songs;* the world premiere of *Ritual Sounds* by the Philadelphia Orchestra in March, 1976, and a repeat performance at Curtis Institute of Music the following season; the world premiere of *Ceremonial* in February, 1978, by the Paul Price Percussion Ensemble and a repeat performance by the Manhattan Percussion Ensemble in April, 1978. *Duos 1* was premiered in Washington, D.C., in November, 1977, by the Contemporary Music Forum at the Corcoran Gallery, and given a second performance by the same group in January, 1980. *Declamation and Song* was commissioned by the New Music Ensemble and premiered by them in April, 1978, at York College in Queens.

In 1979 the League-ISCM presented *Daysongs* at Carnegie Recital Hall, and the same piece was played again in 1980 at one of the concerts of Festival III of the Women's Interart Center. *Ceremonial* was presented at the National Conference of the ASUC in Memphis in March, 1980, and *Ritual Sounds* was performed in Carnegie Recital Hall in April, 1980, under the baton of Arthur Weisberg at an Opus One Records showcase concert. Both *Ritual Sounds* and *Daysongs* have been issued on the Opus One Label.

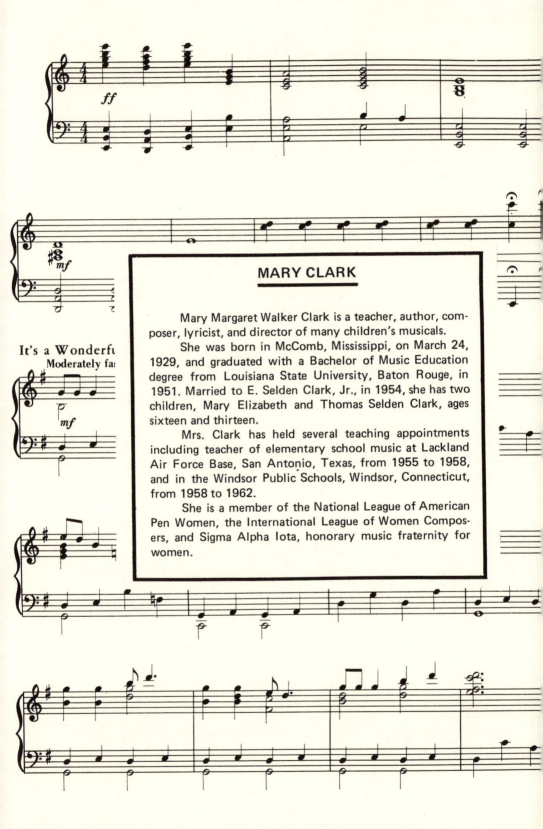

It's a Wonderfu[...]
Moderately fa[...]

MARY CLARK

Mary Margaret Walker Clark is a teacher, author, composer, lyricist, and director of many children's musicals.

She was born in McComb, Mississippi, on March 24, 1929, and graduated with a Bachelor of Music Education degree from Louisiana State University, Baton Rouge, in 1951. Married to E. Selden Clark, Jr., in 1954, she has two children, Mary Elizabeth and Thomas Selden Clark, ages sixteen and thirteen.

Mrs. Clark has held several teaching appointments including teacher of elementary school music at Lackland Air Force Base, San Antonio, Texas, from 1955 to 1958, and in the Windsor Public Schools, Windsor, Connecticut, from 1958 to 1962.

She is a member of the National League of American Pen Women, the International League of Women Composers, and Sigma Alpha Iota, honorary music fraternity for women.

31

MARCIA COHEN

Marcia Cohen was born in August, 1937, in Chicago. Her professional and musical education took place in and around her home town. She studied piano with Lillian Raphling, at the Chicago Conservatory from 1947 to 1952, and at the Aspen Music Festival in 1954. Her composition work with composers Leslie Bassett, Eugene Weigel, Leon Stein, Donald Jenni, and Alan Stout was undertaken at the Universities of Michigan, Illinois, DePaul University, and Northwestern University; she received degrees from Roosevelt University, Chicago in 1958 and Northwestern University in 1969.

Ms. Cohen's compositions have been accorded several honors, among them awards from Pi Kappa Lambda Honorary Music Society in 1969 and Bennington College Composers Conference in 1969. She also served as artist-in-residence, in the Lincolnwood, Illinois, schools in 1972 and currently serves on the Executive Board of the International League of Women Composers.

She has been particularly active in music journalism and cultural programing for radio. In 1969 and 1970, she served as associate editor for *Clavier* Magazine and she was the originator and coordinator for the New Music from Chicago series, 1974 to 1977, the director of Cultural Affairs, City of Pensacola, Florida, 1978 to 1979 and is at present host and associate producer, "Studio A," for WSRE-TV.

Ms. Cohen is married to a physician and has two children.

FRANCES DANFORTH

Frances Louis Adams Danforth was born in Chicago, Illinois, where she studied piano until a move to New York at age eighteen. In New York, she studied piano with Eugene Heffley and Leslie Hodgeson, and composition with Robert Russell Bennett. One year later, she came to Ann Arbor and enrolled at the University of Michigan, earning an A.B. degree in literature and music and a year later a Bachelor of Music degree with a major in piano.

After her marriage to Percy Owen Danforth, an architect, the couple lived in Ann Arbor and Monroe, Michigan, where she taught piano privately. In Monroe, Mrs. Danforth started the Piano Repertoire Club and contributed to the furtherance of music education, earning substantial community recognition for her work. It was this work, together with her compositions, that qualified her to be listed in *Who's Who of American Women.*

She spent many summers attending Michigan State University and the University of Maryland before enrolling at Eastern Michigan University where she earned a M.A. degree in music literature and composition, studying there with Dr. Edith Borroff and Dr. Anthony Iannaccone. Additional work in electronic music with John Carlson of the University of Michigan and Dr. Iannaccone was followed by studies in experimental sounds with George Caccioppo.

Mrs. Danforth was awarded a "Teacher of the Year" award in 1978 by the Michigan Music Teachers Association. Among her most notable works are *Suite for Piano,* premiered in 1972 at Eastern Michigan University, which won a first prize in a national "Original Composition Contest" in 1973; and a wind trio, *Theme and Variations,* which won an honorable mention in a similar competition in 1974. A piece for marimba solo with multiple percussion won an honorable mention in a contest sponsored by the Percussive Arts Society in 1978. A piano solo, *Karelian Light,* was an honorable mention in a contest at Oxford, England, in 1979.

ROYCE DEMBO

Royce Dembo was born to Gertrude and Nathan Benderson on March 19, 1933, in Troy, New York. She studied composition and piano at the Eastman School of Music, Syracuse University, and Ithaca College. In 1953 she married Lawrence Dembo and lived in Taiwan for two years, where she taught music in the Chinese and American School. She then moved to Los Angeles where she took courses in composition at University of California at Los Angeles and resumed her composing. In 1965 she moved to Madison and in 1970 she received her Master of Music degree in composition at the University of Wisconsin. Since then she has taught piano, theory and composition privately and has done extensive composing for all musical forms and instrumentation.

Two complete concerts of her own music have been broadcast statewide and she was recognized as a Wisconsin composer in the Bicentennial issue sponsored by the National Music Council. Her works have also been heard in Taiwan, Indonesia, and Scotland. Two major Wisconsin dance companies have choreographed her music and in 1979 *The Story of Beowulf,* a music drama for early instruments and narrator, was commissioned and produced through a grant from the Wisconsin Arts Board and the National Endowment for the Arts. Her recent work, *Sextet for Woodwind Quintet and Piano,* was performed and broadcast in March, 1980, as part of the celebration for the opening of the Madison Civic Center. She is presently working on a two-act opera based on the Psyche myth.

EMMA LOU DIEMER

(ASCAP)

Emma Lou Diemer was born in Kansas City, Missouri, on November 24, 1927, and received some of her early training in composition, piano, and organ at the Conservatory there. Her determination to be a composer was crystallized in high school, and her undergraduate and graduate degrees in composition were earned at the Yale School of Music and the Eastman School of Music. Other study in Brussels on a Fulbright scholarship and at the Berkshire Music Center was interspersed by teaching positions in Missouri and Tacoma, Washington.

Following receipt of the Ph.D. from Eastman, she spent two years as composer-in-residence in the Arlington, Virginia, schools under a Ford Foundation Young Composers Grant, and stayed in the Washington, D.C., area to teach theory and composition at the University of Maryland from 1965 to 1970. Since 1971 she lived in Santa Barbara, California, and is professor of theory and composition at the University of California campus there.

Her creative output has continually and consciously balanced two types of work: symphonies, concertos, and concert pieces; and music for church and school. Her catalogue includes over one hundred publications, ranging from orchestral overtures and electronic pieces to organ and choral works; a number of works were recognized by awards and commissions from several musical organizations.

(5)

mp

←(Ped.)→   Ped.

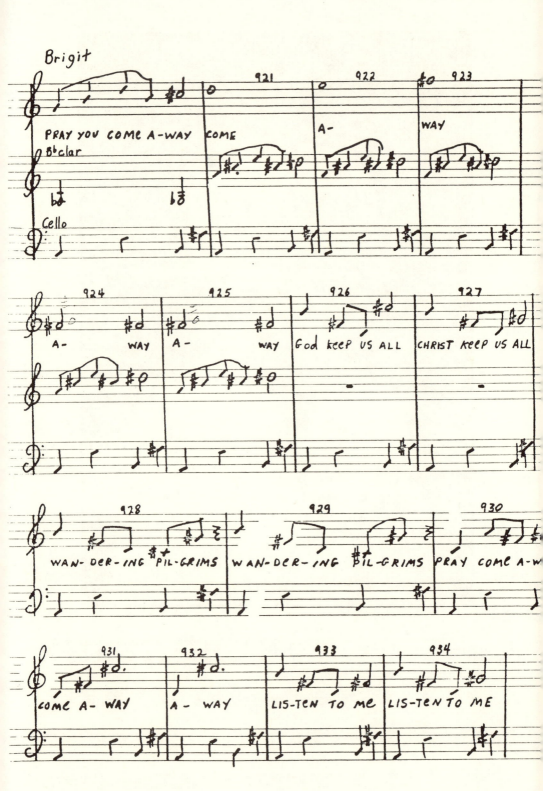

40

JOANNE FORMAN

Joanne Forman was born on June 26, 1934, in Chicago, Illinois. She grew up there and in Michigan, Florida, Mississippi, Indiana, and California, beginning piano study at age seven and theory studies at age fourteen. She attended Los Angeles City College, Los Angeles State College, University of California at Berkeley, University of California at Los Angeles, Merritt College, and the University of New Mexico, but managed to escape unscathed and without a degree. She has traveled extensively in the United States, Mexico, and Asia, and regards herself primarily as a composer of operas, for which she writes her own librettos.

She is the founder and director of the Downeast Chamber Opera founded in Maine in 1978 and the Southwest Chamber Opera founded in Albuquerque in 1980. She is also a playwright, puppeteer, teacher, and journalist. She is a recipient of a National Endowment for the Arts Composer's Fellowship; of a grant from the Maine State Commission on the Arts and Humanities; three grants from "Meet The Composer"; and Fellowships from the Ossabaw Island Foundation and the International Women Writers Guild. Ms. Forman is a member of the International League of Women Composers, the New Mexico Composers Guild, the Maine Writers and Publishers Association, and the Rio Grande Writers Association. She has one daughter, no telephone, car, television, or radio, and likes to take long walks and swim. She reads extensively and lives in a 200-year-old adobe in Taos, New Mexico.

JANE FRASIER

(BMI)

Jane Frasier was born in 1951 in Loveland, Colorado, and attended Fort Collins High School in Fort Collins, Colorado, graduating in 1969. Jane studied piano and clarinet, participating in band, orchestra, and choir throughout school. Honors in high school included All-State Band, 1968 and 1969; state vice president of Junior Music Clubs, and participation in the All-Student Groups Band Tour of Europe in 1969.

Jane attended the University of Northern Colorado in Greeley, graduating in 1972 with a B.A. in music education.

Following graduation, Jane obtained a position as band and choir teacher in Lyman, Wyoming, and taught music on all levels 1973 through 1978. She then returned to University of Northern Colorado to study theory and composition, receiving a Master of Music degree in 1977. Jane was elected into Pi Kappa Lambda, honorary music fraternity, as a graduate student. From 1976 to 1978, whe was music instructor in the Ovid, Colorado public schools, teaching band and choir in grades four through twelve.

She was a member of the Contemporary American Composers' Cooperative and continues as a member of the International League of Women Composers. Several of her works have been performed at the University of Northern Colorado, including music written for an educational film. As a teacher, Jane wrote original pieces and arrangements which were performed by students. She will be listed in the 1980 edition of *International Who's Who in Music* and *Musicians' Directory.*

Currently Jane is a library assistant at the University of Northern Colorado Library in Greeley. She is also actively composing, teaching woodwinds privately, and playing clarinet in the Loveland Municipal Band. One of her main projects is compiling a discography of women composers.

43

SARAH MARGARET FULLER-HALL

Sarah Margaret Fuller-Hall was born in South Boston, Virginia, on March 11, 1959. Her musical training began with piano lessons at the age of ten. She began composing three years later in the form of assignments for her piano instructor. While studying sonata-allegro form, she composed a sonatina which placed fourth in a composition contest for high school composers at East Carolina University.

Sarah began playing french horn when she entered the tenth grade. It was at this time that composing music became her main pastime under the supervision of her band director and composition teacher, Robert T. Wall. Besides a number of small works, she composed a three movement suite for concert band which was performed at the high school band's spring concert, the first public performance of any of her work. She went on to compose more works for band, as well as compositions and arrangements for the marching band, jazz band, and choral ensemble.

Sarah entered Appalachian State University in the fall of 1977 as a music major. She has been studying composition with Scott Meister, head of composition at the university, Dr. Max Smith, and Dr. Robert Ward. Sarah has had numerous works premiered by college ensembles.

Although Sarah now majors in history, she is still actively studying music and continues to compose. She is the first vice president of the Epsilon Theta chapter of Sigma Alpha Iota Music Fraternity for women, and is a member of the League of Women Composers, American Women Composers, and the Music Educators' National Conference.

In December, 1979, Sarah married Gregory Hall from Lenoir, North Carolina, then a graduate assistant at Appalachian State University.

Introduction: Moonrise

KAY GARDNER

(ASCAP)

Born in Freeport, New York, on February 8, 1941, Kay Gardner played her first composition in public recital at age four. Her first major work, the musical score for a play, *Tcartsba*, was premiered in 1960 at the University of Michigan where she was studying instrumental conducting. Not encouraged in composing or conducting, Gardner left school, married, and had two daughters. During the next eleven years she researched and performed women's folk music and played flute in symphony orchestras nationwide.

In 1968 she founded, was music director, and flutist of the Norfolk Chamber Consort in Virginia, now in its eleventh season, an ensemble of sixteen professional musicians giving chamber concerts emphasizing contemporary and avant-garde music. John Cage was honorary vice president of this ensemble. Gardner taught from 1968 to 1972 at Norfolk State University and Old Dominion University. On leaving her marriage in 1972, she entered the State University of New York at Stony Brook where she earned a Master of Music degree in 1974, and studied flute with Samuel Baron.

Gardner's compositions, usually cyclical with sections for improvisation, are characterized by melody, ethnic modes and scales, and occasional avant-garde and electronic effects.

In 1974, in New York City, she became involved in record production, eventually recording her own works, including *Mooncircles,* in 1975. In 1977 she went to Denver to study orchestral conducting with Antonia Brico.

Gardner made her conducting debut in 1978 at the National Women's Music Festival, Champaign, Illinois; in the same year she recorded her second disc, *Emerging* and cofounded the New England Women's Symphony, Boston, a professional orchestra presenting compositions by women conducted by women. In summer, 1979, she placed sixth in the National Adult Conducting Competition in Wisconsin, directing Julia Perry's *A Short Piece for Orchestra* as chosen repertoire.

Kay Gardner currently tours three and one-half months annually, giving solo concerts, workshops, and lectures internationally. She writes a regular column, "Colla Sinistra," for *Paid My Dues* (Chicago), challenging fashions and theories of the patriarchal musical establishment. Her workshop, "Music and Healing" has helped to develop her latest works exploring the healing potential of specific tones, keys, modes, and harmonies.

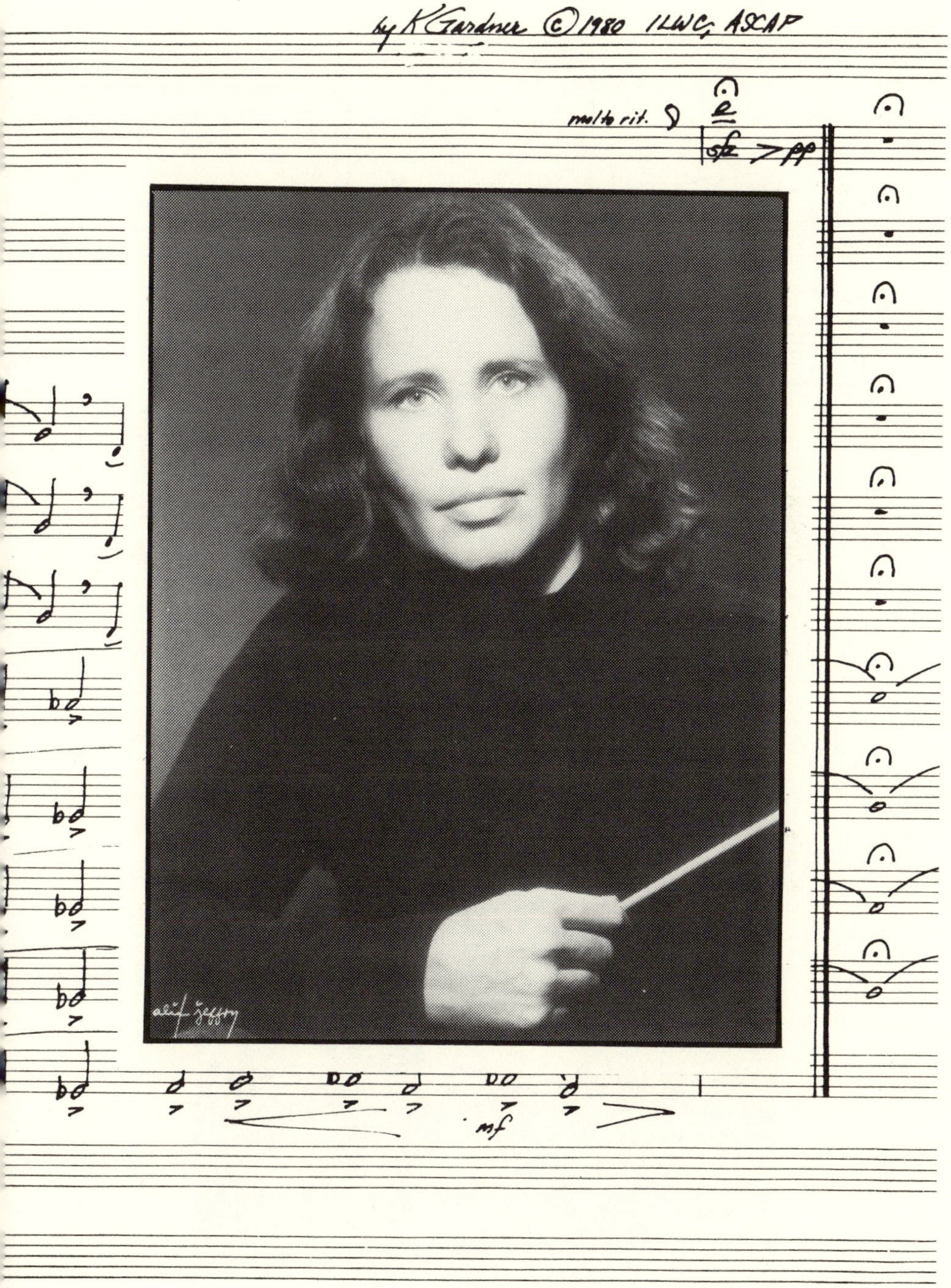
by K Gardner © 1980 ILWC, ASCAP
molto rit.
sfz > pp
mf

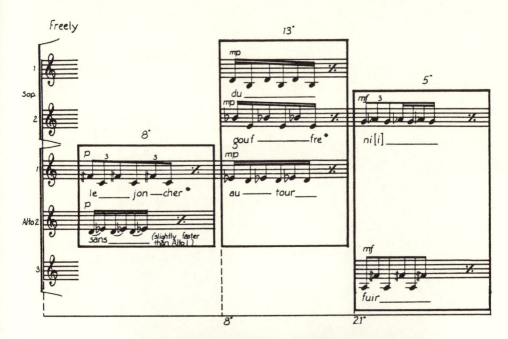

48

A native of New York City, Janet Gilbert completed her undergraduate studies in music at Douglass College and was awarded a B.A. in 1969. She earned an M.A. in composition at Villa Schifanoia, Florence, Italy, in 1972 and received the Doctor of Musical Arts degree from the University of Illinois in 1979. Her principal teachers of composition were Salvatore Martirano and Ben Johnston.

As an electronic music composer she has worked at the following studios: Pisa Computer Center, Columbia-Princeton Electronic Music Center, University of Illinois Experimental Music Studios, Bregman Electronic Music Studio at Dartmouth College, and the Middlebury College Electronic Music Studio. She is currently visiting assistant professor of music at Middlebury College where she teaches electronic music, theory, and composition.

While living in Champaign, Illinois, Ms. Gilbert was a member of the New Verbal Workshop, a group of six professional musicians devoted to exploring the possibilities of "speechmusic"—verbal improvisation controlled by musical/poetic structures. Her enthusiasm for political theater led her to found the Champaign Living Newspaper in 1979.

Her compositions have been performed recently at Bates College where she was guest composer, the Middlebury College Thursday Series where the program consisted of her own works including the premiere of a new choral piece, and at the ASUC Conference in Memphis. Works have been performed at the Art Institute of Chicago, New Music from Chicago, 1977, the NOW Concert in New York City in 1976, a Midwest Composers Symposium in 1976, the Depot Theater and Krannert Center from 1974 to 1979, and WILL Radio, Urbana. Her catalogue of works lists multimedia pieces, choral and solo works with tape, and instrumental compositions. Her current project is a theater piece based on Alfred Jarry's *The Supermale*.

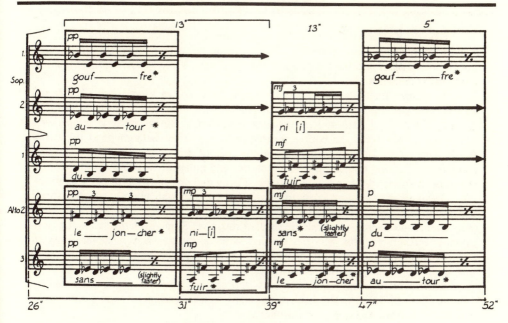

* Syllables can be changed to different pitches during repetitions.
 If only one syllable, begin at different parts of pattern.

BEVERLY GLAZIER

Beverly Kaplan Glazier was born in Syracuse, New York, on May 8, 1933, the granddaughter of Cantor Abraham Elstein, whose home and congregation provided the Hebrew modes and the melodies of the synagogue that were her earliest ideas of a musical framework.

It proved difficult for her to be taken seriously as a composer. When she entered college, it was to study elementary education after which marriage to Louis Glazier, C.P.A. and attorney, immediately followed. Since military service was obligatory at the time, the couple journeyed to an Army assignment at the Army Audit Agency in Detroit. While there she taught first grade in Highland Park, concurrently taking courses in the humanities and music at Wayne State University, which both stimulated her creative urge and provided enrichment for her students.

Two years later she taught in North Syracuse schools and shortly thereafter began her family of three children. She continued to compose and, as the children grew older and more independent, studied music at Syracuse University at a continually accelerated rate. She has studied with composers Bette Kahler, Howard Boatright, Brian Israel, and Joseph McGrath. A middle-aged woman among students the age of her daughters, she has loved every minute.

Most recently, her liturgical music won a prize from a contest sponsored by Temple Sinai of Sharon, Massachussetts. Her liturgical and secular vocal and instrumental music have had many performances.

51

DORIS HAYS

(ASCAP)

Composer/pianist Doris Hays is a recording artist for Finnadar/Atlantic Records. Her album, "Adoration of the Clash," begins with *Sunday Nights,* and uses tone clusters and the hymn-tune melodic and bass line fragments characteristic of much of her music since 1975. In this 'new folk-classical' style is her string quartet *Tunings,* which the Manhattan String Quartet played at its New York premiere in March, 1980, broadcast over National Public Radio. Another set of works, including tape music and an orchestra piece, called *Southern Voices,* was supported by a grant from the National Endowment for the Arts, and uses rhythms and melodies from southern speech that are transcribed or electronically altered. Her largest multimedia concert, "Sensevents," featured in the Lincoln Center Festival Out-of-Doors in 1976, included electronic music on endless cassettes activated by foot switches in the audience.

A native of Tennessee, Doris Hays studied in Chattanooga with Arthur Plettner and Harold Cadek, spent three years at the Munich Hochschule for Music as a Fellow of the Bavarian Ministry of Culture, and earned a Master of Music degree from the University of Wisconsin. Her teachers included Hilde Somer and Paul Badura-Skoda. She has taught at Queens College, Cornell College, and the University of Wisconsin. She has concertized and given workshops at numerous colleges, festivals, and broadcasting stations in Europe and the United States, including the Como Festival, International Composers Week in Holland, May Festival of the Residence Orchestra at The Hague, and the Syracuse Festival of American Piano Music. She was consultant in new music to the Silver Burdett *Music* text series. She organized the eleven-concert series "Meet the Woman Composer" at the New School in 1976, and the Conference on 20th Century String Quartets by Women Composers in New York City, held in March, 1980. Her articles and reviews have appeared in *Music Journal,* the *Village Voice, Ear,* the *Wisconsin Revue,* and *Common Sense.*

Doris Hays moved to New York City in 1969, and commutes to projects in the South.

ADEL HEINRICH

Adel Heinrich was born in Cleveland, Ohio, on July 20, 1926. She received a B.A., magna cum laude, from Flora Stone Mather College of Case-Western Reserve University, Cleveland, Ohio where she was elected to Phi Beta Kappa and awarded the Ranney Scholarship and the Clemens Award in Music. She received an M.S. in music from Union Theological Seminary, New York City where she was awarded a half-tuition scholarship the second year, and a Doctor of Arts in Music from the University of Wisconsin at Madison, for which she gave seven recitals on organ and wrote a 381-page dissertation on Bach's *Die Kunst Der Fuge,* with performance of the work attached to the thesis illustrating analysis. She is presently associate professor of music and college organist at Colby College, Waterville, Maine, and participates in the annual Church Music Institute.

Dr. Heinrich performs from ten to fifteen recitals a year, including recitals given at Middlebury College, Vermont; Portland Symphony Hall; the Flagler Museum in Palm Beach, Florida; at Bowdoin College, Maine; Brown University, and at Saint Michael's College, Vermont.

Three and one-half full programs of her music have been performed, including three major works (forty-five minutes) featured in Spectra 1 in 1979, a program sponsored by the National Endowment for the Arts and Westbrook College, Maine, that emphasizes women in the creative arts in Maine. A complete program of her compositions, with dance, based on Shakespearean texts was performed in the Strider Theatre of Colby College.

Dr. Heinrich received the 1969 Award of Merit for a performance of her choric-dance, *Alleluia, Alleluia!* for double chorus of SATB and SSAA, soprano solo, violin, piano or organ, and modern dance. She has served as assistant conductor of the Colby Community Symphony Orchestra for ten years, preparing and conducting two programs each season; she is listed in numerous biographies, including *Who's Who in the East* and several international listings, and has had numerous choral arrangements and a *Carol Drama* published by the Boston Music Co.

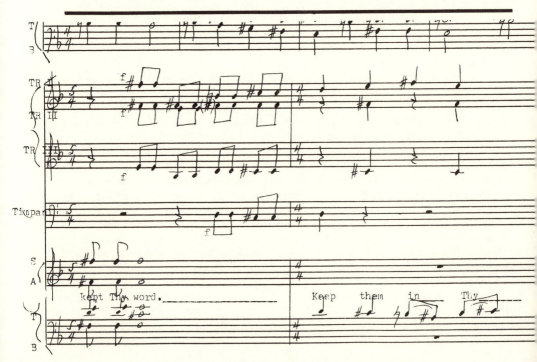

KATHERINE HOOVER

(ASCAP)

Katherine Hoover, born in 1937 in Elkins, West Virginia, has pursued an active career as a flutist and composer in New York for many years. She received her Performer's Certificate in flute from the Eastman School under Joseph Mariano concurrently with a Bachelor's in Music Theory, and later studied flute with William Kincaid in Philadelphia. She also received a master's degree in music theory from the Manhattan School of Music, where she presently teaches both theory and flute.

As a composer, Ms. Hoover is the recipient of a National Endowment Composer's Grant and an ASCAP Award, and she has been published by Carl Fischer, Inc. She has fulfilled commissions for the Rogeri Trio, Ariel, the New York Bassoon Quartet, and the New York Kantorei. Her *Homage to Bartók* was chosen by the BBC for taping and broadcast by the Dorian Wind Quintet. Her *Sinfonia* for bassoons and *Trio* (1978) are recorded on the Leonarda label.

Ms. Hoover has performed with many leading organizations in New York, including the Stuttgart Ballet, the Caramoor Festival Orchestra, American Ballet Theatre, the New York City Opera, New York Grand Opera, the Mostly Mozart Orchestra, and many Broadway shows. She has also appeared many times under the auspices of the Concert Artists Guild, and has made numerous radio and television appearances. Ms. Hoover has recorded for CRI, Grenadilla, Sonar, and Leonarda records.

In 1977, Ms. Hoover was asked by the Women's Inter-art Center to design a program that would help women composers. The result has been the highly successful series of Festivals I, II and III of Women's Music, with concerts, professional tapings, and broadcasts of music by over fifty-five historical and contemporary women composers.

The *Trio* was selected by the judges of the Kennedy Center-Friedheim Contest as one of the ten outstanding American chamber works premiered during the 1978-79 season.

Hsu, Wen-ying was born in 1908 in Shanghai, China, and graduated from McTyeire High School in 1928. She studied three years in Yenching University, Peiping, and got married. In 1948 she moved to Taiwan with her family and started to teach piano and to compose. In 1954, she entered George Peabody College, Nashville, where in 1955, she received a bachelor's degree in composition with honors and became a member of Sigma Alpha Iota. She returned to Taiwan and was featured as a composer in a concert in 1956 presented to a full house of 2,000.

With a fellowship from China Foundation and a Scholarship from SAI, she entered New England Conservatory in 1958 to study composition. In 1959, she received a master's degree in musicology. Her particular interest in Chinese music theory led to her return to Taiwan to continue research.

She entered University of California, Los Angeles, in 1963 to study composition, and composed an opera, *Cowherd and Weaving Maiden,* in the spring of 1964; subsequently she transferred to University of Southern California. The School of Music there presented her in a program of her compositions in 1966. She stopped studying and resumed her research.

"Origin of Music in China" was delivered at the Society of Ethnomusicology in 1971 and was published in *Chinese Culture,* a quarterly in Taiwan, in 1972. Her book of research, *The Ku-ch'in,* was published in Taiwan in 1976 and now is in its second edition.

She has won many prizes in poetry and a book of translations of Chinese poems will be published soon.

She is a member of Sigma Alpha Iota, National League of American Pen Women, National Association of Composers, National Federation of Music Clubs, American Music Center, American Women Composers, American Society of University Composers, American Musicological Society, Society of Ethnomusicology, International Musicological Society, College Music Society, Poetry Society of Southern California, California Federation of Chaparral Poets, National Society of Poets, American Association of University Women, and Music Teachers Association of California. Her name is in the *International Who's Who in Music, International Register of Profiles, Dictionary of International Biography, World Who's Who of Women, Personalities of the West and Midwest,* and the American Biographical Institute's *Book of Honor.*

WINIFRED HYSON

(ASCAP)

Winifred Hyson earned her A.B. in physics, magna cum laude, at Radcliffe College, where she was elected to Phi Beta Kappa. She studied music theory and composition at the American University under Esther Ballou and Lloyd Ultan, and has studied piano with Evelyn Swarthout and Roy Hamlin Johnson. Her compositions, which have won numerous awards, are performed frequently in the Washington metropolitan area, and in music festivals around the country.

Ms. Hyson is a nationally certified teacher of piano, music theory, and composition. Formerly vice president of the Maryland State Music Teachers Association in charge of teacher certification, she was appointed in 1974 by the executive board of that organization to initiate a program for the instruction of music theory to Maryland students. Under her direction, a curriculum was developed covering all phases of music theory; a six-level syllabus for teachers was published, and suitable testing procedures devised. In 1980, music theory tests, prepared under her supervision, were administered to more than four hundred students between the ages of six and eighteen.

Hyson's song cycle, *Songs of Job's Daughter,* was selected as the required composition for sopranos in the 1980 Sterling Staff Competition, sponsored by Mu Phi Epsilon, of which she is a member.

As chairman of the Composers Group of the Friday Morning Music Club of Washington, Ms. Hyson has successfully promoted broadcast of the works of composer members on a regular basis by a local good music station.

Hyson is a member of ASCAP. Her compositions are published by Elkan Vogel and Neil A. Kjos, Jr.

LORETTA JANKOWSKI

Born in New Jersey on October 20, 1950, Loretta Jankowski has been involved seriously with music since she began piano study at the age of ten. In addition to her public school work and participation as bassoonist in various ensembles, she served as piano accompanist of the chorus, and she attended the preparatory division at the Juilliard School for six years with studies in musical theory and composition. During her years of undergraduate study at the Eastman School of Music she was awarded a two-year scholarship by the Polish Alliance Club of Rochester. Her composition teachers there were Samuel Adler, Warren Benson, and Joseph Schwantner, and she was chosen as winner of Eastman's Bernard Rogers Composition Award.

As a graduate student in composition at the University of Michigan, Ann Arbor, she studied with William Albright and with George Wilson in electronic music. She was awarded the Master of Music degree in 1974. During her doctoral studies at Eastman she continued composition studies with Samuel Adler, Warren Benson, Joseph Schwantner, and also with William Penn. She was awarded a Ph.D. degree in 1979.

Loretta Jankowski participated in the Dartington Summer School of Music, Dartington, England in 1972 and studied with Harrison Birtwistle and Morton Feldman. In 1973, from September through December, she received a scholarship from the Polish Government for studies in Cracow, Poland, at the Higher School of Music under Marek Stachowski.

Her compositions have demonstrated a wide range of instrumentation. These include *Icons: Fragments of a Poem* for soprano, alto flute, harp, cello, and vibraphone (1971); *Declarations* for cellist and three percussionists (1972); *Flute Sextet* for two piccolos, two flutes, alto flute, and bass flute, which was performed at the Museum of Modern Art, New York, August 15, 1975, in a concert sponsored by the League of Women Composers; *Strephenade* for electronic tape (1973), which was performed at the Theatre Jacques Coeur, Bourges, Belgium, as part of the Fifth International Festival on Experimental Music; *Todesband* (1973), winner of the American Band Association - Ostwald Band Composition Contest of 1976, which was performed by the U.S. Bicentennial Band; *Inside the Cube, Empty Air* (1975) for thirty women's voices and various renaissance instruments, commissioned by Hood College, Frederick, Maryland; *Or* (1976) for chamber orchestra; *Lustrations* (1978), which was premiered by the Chicago Symphony Orchestra; and *A Naughty Boy* (1979) for soprano, clarinet, and piano, which was premiered at Alice Tully Hall, Lincoln Center, New York.

Loretta Jankowski taught theory and composition at Northern Illinois University in DeKalb, Illinois. She is currently teaching theory and composition at California State University, Long Beach.

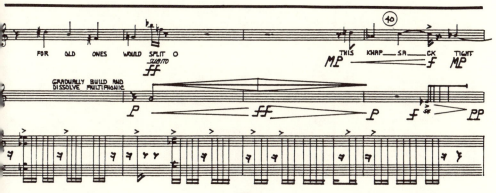

VIRGINIA KENDRICK

(ASCAP)

Virginia (Bachman) Kendrick was born in Minneapolis, Minnesota April 8, 1910. At the age of seven her ability to compose was discovered and encouraged by her piano teacher, Isabella B. Parker. At age eleven she was presented in a solo piano recital of works from Chopin, McDowell, Beethoven, Grieg, and Mozart. While at West High School, Virginia furthered her study of musical composition and participated in several city-wide original composition contests.

She continued her education at the University of Minnesota from 1928 to 1933, studying piano and composition with well-known teachers. In 1934 she married W. D. Kendrick. The Kendricks have three sons, Warren, Ned, and David, and two daughters, Nancy and Susan. Ten grandchildren complete the family.

Since 1958 Mrs. Kendrick has been pianist for the Andahazy Ballet Company, organ music consultant for Schmitt Music Company of Minneapolis, and has been organist for Christian Science churches in the Minneapolis area. As a ballet pianist, she has played accompaniment for many visiting guest teachers: Audrey Keane and the Metropolitan Opera Ballet; Margo Fonteyn, Ballet West; George Zorich, Anton Dolin, and members of the Royal Swedish Ballet.

Her compositions deal with topics relative to her love of nature, for example, *April Whimsy* and *White Sky,* and her delight in her children, for example, *Little Miss Whuffit, Hush Little David,* and *Wealth of Mine.* More recent efforts are sacred solos written between 1976 and 1980. Eight of her songs have been arranged with harp accompaniment by Minnesota Orchestra harpist, Anne Ransom.

Mrs. Kendrick's compositions have been most favorably reviewed in many publications. None of her songs are long—most are from two to three minutes long—and they are suitable for sacred or secular occasions.

Virginia Kendrick is a member of Sigma Kappa and Mu Phi Epsilon, and her biography is published in *Who's Who of American Women, World Who's Who of Women, Who's Who in the Midwest,* and is also included in the *International Who's Who in Music and Musician's Directory.*

64

SUSAN COHN LACKMAN

Susan Cohn Lackman was born in Tsingtao, China, July 1, 1948, the daughter of a naval officer. Despite frequent moves, Dr. Lackman began studies at the age of three, and started composing by her eighth birthday. After a mostly conventional childhood, she entered Temple University's College of Music, from which she graduated with honors as a Bachelor of Music Education, with concentration in piano, voice, theory, and English, in 1970. Her Master of Arts degree was taken at the American University, where she expanded her technique in composition to include the avant-garde. During the work for her Ph.D., taken at Rutgers University, Susan's style has become most consistently a lyric contrapuntalism. She has completed composition studies with Robert Moevs and Rolv Yttrehus, and has received guidance from others. At present she is teaching and directing the chorus at a small New Jersey college.

Mrs. Lackman has published in several leading music journals, and she has served a stint as music critic for an arts newspaper. Her honors include various university fellowships, Fellow of the Wolf Trap Composers' Forum, Sigma Alpha Iota Sword of Honor, among others. She is a member of Sigma Alpha Iota, the League of Women Composers, Music Educators' National Conference, American Musicological Society, and College Music Society. Dr. Lackman is also cited in *Who's Who in Music and Musician's Directory* and *Who's Who of American Women.*

ANNE LeBARON

Anne LeBaron was born in 1953 in Baton Rouge, Louisiana; she received the B.A. degree from the University of Alabama, and the M.A. degree from the State University of New York at Stony Brook, and was then awarded a fellowship to study at Columbia University in the doctoral program. She has studied composition with Fred Goosen, Daria Semegen, Bülent Arel, and Chou Wen-chung.

Her works, written for virtually every contemporary genre and performed throughout the United States, have received many national and regional awards, including a BMI Student Composer Award, an ASCAP Foundation Grant to Young Composers, the Bearns Prize, the David Bates Award, the Arnold Salop Memorial Award, and a Mu Phi Epsilon Award. Her music has been broadcast over WPKN, KPFA, KFCF, KPFK, WBAI, WBHM, and WLRH. She has been a fellow at the MacDowell Colony, at Yaddo, with the Composers' Conference at Johnson State College in Vermont, and has also been featured as guest composer at the University of Texas in Austin. In 1980 she won a Fulbright scholarship, and received a partial stipend from the Internationales Musikinstitut to attend the International Vacation Courses for New Music in Darmstadt.

Her activities as a harpist are numerous, with specialization in the performance of contemporary music and free improvisation. This year she produced a recording of trio improvisations entitled Jewels on the label *Trans Museq,* involving strings, harp, guitars, and mandolin.

She has taught a summer theory course at the University of Alabama, an undergraduate course in music fundamentals at State University of New York/ Stony Brook, and assisted the directors of the Electronic Music Studios at State University of New York/Stony Brook. She was recently employed as artist-in-residence in Decatur, Alabama, where she worked with educational institutions and in the community as a composer and performer. She is residing in West Germany as a Fulbright scholar during the 1980-81 academic year, and is now composing a musical drama based on the legend of Orpheus in collaboration with the writer Edwin Honig. The scoring for this work includes chamber orchestra, two small choruses, electronic tape, and four characters.

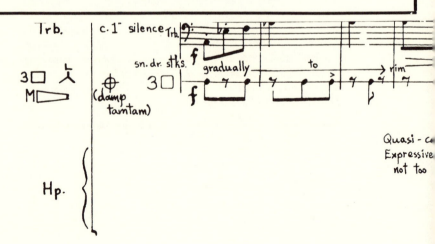

RUTH LOMON

(BMI)

Ruth Lomon was born in Montreal, Canada, on November 8, 1930. She attended McGill University and the Conservatoire from 1946 to 1951. During this period she made her debut with orchestra playing Bach's *D minor Piano Concerto,* won several awards for solfège, and was active as a composer, having written songs and a string quartet. She continued her musical training at the New England Conservatory with composition studies under Carl McKinley and Francis Judd Cooke, and piano studies with Miklos Schwalb. During this time compositions including piano works, a horn trio, and songs were performed at Jordan Hall, Boston, and on WGBH.

In 1964 Ms. Lomon attended the Darmstadt summer courses, and the composition classes of Witold Lutoslawski at Dartington, England. Her *Five Songs on Poems of William Blake* were performed at the Dartington festival.

Ms. Lomon has many compositions for small chamber music ensembles which are performed regularly in America and England. Her compositions for piano duo and duet are in the permanent repertoire of several touring piano teams. Her harp works have received critical acclaim. Her larger works include a forty-minute *Requiem* for SATB chorus and brass, with soprano solo accompanied by woodwinds, which was performed in part in 1978, and a bassoon concerto in three movements.

In 1977 Ms. Lomon was a Yaddo Fellow. The following year she received a grant from the Helene Wurlitzer foundation. She performs in a piano duo and duet team with Iris Graffman Wenglin. Their repertoire includes programs of works written by women which they have performed at universities, for WGBH, and WNAC-TV. She also teaches composition, theory, and piano in Lexington, Massachusetts, where she lives with her physicist husband, Earle, and their three children.

Ms. Lomon is published by Arsis Press.

MARY MAGEAU

(ASCAP)

Mary Mageau, an American composer, began formal study in composition with Leon Stein in the Bachelor of Music degree program at DePaul University, Chicago. She received a Master of Music degree in composition from the University of Michigan at Ann Arbor in 1969, where she studied privately with Leslie Bassett and Ross Lee Finney. Ms. Mageau graduated with honors from both universities and was awarded a further opportunity in 1970 to study composition with George Crumb in the Berkshire Music Center Composer's Fellowship Program at Tanglewood.

Mary Mageau's works have received a number of awards and prizes, among them: a 1968 Composer's award in the competition sponsored by the University of Hawaii, the Louis Moreau Gottschalk Centenary Competition silver medal in 1970, the 1972 Minnesota Composer's Competition, an honorable mention from the Los Angeles Cello Club, and a grant from the Australia Council. She has also had works recorded by Sound 80, Minneapolis, the Australian Broadcasting Commission, and the BBC Radio, London. Ms. Mageau's music has been performed internationally at numerous festivals in North America, Hawaii and Australia.

In addition to composing, Mary Mageau is currently an active performer and lecturer. As a chamber music pianist, Ms. Mageau has appeared in concerts and recitals both in the United States and Australia. From 1967 to 1969 she was harpsichordist with the University of Michigan's Collegium Musicum and Contemporary Directions Ensemble and is one of the founding members of the Brisbane Baroque Trio. As a lecturer, Ms. Mageau taught at Scholastica College, Duluth, Minnesota, the University of Wisconsin, Superior, and the Kelvin Grove and North Brisbane Colleges of Advanced Education in Queensland, Australia. She has also conducted lecture demonstrations and workshops throughout the American Midwest and Queensland. Mary Mageau is a member of ASCAP, the International League of Women Composers and the Composers Guild of Australia.

In 1974 Ms. Mageau accepted an Australian guest lectureship and since her marriage to Kenneth White, a Brisbane architect, she has become a permanent Australian resident. Mary Mageau currently works from her studio in Saint Lucia.

ADA BELLE GROSS MARCUS

(ASCAP)

Ada Belle Gross Marcus, pianist-composer, and faculty member of the Chicago Conservatory College in piano, theory and composition, has a Master of Music degree from De Paul University. She was born in Chicago, Illinois, on July 8, 1929. She has concertized extensively throughout the Midwest, appearing in her prize-winning capacity as soloist with symphony orchestras, in recitals, and on television. She is a prolific composer, having written many compositions in the contemporary style, including piano, vocal, choral, chamber, concerti, operatic, and orchestral works. At De Paul she was a protégée of Sergei Tarnowsky in piano and Dr. Samuel Lieberson in theory and composition. She also studied composition with the great Russian, Alexander Tcherepnin as well as Leo Sowerby, and Dr. Karel B. Jirak. She also participated in electronic workshops at De Paul University.

Ms. Marcus' father, Theodore Gross, was an opera singer and music coach. A child prodigy, she began composing when she was only four years old.

Ms. Marcus is a member of ASCAP, American Music Center, Chicago Artist's Association, Musician's Club of Women (affiliate of the National Federation of Music Clubs), International Society for Contemporary Music, Chicago Federation of Music, League of Women Composers, American Women Composers and the American Society of University Composers. She is included in *World Who's Who of Women* and *Who's Who of American Women.* She is also included in the following publications: *Music of the Last Forty Years* (Fromm Music Foundation at Harvard University); *Encyclopedia of Modern Music* (West Germany); *Women in American Music: A Bibliography of Music and Literature; Women Composers' Works: For Solo Voice; International Who's Who in Music and Musician's Directory.*

Ms. Marcus composed the original music for a movie currently showing in over twenty countries. Her ISCM prize-winning composition *American Song Cycle,* based on a text by Robert Frost, was recently presented on WTTW-TV in Chicago. She performed her piano works and was interviewed on WNYC Radio, New York in 1978, in a program funded by the New York Council of the Arts.

MARGARET MEACHEM

Margaret Meachem was born in Brooklyn, New York, on January 1, 1922. She received her B.A. from Bennington College, where she studied with Paul Boepple in sixteenth-century counterpoint. At Williams College she continued her study of counterpoint and harmony with Robert Barrow, and then worked for her masters at the University of Massachusetts at Amherst where she studied composition with Charles Russell and Philip Bezanson. Later work included studies of electronic music with Joel Chadabe and composition with Nadia Boulanger. She studied flute originally with Louis Moyse and more recently with Julius Baker.

In 1975 she received a fellowship from the Composers' Conference where she also taught Orff and improvisation to the Green Mountain Fiddlers.

She has taught flute privately for fifteen years, and also taught for two years in the Dorset, Vermont, elementary school, five years at Pine Cobble School in Williamstown, and three years at North Bennington, Vermont. She is currently teaching flute, theory, and Orff classes privately at the Pittsfield Community Music School, and at Berkshire Community College.

JOYCE ELLIN ORENSTEIN

Born in Chicago, Ms. Orenstein began studying piano at the age of nine. She attended the University of Chicago and Stanford University and received a B.A. in English from the University of California, Los Angeles, in 1961. Following graduation, she continued to attend music classes there and studied with Leonard Stein. After moving to New York, Ms. Orenstein studied composition with Mario Davidovsky both before and during graduate work at the City College of the City University of New York, where she received her M.A. in music composition in 1974. Ms. Orenstein received the City College's Mark Brunswick Award in composition in 1970 and 1971. She has also been the recipient of fellowships to the Composers' Conferences at Bennington College, Bennington, Vermont, in 1970 and 1971, and at Johnson State College, Johnson, Vermont, in 1974.

Ms. Orenstein's compositions have been performed at Carnegie Recital Hall and the City College in New York, the Eastman School of Music, the Composers' Conferences at Bennington College and Johnson State College in Vermont, and at Rutgers University and Somerset County College in New Jersey.

ALICE PARKER

(ASCAP)

Alice Parker, American composer and conductor, was born in Boston, Massachusetts, and is a graduate of Smith College and the Juilliard School of Music. In May, 1979, she received the honorary degree, Doctor of Musical Arts, from Hamilton College.

She composes only on commission for performance, and her lengthy list of works testifies to her success at writing music in an idiom which is rewarding both to performers and audiences. Recent works include an Advent cantata, *The Day-Spring; Love Songs,* for chorus and piano; *O Sing the Glories* and *The Song of Simeon,* anthems; and *Echoes from the Hills,* a song cycle to poems of Emily Dickinson, for soprano and chamber orchestra. Three full concerts of her music were given at an Alice Parker Festival in Holland, Michigan, involving community, church, and high school choirs, and the Grand Rapids Symphony Orchestra.

Other works receiving performances in recent seasons are the operas *Family Reunion* and *The Martyrs Mirror,* both in Canada; and *Singers Glen,* in Pennsylvania, Kansas, Maryland, and Virginia. She conducted the cantatas *Journeys: Pilgrims and Strangers* in Michigan and California; *A Sermon from the Mountain* at Boston University; and *Melodious Accord* in Michigan, Texas, and Ohio. *Gaudete: Six Latin Christmas Hymns,* commissioned by the Atlanta Symphony, was heard at many Christmas programs. Her many arrangements of folksongs, hymns, and carols in collaboration with Robert Shaw are well established in the choral repertory in this country and abroad.

Her schedule regularly includes performances and workshops throughout North America. She conducts honors choruses in many parts of the United States. Her classes in composition and choral arranging are highlights of these tours.

Miss Parker's compositions are published by Hinshaw Music, Inc., E. C. Schirmer, Carl Fischer, and Lawson-Gould. She is the author of *Music Reference Crammer* (New York: Doubleday, 1964) and a guide to choral arranging through improvisation: *Creative Hymn Singing.* She has received composer's grants from the National Endowment for the Arts and ASCAP, and is an honorary member of Sigma Alpha Iota and the Association of Choral Conductors. She also belongs to the American Symphony Orchestra League, the National Opera Association, the American Choral Directors Association, the Hymn Society of America, and the League of Women Composers. She is listed in *Who's Who of American Women, World Who's Who of Women,* and the *Dictionary of International Biography.*

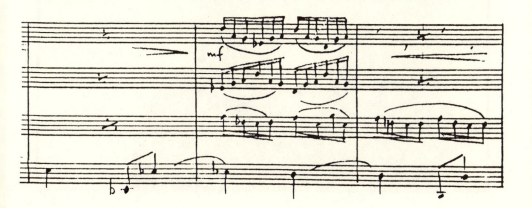

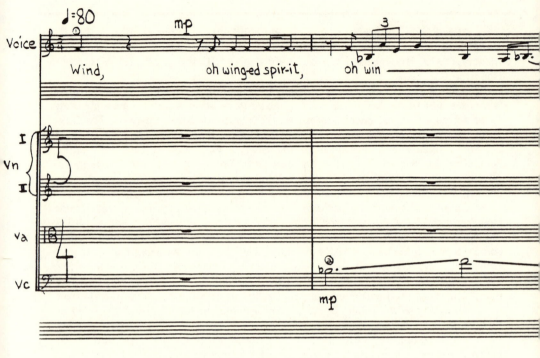

BARBERI PAULL

(ASCAP)

Barberi Paull was born in New York City and has lived in Europe, Israel, and Canada. A prodigy, she spent her early years touring as a concert pianist until a fascination with improvisation led her to become a composer and lyricist.

She undertook composition studies at the Juilliard School with Hall Overton and Jacob Druckman, at the Manhattan School of Music with Charles Wuorinen, and on fellowship at Tanglewood with Bruno Maderna. She also studied music theater with Lehman Engel at the BMI Musical Theatre Workshop, American music and jazz with Billy Taylor, and electronic composition with Jacob Druckman and Elias Tanenbaum.

As director of the Barberi Paull Musical Theatre, Inc., she travelled with a company of artists, presenting mixed media and theater events across the country from 1972 to 1975.

Ms. Paull's awards include the Delius Composition Award for *Antifon,* a Rockefeller grant for *O Wind,* Segall and Exxon prizes, and grants from ASCAP and CAPS. She has received commissions from the Presbyterian Church, the Walnut Street Theatre, the Norwegian and Denmark dance companies, and Feather.

After 1975, Barberi Paull expanded her musical theater into commercial projects, scoring for film and writing jingles and cabaret/popular music. She appears in lecture/concerts through states' Arts Councils and is a frequent guest director of children's theater and creative play projects.

Listed in *The World Who's Who of Women, Baker's Biographical Dictionary of Musicians,* and *Who's Who of American Women,* Ms. Paull serves on the Executive Board of The League of Women Composers. She is also actively engaged in projects sponsored by the American Guild of Authors and Composers and the American Music Center.

ALEXANDRA PIERCE

(ASCAP)

Alexandra Pierce, composer, pianist, music theorist, and movement teacher, was born in Philadelphia in 1934. She was educated at the University of Michigan, the New England Conservatory, Harvard, and Brandeis where she earned her Ph.D. in theory and composition. Formerly on the faculty of Antioch College, she is now professor of theory and piano at the University of Redlands. Her music since 1974 is published by Seesaw Music Corporation.

ELIZABETH PIZER

Elizabeth Pizer is a composer, pianist, improvisor, accompanist-coach, and musicologist. Originally from Watertown, New York, she was born into a musical family, and began playing the piano at the age of two and one-half. She studied the piano privately for sixteen years. Elizabeth began notating original musical themes when she was eight and, by the time she reached the age of seventeen, knew that composition would play an important role in her life.

Elizabeth pursued her formal training at the Boston Conservatory of Music, then left the East Coast to settle in the San Francisco Bay area. Here she has established herself as an accompanist-coach, at San Jose State University for the Opera Workshop, with various performing ensembles, teachers' studios, and also on a free-lance basis.

As a performer, Elizabeth specializes in twentieth-century music and improvisation. As a composer, she has written orchestral, chamber, vocal, choral, solo piano, and electronic-tape compositions. She and her husband, Charles, were recently the subjects of a two-hour special broadcast on radio station KPFA (the Pacifica station in Berkeley), where their music in both written and improvised formats was represented. In May 1979, the world premiere of her *Under and Overture for Symphonic Band and Antiphonal Tympani, Op. 37*, composed from 1977 to 1979, was given by the San Jose State University Symphonic Band, William Trimble, conductor. Also in 1979, *Qulisoly* for flute and piano was premiered in a concert presented as part of the New Times series of programs directed by Dr. Dinos Constantinides at Louisiana State University in Baton Rouge. *Five Haiku* for medium-high voice and small chamber ensemble was performed at the ASUC Annual National Conference in March 1980 at Memphis State University. And in May 1980, her *Five Haiku, II* for mezzo soprano and piano was premiered at San Jose State University.

As a musicologist, Elizabeth, with her husband, has established one of the largest private archival collections of performances of contemporary classical music in the United States.

Ms. Pizer is an Executive Board member of the International League of Women Composers, and an active member of American Women Composers, the American Music Center, and the American Society of University Composers. Through contacts with fellow composer-members of these groups, she has received tape recordings of their music for broadcast on radio station KPFA.

She is currently working on an oratorio which is scored for three full choirs, several vocal soloists, and organ.

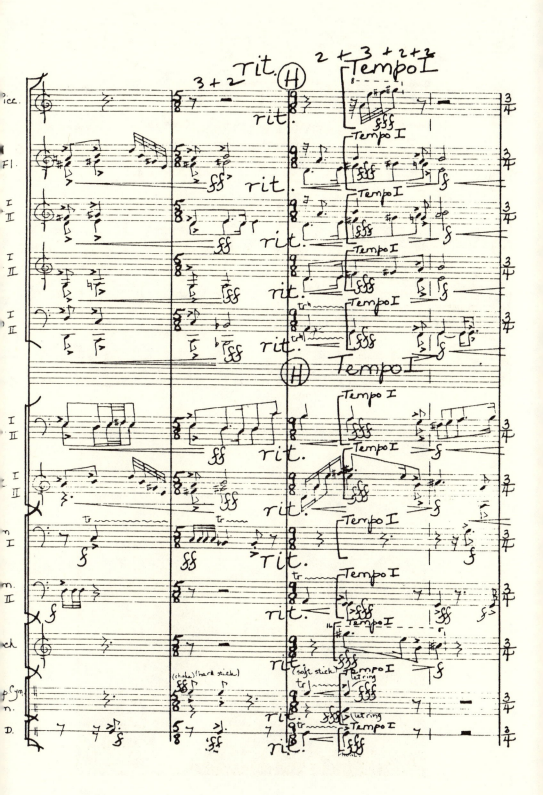

VERA PREOBRAJENSKA

Dr. Vera N. Preobrajenska, born on April 27, 1926, was trained in San Francisco, Oakland, and Berkeley, California. She received her B.A. from San Francisco State University. Her advanced studies were at the San Francisco Conservatory of Music, Mills College Music and Arts Institute, Holy Name College, and the University of California, where she studied with Darius Milhaud, Ernest Bloch, Roger Sessions, Frederick Jacobi, Ernst von Dohnanyi, and Dmitri Shostakovich. She has an M.A. in musical composition, and a Ph.D. in musicology from Bernadean University in Nevada.

Dr. Preobrajenska's professional listings include: *Who's Who of American Women, Who's Who in the World, Who's Who in Music,* as well as the *Dictionary of International Biography.* Dr. Preobrajenska is a member of the American Music Center, and American Society of University Composers in New York, American Women Composers, in Washington, D.C.; Bibliotèque Internationale de Musique Contemporaine in Paris; International League of Women Composers, and the National Association of Composers. She organized the Santa Cruz Chapter (Composers Workshop) of the National League of American Pen Women in Washington.

Her appointments include those of staff ballet-pianist at the University of California at Berkeley, dance department, from 1965 to 1968; and at the University of California at Santa Cruz, ballet division, from 1977 to 1979 and 1980 to the present.

Dr. Preobrajenska's *American Tone Poem,* a symphonic work in three movements, was awarded second prize in the 1980 Biennial Competition for original orchestral music held by the National League of American Pen Women.

"La Vendetta di Luzbel"
Opera in 1 atto e 2 quadri
Testo tratto da "La Creacion del Mundo" di Lope de Vega Carpio - Traduzione e adattamento
Teresa Procaccini
Musica di: Teresa Proc
Andantino 𝅗𝅥=66-72 min. 32
I° Quadro
2 Flauti
2 Oboe
2 Clar. in sib
2 Fag.
2 Corni in Fa
2 Trombe in do
2 Tromb.
Timp.
Suona musica all'interno. All'alzarsi del sipario si vede un trono molto ben adorn
Al lato destro c'è Miguel con spada e scudo e al lato sinistro Luzbel, entrambi co
P. forte
Andantino 𝅗𝅥=66-72
I Viol. II
Viole
Celli
Bassi
col celli

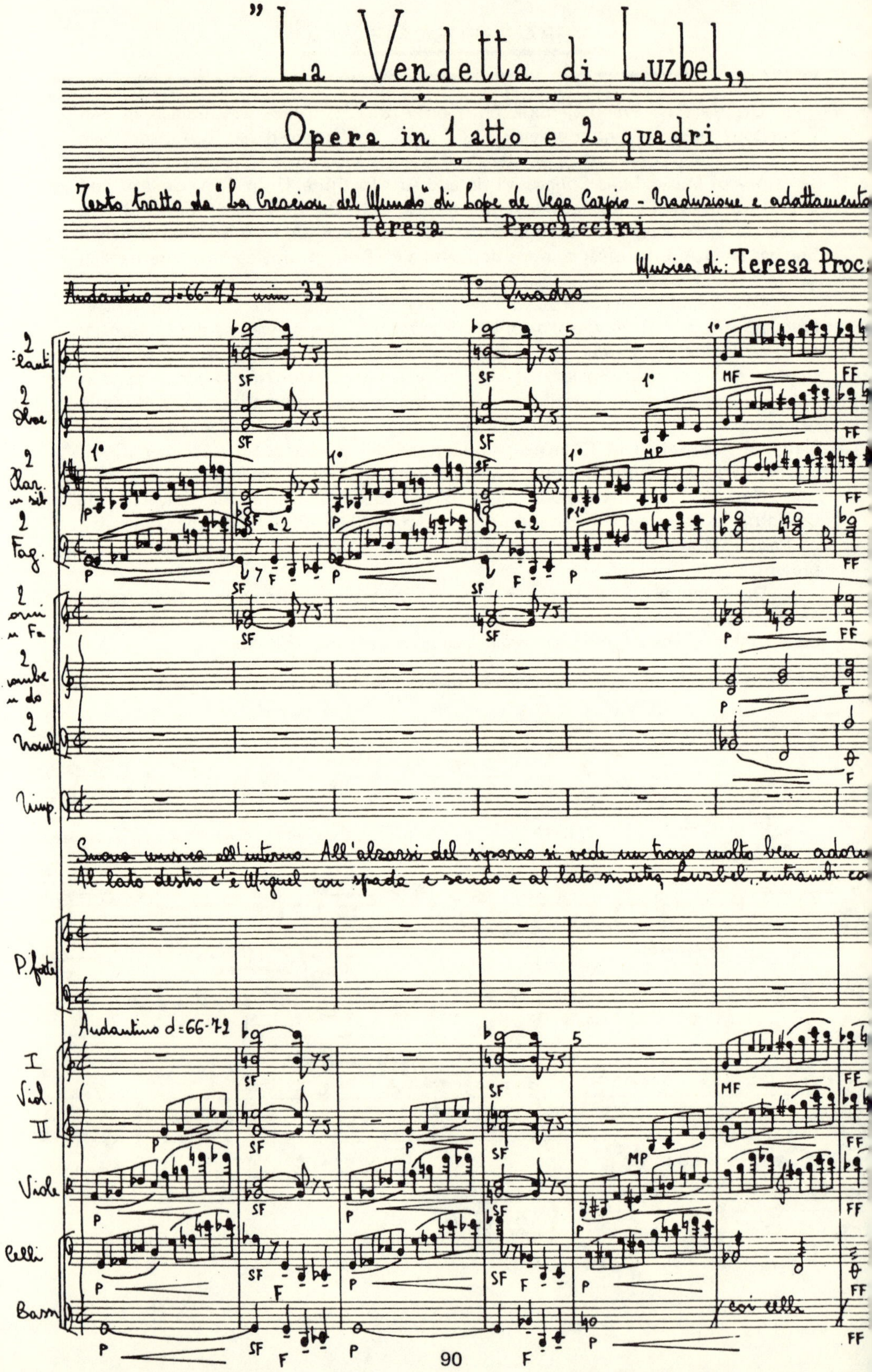

TERESA PROCACCINI

From the age of six Teresa Procaccini showed a marked musical aptitude. At eight years of age she began to compose short pieces for piano and was immediately introduced to the study of piano and composition. In 1952 she received a diploma in the study of pianoforte from the Conservatory of Music "Giordano" of Foggia. She continued studying at the Saint Cecilia Conservatory of Rome with Fernando Germani and Virgilio Mortari and graduated with degrees in organ and composition.

Teresa Procaccini's style and technique of composition show the influence of the French and Italian schools with rhythmic elements of American origin. The composers she feels most related to are Bartók and Stravinsky. The fundamental characteristics of her artistic personality are: 1) the accurate search for a simplicity, more apparent than real, that enables anyone to penetrate with immediacy the spirit of the composition; 2) the intent of making each instrument a protagonist, giving it its own, almost tonal, melodic line; 3) the construction of forms akin in breadth to the classical; and 4) the predilection for woodwinds. Thus, from the interplay of various instruments and themes, a melodic-harmonic-rhythmic-atonal texture is born, and a composition solidly constructed, which is spontaneous and clear to all, and which constitutes the essence of her musical thought.

In 1970 she won the International Competition of Composition "A. Casella" with the woodwind quintet *Clown Music*. During the years 1972 and 1973 she directed the Conservatory of Music in Foggia. At the present time she is a professor of composition at Saint Cecilia Conservatory in Rome and she teaches a course in composition at the "Ottorino Respighi" Academy of Music every summer.

Her compositions are frequently performed in Italy, but most of all abroad. Some of these are published by Sonzogno and Carisch (Milan), Zanibon (Padua), Leduc (Paris). Others are in the process of being published with La De Santis (Rome). Her recordings are issued by La EDI-PAN of Rome.

MARLYCE REED

Marlyce Reed, born January 14, 1955, began studying clarinet at the age of nine. In 1972, she was selected as principal clarinetist for the American Youth in Concert Ensemble which performed at Carnegie Hall and the John F. Kennedy Center as well as abroad in such cities as London, Paris, Salzburg, and Rome. In 1975 she returned to Germany where she studied with composer Gloria Coates and enrolled privately with Edward Brunner, principal clarinetist of the München Rundfunk Orchestra. Her conducting debut took place the following year when she won the Honors Concert Competition at the University of Wisconsin at Stevens Point. Here, she also received the Colman Scholarship for Music and the Albertson Scholarship Award. In 1977 she graduated from the University of Wisconsin with a Bachelor of Music. In the fall of 1977 Ms. Reed began studying composition with Alan Stout at Northwestern University. While enrolled at Northwestern she also became active in electronic and computer music, studying both the analytical and compositional applications of computers to music. Her masters thesis, *Shir Kadosh,* for symphonic orchestra and boys' choir received the Northwestern University Faricy Prize for Creative Composition and in June of 1979, she was awarded a Master of Music from that institutuion. A teacher, composer, and performer at various schools and music camps, Ms. Reed has also worked in arts administration with the Chicago Symphony Orchestra. She is published by Seesaw Music Corporation and Shawnee Press and a collection of her works is on file at the American Music Center Inc. in New York City. Ms. Reed is a member of Pi Kappa Lambda, the International League of Women Composers Inc., American Women Composers, the American Symphony Orchestra League, and the Chicago Society of Composers and is listed in *Who's Who Among Students in American Universities and Colleges.* She resides in Chicago, Illinois.

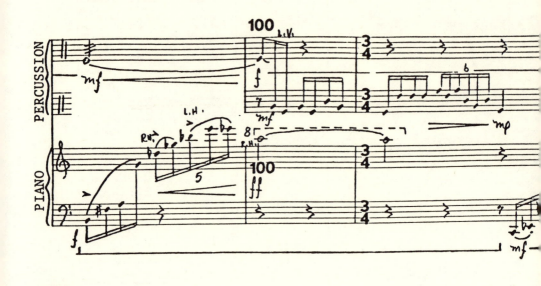

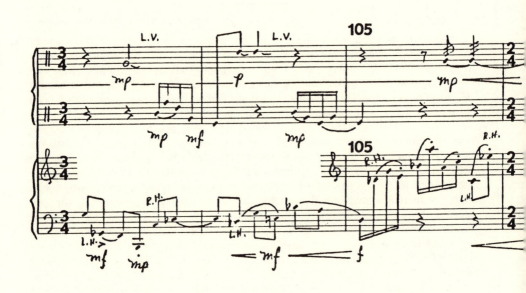

SARAH JOHNSTON REID

Sarah Johnston Reid was born in East Liverpool, Ohio, on January 30, 1948, the daughter of Mabel Voyles Johnston and William Dale Johnston. After completing her work at the Box Elder High School, Brigham City, Utah, in 1965, she entered Abilene Christian University at Abilene, Texas. She received the degree of Bachelor of Music Education with a concentration in oboe from Abilene Christian University in May 1969, and the degree of Master of Music from Hardin-Simmons University in 1971. She was employed as an instructor at Abilene Christian University from 1970 to 1973. In June 1973, she entered the graduate school of the University of Texas at Austin and received a Ph.D. in music theory in 1979.

Ms. Reid is currently chairman of the Department of Music and director of the electronic music studio at Abilene Christian University. Besides composition, she teaches music theory and double-reeds. She also holds positions with the San Angelo Symphony and the Abilene Philharmonic, and is married to Brad Reid, an attorney and Abilene Christian University faculty member.

MARGA RICHTER
(ASCAP)

Marga Richter was born in Reedsburg, Wisconsin, and received her early musical training in Minneapolis, Minnesota. She earned bachelor's and master's degrees at the Juilliard School where she studied composition with William Bergsma and Vincent Persichetti and piano with Rosalyn Tureck.

Her music first came to national attention in the late 1950s through a series of recordings on MGM Records by Maro Ajemian, William Masselos, Menahem Pressler, Izler Solomon, and Walter Trampler. Then, in 1964, the Harkness Ballet commissioned the score for a ballet, *Abyss,* which was performed in most of the major cities of Europe and North and South America during the next few years. It has since been added to the repertoires of the Joffrey and Boston Ballet Companies. A second ballet commissioned by Harkness, *Bird of Yearning,* was first performed in Cologne in 1969.

Beginning in 1968 and continuing throughout the next decade she wrote a series of pieces called *Landscapes of the Mind.* The first is a large piano concerto, directly inspired by two paintings by Georgia O'Keeffe and the instrumental music of India. *Landscapes II* is for violin and piano and *Landscapes III* is for piano trio. All of these pieces, as well as three others written during the same period *(Blackberry Vines and Winter Fruit, Music for Three Quintets and Orchestra* and *Requiem)* make use of the same or related thematic material and thus provide a ten-year continuity of musical thought.

Since 1975 her music has appeared with increasing frequency on orchestral and recital programs. Among orchestras programming her works are the Minnesota Orchestra, the Milwaukee Symphony, the Buffalo Philharmonic, the National Gallery Orchestra, and the Oklahoma, Tucson, Oakland, Madison and Maracaibo Symphonies. Soloists who have recently performed her music include Jessye Norman, Daniel Heifetz, William Masselos, Karen Phillips, Peter Basquin, Vivian Taylor and Leonard Raver.

Ms. Richter has received grants, awards and commissions from the National Endowment for the Arts, the Martha Baird Rockefeller Fund, the National Federation of Music Clubs, Meet-the-Composer and ASCAP. As a pianist, she frequently performs her own compositions.

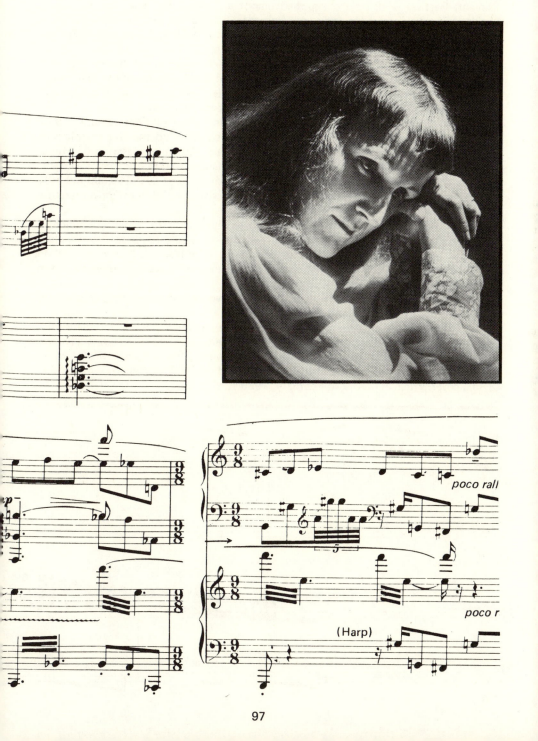

GERTRUD ROBERTS

Gertrud Roberts was born in Hastings, Minnesota, on August 23, 1906, to Austrian parents. She and her husband have two children, Michael Stefan and Marcia Eveline, and have lived in Honolulu since 1947.

One of today's foremost harpsichordists and a pioneer in revival of the instrument, Gertrud is also a distinguished pianist and composer. She received a B.A. degree in music at the University of Minnesota in 1928 and continued her studies in piano at the Leipzig Conservatory from 1930 to 1931. In 1935 and 1936, she studied piano in Vienna with Madam Julia Elbogen.

She began composing at age seven and performing at age twelve. Her first European concert was in Asch, Czechoslovakia in 1931. She heard her first harpsichord at a private concert in Berlin in 1933 while conducting tours in Europe and went back the following year to purchase a German instrument.

Her first public harpsichord concert was in Saint Paul, Minnesota, in 1936. She introduced the harpsichord as a concert instrument to the Hawaiian Islands in the late 1940s and early 1950s, performing each Christmas season at the Honolulu Academy of Art festival for school children (some 10,000 students of all ages). With her own Challis concert harpsichord, she has traveled over 160,000 miles by air for mainland concerts. Her programs always consist of both traditional literature and her own compositions.

On commission, Mrs. Roberts composed music for the Honolulu Community Theatre's *Thieves Carnival* by Anouilh and Shakespeare's *Tempest;* the Honolulu Youth Theatre's *Alice in Wonderland;* the University of Hawaii's theater production of Lorca's *Yerma;* and the Pineapple Companies of Hawaii documentary film *Pineapple Country Hawaii.*

Her catalogue includes three published works and numerous unpublished compositions for harpsichord, voice, and orchestra.

She holds membership in many professional organizations and foundations; is listed in fourteen directories and biographical reference works including *Men and Women of Hawaii, Who's Who of American Women, International Who's Who in Music, International Harpsichord Blue Book,* and others. Mrs. Roberts was featured in a cover article in *Clavier* in February, 1980.

FAST AGAIN (♩ = 132)

PATSY ROGERS

(BMI)

Patsy Rogers was born in 1938 and holds two degrees in composition from Bennington College; she also studied at Columbia University and Smith College. Her principal teachers have been Henry Brant, Louis Calabro, Lionel Nowak, Vivian Fine, and Iva Dee Hiatt.

Rogers has taught music privately—piano, guitar, and composition—and in schools and colleges in New York and New England, including Brooklyn College, the Bank Street School, the Brattleboro School of Music, Antioch/New England Graduate School, Keene State College, the United Nations International School, the New Lincoln School, and the Mannes College of Music. She has also been a free-lance music editor and copyist. In 1979, she was a composer-in-residence at the Chamber Music Conference and Composers' Forum of the East.

Works by Rogers that have been performed recently include a chamber opera for soprano and eleven instruments, performed twice; two ballets for eight musicians, one performed seven times, the other, fourteen; a theater piece for eight musicians which was recorded for taped performance; a choral piece for SAB, piano, and percussion; a trio for flute, viola, and bassoon; a string quintet; a percussion duo; and three songs for soprano and piano set to poems by Adrienne Rich, which received four performances.

Rogers' music is purposefully accessible to the average listener. She was quoted in a recent interview as saying: "I'm interested in affecting people's feelings. I want to make you laugh or cry . . . to react immediately to my music, or to the message of the words I choose to set." Some aspects typical of her music are long melodic lines, rhythmic patterns which are often disjunct but not necessarily complex, and a feeling of momentary tonal centers which have weight but are constantly shifting (a system which she refers to as "floating tonalities").

Rogers is a member of the International League of Women Composers, BMI, the American Music Center, and the Catgut Acoustical Society. She is currently living in New York City.

VALERIE SAMSON

Music has always been at the core of Valerie Samson's life. She was born October 16, 1948, in St. Louis, Missouri, the fourth of eight children. Both of her parents were active musically, and since there were three pianos in the house, as well as various stringed instruments, she played as a matter of course. Creating her own music followed naturally.

She studied music theory at Newton High School, Massachusetts, then earned a B.A. in music in 1970 from Boston University, where she studied with Hugo Norden. She became involved in contemporary music through her weekly radio program on WTBS in Cambridge.

In 1973, she completed an M.A. in music composition at the University of California, Berkeley, where her most important studies were with Andrew Imbrie and Alan Curtis. Besides composing, she researched French baroque modal theories and the use of emotive effects in Lully's operas.

Since 1973, Ms. Samson has been researching contemporary music in Northern California, and has published interviews in *Ear* and *The Composer*. She has lectured on the results of this study, sometimes focusing on women composers, and has presented her compositions in various Bay Area concerts, notably with the Composers' Cooperative.

Since 1977, she has been studying and performing Chinese music with Betty Wong, and more recently with Sam Lau and the Chinese Performing Arts Society, playing primarily the er-hu and jung-wu, which are small and middle-sized two-string violins. Her Chinese music study concerns the relationship of notation practice to performance practice and the use of ornamentation, and she is also tracking the impact of Asian music and ideology on California composers.

ALICE SAMTER

A proud Berliner, Alice Samter considers that she owes her common sense and wit largely to the character and flavor of life in her city. Berlin is also the place of her musical education: piano studies with Else Blatt, Amalie Iwan, and Dr. Starck at the Klindworth-Scharwenk-Konservatorium; improvisation study with Gerhard Wehlé; choral work with Karl Ristenpart; and school music preparation with Prof. Heinrich Martens at the Hochschule fuer Musik. Ms. Samter notes: "I composed very early in life but I could not go public because of unusually adverse circumstances. For many years I was a music teacher at Berlin high schools where I also taught art education as a secondary subject—one has to earn a living somehow."

Her listing of works is voluminous. Many of the works were written on commission and heard on radio programs that were eventually broadcast over many stations.

Ms. Samter's music has received critical notice and acclaim, particularly in regard to her preference for the "farcical, unusual and pointed" statement, and for the "instrumental wit and humor" she so often demonstrates.

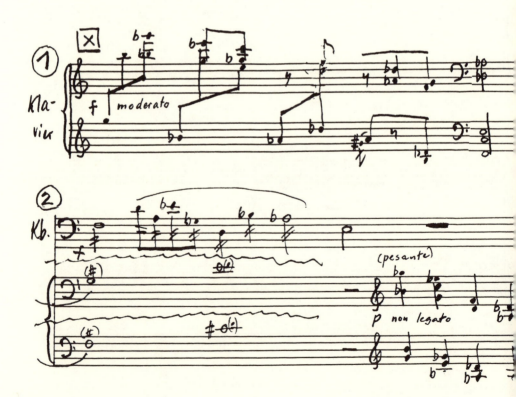

Gently moving

Through the am - ple o - pen door_____ of the peace - ful coun - try

RUTH SCHONTHAL

(ASCAP)

Ruth Schonthal, composer, concert pianist and teacher, is on the faculty of New York University, and is also currently a faculty member of the Westchester Conservatory, where she teaches courses for Mercy College.

Born in Hamburg, Germany, of Viennese parents, she was accepted at age five as the youngest pupil at the Stern Conservatory in Berlin. At thirteen, again as the youngest student, she entered the Royal Academy of Music in Stockholm, Sweden. After moving to Mexico City, she studied composition with Manuel M. Ponce.

In 1946, her talents came to the attention of Paul Hindemith, who arranged for her to study composition on a scholarship at Yale University, where she was awarded the Bachelor of Music degree in 1948. She studied orchestration with Richard Donovan and Paul Creston, and piano with Mme. Simon Barere and Sascha Gorodnitzky.

Ruth Schonthal won first prize in piano at the Conservatorio Nacional in Mexico, and third prize in the Triannual Delta Omecron International Competition for her *String Quartet*. She holds many ASCAP Standard Awards, was nominated for the 1979 Kennedy Friedheim Award for *In Homage of . . .* (24 Preludes), and was a finalist, with *The Courtship of Camilla,* in the 1980 New York City Opera Competition for a one-act opera by an American composer.

Her music has been widely performed in the United States—in concert halls such as Alice Tully Hall at Lincoln Center, Carnegie Recital Hall, Kaufmann Auditorium, McMillin Theatre, Composer's Forum and Jacob's Pillow and abroad—in Belgrade, London, Mexico City, Paris, and elsewhere.

She appeared on TV's "Lee Graham Presents," in a program of piano improvisations, and has been broadcast on WQXR, WNYC and WBAI in Robert Sherman's "Listening Room," Martin Bookspan's "Composer's Forum," and the Alan Weiss program, "Artists in Concert."

Oxford University Press is planning to publish a complete library of her music, and two recordings were released in 1980: Leonarda Productions presented her *Totengesange,* with soprano Berenice Bramson, and Capriccio Records featured her piano works, with pianist Gary Steigerwalt.

barn,

and hor · ses

feed · ing,

And haze _____ and vis · ta,

mp *pp*

sfz *fp* *pp*

ancora più lento

dolce *p* *p* , *pp*

and the far ___ ho · ri · zon fad · ing a · way. _____

dolce ,

p *pp*

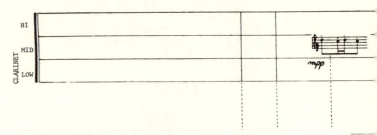

DARIA SEMEGEN

(BMI)

Daria Semegen was born in 1946 in Bamberg, West Germany, and began writing music and studying the piano at age seven. She subsequently studied composition at the Chautauqua Institution and received a Master of Music degree in 1968 from the Eastman School of Music where she studied with Samuel H. Adler and Burrill Phillips. In the academic year 1968-69 she was a Fulbright scholar in Warsaw, Poland studying composition with Witold Lutoslawski and electronic music at the Warsaw Conservatory lab. She received a Yale University Fellowship and returned to the United States in 1969 to attend Yale where she studied composition and electronic music with Bülent Arel and theory with Alexander Goehr and earned a Master of Music degree in 1971. She continued electronic music work during the summer of 1971 at the Columbia-Princeton Electronic Music Center and received a fellowship to the School of the Arts, Columbia University for postgraduate studies.

During the four years she spent at Columbia, she studied with Vladimir Ussachevsky and was on the teaching staff of the C-PEMC. She worked as sound engineer in the World Music Collection at Columbia and as technical assistant to Ussachevsky and Otto Luening in creation of electronic music materials for disc recording. In January, 1974, she joined the Department of Music at the State University of New York at Stony Brook teaching composition/theory, serving as a director of the Electronic Music Studios and designer of the recording studios project.

Her composition awards include two BMI Awards, three National Endowment for the Arts grants; Chautauqua, MacDowell Colony, and Tanglewood fellowships; prizes from Yale University, University of Maryland, and Mu Phi Epsilon; two State University of New York Research grants, a National Academy of Recording Arts & Sciences grant, and the ISCM 1975 International Electronic Music Competition prize. Her works have been played and broadcast in the United States and throughout the world. In 1977 she was guest composer at Eastman School of Music in an event honoring three women composers and has been panelist at electronic music festivals at Jersey City State College and Bowling Green State University. She served twice on the judging panel of BMI Awards and on the CAPS selection panel.

Her memberships include the Audio Engineering Society, American Composers Alliance, International League of Women Composers, BMI, ASUC, MOE. Her articles have been published in *Music Journal,* the arts journals, *Signs* (University of Chicago), and *Heresies,* and in other publications.

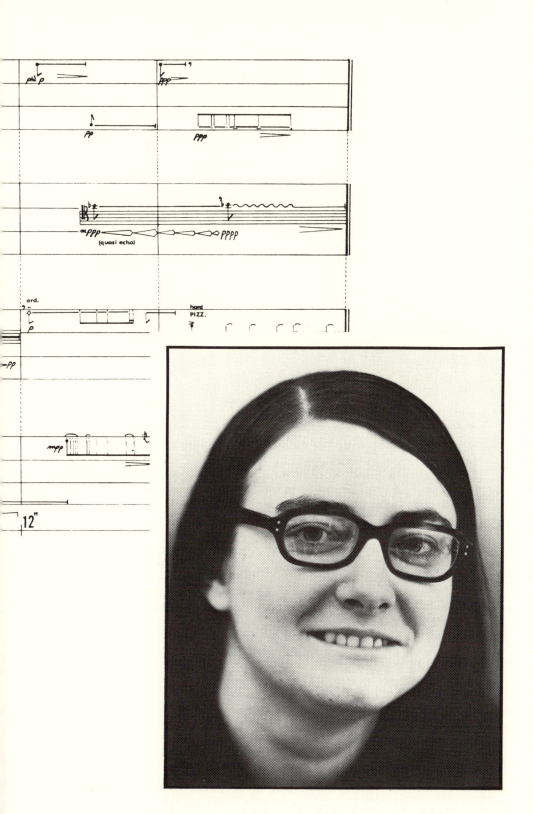

109

ANN L. SILSBEE

Ann Silsbee received her A.B. degree from Radcliffe College, her Master of Music degree from Syracuse University, and a Doctor of Musical Arts degree from Cornell University in composition, where she studied with Karel Husa. She has been a member of the music faculties at the State University of New York College at Cortland, and at Cornell University, teaching music theory and piano, and has appeared as pianist in many solo and chamber music concerts featuring music of the twentieth century, including her own. She was a participant in the 1974 Darmstadt Ferienkurse für Neue Musik. She has written in a variety of media, her output including many chamber works, both vocal and instrumental, as well as works for orchestra, chorus and solo instruments.

Composition awards include two fellowships to the Composers Conference in Vermont and a Composer Fellowship-Grant from the National Endowment for the Arts in 1979, to write *De Amore et Morte* for Neva Pilgrim and the Society for New Music, in Syracuse. She received a second prize in the Burge-Eastman Competition in the fall of 1978 for her piano work, *Doors,* which was recently recorded by David Burge for CRI. A month's residence at Yaddo in 1979 resulted in two new works, *Runemusic,* for solo cello, and *Pathways,* for chamber orchestra. Most recently, her new *Quartet* (1980) for clarinet, violin, cello and piano received its premiere in a five-concert tour by the Society for New Music of Syracuse, as part of a large-scale celebration of women artists. She was also featured on a panel of women composers at Hamilton, Everson Museum in Syracuse, and as speaker at Colgate University. Her works have been played in concert and over the radio in France, Germany, and in the United States.

NETTY SIMONS

(BMI)

One of America's foremost women composers, Netty Simons has won praise for her compositions from colleagues, critics, and performers alike. Audiences in London, Paris, Tokyo, Osaka, Melbourne and throughout the United States have enjoyed her works and the *Pied Piper of Hamelin* was a bestseller on CRI Records. Iannis Xenakis described her music as "sensitive, poetic"; Raymond Ericson in the *New York Times* found that her *"Illuminations* (for two pianos) was mesmerizing"; and conductor/composer Stanislaw Skrowaczewski commented after a performance of one of Miss Simons' works "I enjoyed the whole, exciting 'spectrum sonorum.'"

Netty Simons was born in New York City, where she still lives with her husband. She attended New York University's School of Fine Arts, and was later awarded a scholarship at the Juilliard Graduate School. She also studied privately with Stefan Wolpe. For many years, Netty Simons was the producer of highly successful programs of contemporary music at radio station WNYC in New York and WUOM at the Universtiy of Michigan.

Netty Simons' early works were marked by great economy of means and imaginative control of color. Her more recent graphic scores have enjoyed great popularity with performers and audiences alike, and her opera *The Bell Witch of Tennessee* makes exciting use of an American folk tale.

Netty Simons is the recipient of a Ford Foundation Recording-Publication Award.

JEANNE SINGER

(ASCAP)

Jeanne (Walsh) Singer, a native New Yorker, majored in music at Barnard College, graduating magna cum laude and Phi Beta Kappa. Her teachers in theory, analysis, and composition included Seth Bingham, William Mitchell and Douglas Moore. She studied piano privately with Nadia Reisenberg and received the Artist Diploma from the National Guild of Piano Teachers.

Mrs. Singer is an active concert pianist, private teacher, and lecturer. She is often engaged to present her own works in public and has been on numerous radio and TV broadcasts. Her compositions have been performed throughout the United States and in countries abroad. Several all-Singer concerts of vocal and instrumental music have been sponsored in New York and Boston. In South America, the National University of Colombia presented an all-Singer concert at the National Museum of Colonial Art in Bogotá, Colombia, March 1980.

She has received commissions from choral groups, chamber ensembles, and poetry organizations. Many contemporary poets have asked her to set their poems. Her vocal music is based mainly on the poetry of living Americans.

Since 1971, Jeanne Singer has received over thirty national awards and prizes from the National Federation of Music Clubs; the Composers Guild; the National League of American Pen Women; Composers, Authors & Artists of America; the New York Poetry Forum; and annual ASCAP Awards since 1978.

Jeanne Singer served as national music chairperson for the National League of American Pen Women; as vice-president of Composers, Authors & Artists of America, and as executive vice-president of Community Concert Association of Great Neck. She is music advisor to the North Shore Community Arts Center. She is a Life Fellow of the International Biographical Association and a member of "The Bohemians" (a New York Musicians Club); the International Platform Association; the American Women Composers; and the American Music Center. She is listed in numerous reference books including *Who's Who of American Women; International Who's Who in Music;* and *Dictionary of International Biography.*

Jeanne Singer is also an internationally recognized authority on Siamese cats, having bred prize-winning Siamese for thirty years. She was president of the National Siamese Cat Club for eighteen years. Her many published articles about the breeding and genetics of Siamese have had world-wide distribution.

Andante expressivo

Bb Clarinet

SUSAN SMELTZER

Susan Smeltzer, born in 1941 in Sapulpa, Oklahoma, was a child prodigy and is considered by outstanding critics and scholars as an "uncommonly gifted pianist," "novel," and a "genius of our times." Early training was in Tulsa University in Oklahoma and Oklahoma City University, where she earned her Bachelor of Music degree in 1964. Her artistic training was at the University of Southern California, where she earned her Master of Music degree in 1967, and studied under Lillian Steuber, with master classes under Gregor Piatigorsky and Mme. Lhevinne. A winner of over twenty competitions, the artist studied at the Akademie für Musik as a Fulbright scholar under Dr. Dichler in 1969.

At age five, she composed a book of marches. *Furious Wind,* for piano, was performed on KVOO, Channel 2 in Tulsa, Oklahoma when she was ten. Honors continued to come her way and in 1958, she won the top prize in composition at Western State College Music Festival, Gunnison, Colorado with her elaborate work for piano, *El Matador.*

In 1976, she wrote a large, demanding work, *Twelve Mood Pictures,* in seven weeks for Vladimir Horowitz. *Reverie,* written when she was nineteen, was dedicated to Artur Rubinstein.

She received the *Distinguished Alumni Award* in 1976 from Oklahoma City University. Her works are currently performed throughout the United States, including performances over WQXR in New York with critic, Robert Sherman, on the "Listening Room" and "Artists in Concert." A composer of over forty works, twenty poems, eleven paintings, and a designer, Susan Smeltzer is also a distinguished teacher and adjudicator.

Her patriotic work, *The Bald Eagle March* will be listed in a presidential library, and she wrote *The Brotherhood March* for her cousin, G. William Miller, secretary of the treasury of the United States. Her biography appears in *International Who's Who in Music* and *World Who's Who of Women.* Her hobbies include painting, poetry, cycling, geneology, and medicine.

JULIA SMITH

(ASCAP)

A native of Denton, Texas, and educated at North Texas State University, the Juilliard School, and New York University, Julia Smith has composed in virtually all musical media except electronic tape. Her catalogue includes works for orchestra, choral music with orchestra and band, six operas (all performed), piano solo, two-piano, chamber music, band, vocal, songs, and educational works.

Dr. Smith's orchestral music has been performed by the CBS Symphony conducted by Howard Barlow and Bernard Herrmann, WOR Symphony, conducted by Alfred Wallenstein, Orchestrette of New York, New York Philharmonic "Pops," the orchestras of Columbia University, Dallas, Houston, Fort Worth, Oklahoma City, Duluth, Cleveland, Toledo, San Francisco, Santa Fe, Baltimore, Norwalk, and other orchestras here and abroad.

Her six operas have received performances at various times by the Fort Worth Opera Association, the Opera Guild of Greater Miami, the Piccolo Company in Detroit, by opera companies in Charlotte, North Carolina, Lancaster, Pennsylvania, by the Birmingham Civic Opera, Syracuse Opera Theater, and numerous college and university opera workshops.

In 1963 Julia Smith was named one of ten leading women composers by the National Council of Women of the United States. In 1970 she was recipient of the Distinguished Alumnus Citation from her alma mater, North Texas State University.

A composer, pianist, author, teacher, and lecturer, Dr. Smith is well known for her books on *Aaron Copland* (Dutton, 1955) and *Carl Friedberg* (Philosophical Library, 1963). Her efforts to win recognition for American women composers resulted in the publication of the first *Directory of American Women Composers,* issued by the National Federation of Music Clubs in 1970. In 1972 and 1973 she arranged two thirteen-week series of broadcasts over seventy-two radio stations in the United States which programmed recordings of forty-six American composers, twenty-four of whom were men, twenty-two, women.

A composer-member of ASCAP, Dr. Smith is a National Honorary Member of Sigma Alpha Iota, a leading music fraternity. She has served the last three presidents of the National Federation of Music Clubs over a ten-year period as first chairman of American Women Composers and as chairman of "Decade of Women," working to provide greater exposure and more performances for women composers and conductors. She resides in New York City.

Vivace (♩ = 132)

(con pedale)

HELEN STANLEY

Helen Stanley, born in Florida, became interested in microtonal music while a teenage student of Hans Barth, who patented the first "portable quarter-tone piano." She holds Bachelor of Music, B.S. and Master of Music degrees. She received her master's degree as a student of Ernst von Dohnanyi.

Her microtonal composition led to early involvement in electronic music. When she was listed in *Repertoire International des Musique Electroacoustiques* (M.I.T. Press, 1968) she was one of only three composers in electronic music listed in Florida at that time, and the only one listed in the northeast portion of that state.

Active in keyboard improvisation since childhood, she draws upon the improvisational skills of the pianist in her *Duo-Sonata for Tape Recorder and Piano* premiered by the composer in 1970.

Rhapsody for Electronic Tape and Orchestra, the 1972 composition commission by the jointly funded Florida State Music Teachers Association-Music Teachers National Association award, expresses the urge to interrelate the areas of nature, electronic music, and live performance. Incorporating source birdsong tape material gathered in the field by ornithologist Sam Grimes, a challenging statement by the electronic synthesizer is answered by the human orchestra. Transmuted sounds of nature are heard. Interaction between the electronic, natural, and human elements progresses until the separate statements rush to coalesce.

Helen Stanley's Bicentennial musical activities were varied and included the selection of some of her works for the Federated Music Clubs' circulating radio tapes; the commission to arrange a new setting of the *Battle Hymn of the Republic* for two choirs, organ and optional flute, trumpets and percussion and also to conduct its July fourth premiere; and the premiere performance of a song with the composer at the piano, at an International Conference on the Arts and Communications in Washington D.C.

Her current activities include preparing a book of modal pieces for early piano study. Helen Stanley's biographical listings in addition to the *Repertoire International* are found in *Who's Who of American Women, International Who's Who in Music, Dictionary of International Biography,* and the *Directory of American Women Composers* issued by the American Federation of Music Clubs.

GLORIA WILSON SWISHER

(ASCAP)

Gloria Wilson Swisher was born March 12, 1935, in Seattle, Washington. She graduated from the University of Washington as a piano major, summa cum laude, in 1956. In the 1956-57 academic year she was a Woodrow Wilson Fellow at Mills College, and received an M.A. in composition from Mills in 1958. In 1960, she received a Ph.D. in composition from the Eastman School of Music. She studied composition with Howard Hanson, Bernard Rogers, Darius Milhaud, and John Verrall; she studied piano with Egon Petri, Armand Basile, and Berthe Poncy Jacobson.

She was an instructor at Washington State University in 1960 and 1961 before her marriage in 1961 to Donald P. Swisher, a foreign service officer. From 1961 to 1968 she lived abroad, in Caracas, Veracruz, Yokohama, and Niigata. After returning to Seattle in 1968 she resumed teaching, and is now professor of music at Shoreline Community College, where she has taught since 1969.

She is a member of the International League of Women Composers; American Women Composers; ASCAP; American Music Center; Sigma Alpha Iota, for which she has been chairman of the International Music Fund since 1974; Music Educator's National Conference; Ladies Musical Club of Seattle; Phi Beta Kappa; and the Japan-America Society. She and her husband, now an attorney, are the parents of two sons, Donald William (1963-65), and Stephen Alexander (1965-).

NANCY VAN DE VATE

(ASCAP)

Nancy Van de Vate, born in Plainfield, New Jersey, now resides in Honolulu. She studied piano with Anton Rovinsky in New York before beginning her undergraduate work at the Eastman School of Music as a Rochester Prize Scholar and student of Cecile Genhart. She completed her undergraduate work at Wellesley College, receiving the A.B. in 1952, then continued her study of piano with Bruce Simonds of the Yale School of Music. She subsequently shifted the focus of her study to composition, completing the Doctor of Music degree in composition from Florida State University in 1968. In 1972 she was a participant in the eight-week Summer Institute of Electronic Music at Dartmouth College and the University of New Hampshire.

Ms. Van de Vate has been a faculty member at nine colleges and universities throughout the South and in Hawaii. She is presently associate professor of music at Hawaii Loa College where she also served as Dean of Academic Affairs during 1979.

The composer has received ASCAP Standard Awards annually since 1973 and has been a Resident Fellow at Yaddo and Ossabaw Island. Her many awards include first prize in the 1979 Los Alamos Chamber Music Competition, first place award in the 1975 Delius Composition Contest and third prize in the 1975 Stowe Chamber Music Competition. She has received three awards from "Meet the Composer" and commissions from the Music Teachers National Association, The University of Redlands New Music Ensemble, the Knoxville, Tennessee, Choral Society and others. Her music is regularly performed throughout the United States and abroad, and her articles have appeared in *Musical America, Symphony News, Pan Pipes,* and *The International Musician.*

From 1965 to 1968 and again from 1970 to 1973, Ms. Van de Vate was secretary of the Southeastern Composers League and editor of its newsletter, *Music Now.* From 1973 to 1975, she was president of that organization. In 1975 she founded the International League of Women Composers and still serves as its chairperson.

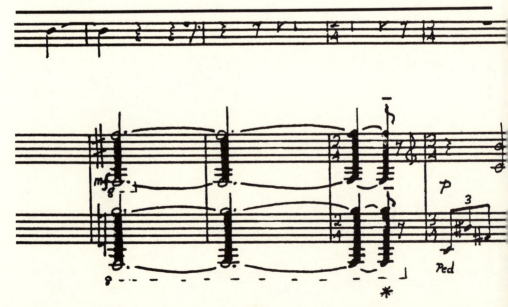

LUCIE VELLÈRE

Lucie Vellère was born in Brussels in 1896 and died there in 1966. She was six years old when her father, an enthusiastic teacher, started teaching her musical theory and piano. She later studied the violin with E. Chaumont, harmony with P. Miry, and composition with Joseph Jongen.

She won a number of prizes including the only prize awarded in a competition organized in 1957 by the American section of the International Council for Women for *Air de Syrinx,* a work for a cappella choir with words by Claudel. In the same year, she was awarded a prize by the Province of Brabant for her *Petite symphonie pour cordes.*

Lucie Vellère created about 100 works. She belonged to no particular school of composition and it was her rare privilege to be able to express herself freely and in widely differing forms. She composed mainly for solo instruments and for voice, always showing regard for their inherent qualities, personality, and possibilities. She also wrote compositions for the orchestra, with and without solo performances, as well as for chamber groups, for string and wind instruments—difficult art where a cleverness of writing, a profundity of feeling and a rhythmical invention are revealed that surprised more than one listener.

Lucie Vellère's output, covering a span of forty-five years, bears the imprint of a warm and sensitive personality. Without references to any particular school of composition, her works were never banal and reflect the taste, distinction, sensitivity, poetry, and sincerity of an outstanding musician.

$\textbf{.} = 50^{\pm}$

Piano

f

(no Ped.)

Ped.

(hold

ELIZABETH VERCOE

(BMI)

Active as a composer since 1963, Elizabeth Vercoe has written for a variety of instrumental and vocal ensembles including music for orchestra, chamber groups, voice and instruments, and piano alone. An impressive portion of her music has been performed and published.

A native of Washington, D.C., she has received a B.A. from Wellesley College, a Master of Music from the University of Michigan and a Doctor of Arts in Music from Boston University, studying with composers Leslie Bassett, Ross Lee Finney, and Gardner Read. She has been on the faculties of Westminster Choir College and Framingham State College, worked for WUCM-FM in Ann Arbor and the Kodaly Institute in Boston, performed as pianist in concerts of her music, and written radio programs for the American Society of University Composers. She has been music critic for the *Concord Journal* since 1979.

Since 1974 she has written *Fantasy for Piano,* a string duo, a violin concerto, an aphoristic set of piano pieces entitled *Six Gratitudes,* two song cycles for soprano, piano, and percussion entitled *Herstory I & II,* and a solo cello piece called *Sonaria for Cello Alone.* She was commissioned in 1980 by pianist Vivian Taylor to write a piece for solo piano.

In 1978 she received the Hubert Weldon Lamb Prize in composition from Wellesley College, first prize in composition and theory from Boston University, and was elected to Pi Kappa Lambda, the national music honor society. In 1979 her song cycle, *Herstory I,* was chosen in a competition sponsored by WGBH-FM in Boston to be recorded by the Boston Musica Viva for broadcast on National Public Radio. The second cycle, *Herstory II,* was premièred in 1980 by Alea III under the direction of Theodore Antoniou as one of the finalists for the Politis Composition Prize.

Her *Three Studies* for piano, *Balance* for violin and cello, and *Fantasy* for piano are published by Arsis Press. The *Fantasy* has also been recorded on the Coronet label by Rosemary Platt.

Elizabeth Vercoe is a composer member of the American Music Center, the League of Women Composers and the American Society of University Composers, and is affiliated with Broadcast Music Incorporated (BMI).

GWYNETH WALKER

Gwyneth Walker is a resident of New Canaan, Connecticut. A graduate of Brown University and the Hartt School of Music, she has studied primarily with Arnold Franchetti. After several years as an assistant professor of theory at the Oberlin College Conservatory of Music, she has recently left teaching in order to compose on a full-time basis.

Ms. Walker's compositions have been widely performed. Among the more well-known works are: *Fanfare for the Washington Festival Orchestra,* premiered in D.C. in 1978 and *Sonata for Flute and Piano,* also premiered in Washington D.C. in 1978.

Her choral works have appeared in numerous concerts, the most memorable of which were the presentation in 1979 of *The Radiant Dawn* by the University of Notre Dame Chorale and the première of *As the Stars Had Told* on Christmas, 1979 by the University of Delaware Concert Choir.

Having spent her years of graduate study in Hartford, Ms. Walker has often collaborated with the musicians of this locale. She has lectured at the Hartford Musical Club and attended concerts of her works sponsored by this organization. In addition, her compositions are regularly performed by the faculty and students of the Hartt School of Music. She has especially enjoyed composing works for the guitar department.

Ms. Walker has written many songs, setting preexistent poems to music or occasionally providing her own text. *Though Love Be a Day,* a cycle for high voice and piano, was recently premiered in Oberlin, Ohio. *My Love Walks in Velvet* is a popular wedding song with an original text.

When not composing, Ms. Walker, a former tournament tennis player, can be found playing tennis, biking, swimming, running or walking near her Connecticut home.

JOELLE WALLACH

(BMI)

Joelle Wallach was born in New York City, and grew up in New York and Morocco. She began her musical studies early with private study and at the Juilliard Preparatory School, and excelled in the study of piano, voice, theory, and composition while also studying the violin and bassoon. Her studies continued at Sarah Lawrence College and at Columbia University, from which she holds respectively, bachelor's and master's degrees in musical composition. Composers with whom she has studied include Meyer Kupferman, Jack Beeson, and Mario Davidovsky.

Ms. Wallach's compositions have been performed and broadcast in many parts of the United States and Europe, and her choral work *On the Beach at Night Alone* won a major prize from Sigma Alpha Iota in 1980.

Ms. Wallach is an active performer as well as composer and has done substantial work in improvisation for dancers. A gifted teacher, she currently teaches both privately and for the State and City Universities of New York.

ELINOR REMICK WARREN

(ASCAP)

Elinor Remick Warren, born in Los Angeles in 1906, began composing and also music lessons at the age of five. While still in high school her compositions were first published by leading New York music publishers. Her studies in piano and composition continued in New York with distinguished teachers, and later in Paris with Nadia Boulanger. For several years she toured the United States as pianist and assisting artist with leading opera and concert singers, all of whom featured her songs. Her compositions are widely performed in the United States, Canada, and Europe, and *Abram in Egypt* was the featured work of the Israel Music Festival of 1976. She holds an honorary doctorate in music from Occidental College, and has received many commissions, awards, and honors. Her catalogue consists of more than 180 compositions for orchestra, voice, chamber music, chorus, piano, and major choral works with orchestra.

VALLY WEIGL

(BMI)

Austrian-born Vally Weigl studied piano with Richard Robert, musicology at Vienna University with Guido Adler, and composition with Karl Weigl, whom she later married. Upon completing her studies she assumed teaching responsibilities as Professor Robert's assistant and at Vienna University's Musicology Institute. She worked summers with visiting students near Salzburg during the music festivals.

In 1938, the Weigls moved to New York City, continuing their composing and performing activities, while Mrs. Weigl taught at the Institute for Avocational Music and the American Theatre Wing. In 1955, after receiving her M.A. from Columbia University, she pursued her lifelong interest in music therapy as chief music therapist at the New York Medical College. Mrs. Weigl also directed research projects at Mt. Sinai Hospital's Psychiatric Division and an old age home in New York City and has contributed many papers to the music therapy literature. She was a faculty member of the New School and has lectured widely in the United States and abroad.

In 1964, she became chairman (later cochairman) of the Friends' Arts For World Unity Committee for which she has organized international cultural programs. She is a member of the American Composers Alliance; the American Music Center; the National Federation of Music Clubs; a Fellow of the MacDowell Colony Association where she has twice been a composer-in-residence; a member of Composers, Authors and Artists of America, and of American University Composers.

Her music has been widely performed and is published by E.C. Schirmer, Theodore Presser, Galaxy Music, Jelsor Music, Broadcast Music, Inc.; her book, *Songs For a Child,* was published by Westminster Press.

In 1973, she was awarded recording grants by the American Composers Alliance and the Mark Rothko Foundation to record her clarinet trio, *New England Suite,* and lyrical cycle, *Nature Moods,* with prominent soloists of the New York area.

She is recipient of a fellowship grant from the National Endowment for the Arts, 1976, for completion of her Carl Sandburg cantata *The People, Yes,* premiered by Robert DeCormier at Carnegie Recital Hall in 1977.

RUTH SHAW WYLIE
(ASCAP)

Ruth Shaw Wylie was born in Cincinnati, Ohio, but moved to Detroit at an early age and remained there until 1943 when she began her first teaching position as head of composition and theory at the University of Missouri.

Her education includes an A.B. degree in Romance languages from Wayne State University, an M.A. in composition from the same institution and a Ph.D. in composition from the Eastman School of Music where she studied with Bernard Rogers and Howard Hanson. Further study was taken with Arthur Honegger, Samuel Barber, and Aaron Copland at the Berkshire Music Center.

She left the University of Missouri to come to Wayne State University in 1949 where she was head of composition until her retirement in 1969 with the rank of professor emeritus. While there, she organized, directed and played piano and flute in the Wayne State University Improvisation Chamber Ensemble which gave concerts throughout the Midwest for several years.

Her honors have been many and include fellowships from the Eastman School, the MacDowell Colony, the Huntington Hartford Foundation, the University of Missouri, Wayne State University and the Berkshire Music Center. Other grants and awards include a Bicentennial Commission/Grant from the Michigan Council for the Arts, an NEA Fellowship/Grant, the Friends of Harvey Gaul Award, Standard Awards from ASCAP, a grant from the Colorado Council on Arts and Humanities, and prizes from Mu Phi Epsilon, Baylor University and the Arizona Cello Society. She has also been granted numerous commissions.

She has written over fifty compositions in all media which have been widely performed throughout the United States.

She is a member of ASCAP, Phi Beta Kappa, American Society of University Composers, American Women Composers, International League of Women Composers, National Association of Composers, Mu Phi Epsilon, and the United States Chess Federation. She is listed in several reference works including *Dictionary of International Biography, International Who's Who in Music,* and *Who's Who of American Women.*

Upon retirement she moved to Salt Lake City and came to Estes Park, Colorado, in 1973 where she now devotes her time to composing, painting, hiking, skiing, golf, and tournament chess.

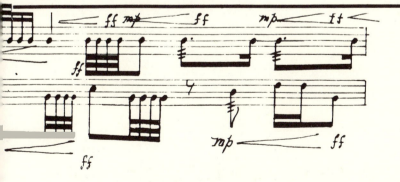

JUDITH LANG ZAIMONT

(ASCAP)

In Judith Lang Zaimont's works, a distinctive signature and fresh insights have synthesized a bold new impressionism that is at once romantic, spirited, and lyrical.

Ms. Zaimont's compositions have received over twenty-five awards, including ASCAP Standard Awards, a BMI Prize, the first prize gold medal in the Louis Moreau Gottschalk centenary competition, the Los Alamos International Competition Award, two Delius Competition prizes, and awards from the National Federation of Music Clubs and the Pittsburgh Flute Club. She is a Woodrow Wilson Fellow in composition, a MacDowell Colony Fellow, and holds degrees from Queens College and Columbia University where she studied composition with Hugo Weisgall, Otto Luening, and Jack Beeson. In 1971, Ms. Zaimont was awarded the Debussy Fellowship of the Alliance Française under which she studied in Paris with André Jolivet.

Her works have been performed throughout the United States, in England, France, Australia, and Germany. Among the groups that have commissioned pieces are the Gregg Smith Singers, Great Neck Choral Society, Cantica Hebraica, Primavera Quartet, and the New York Music Teachers Association. Ms. Zaimont's output includes approximately seventy art songs, chamber music and choral works, and a piano concerto and sacred service for orchestra. Her music is published by Broude Brothers Ltd., Alfred Publishing Company, Walton Music, Tetra Music and Galaxy Music Corporation and it has been recorded on the Golden Crest and Leonarda labels.

As a pianist, Ms. Zaimont toured the United States and made recordings as a member of a duo-piano team. She studied piano at the Juilliard School preparatory division as a student of Leland Thompson, and holds a degree in piano from the Long Island Institute of Music. Her articles on twentieth-century composition techniques, and a "Selective List of Twentieth Century Repertoire for Piano" are included in the *Piano Teacher's Guidebook,* published by Yorktown Music Press in 1980.

Ms. Zaimont is currently on the music faculty of the Peabody Conservatory of Music and her biography is listed in several standard reference works, among them the *International Who's Who in Music, Contemporary American Composers* and *International Encyclopedia of Women Composers.*

MARILYN ZIFFRIN

(ASCAP)

Marilyn J. Ziffrin was born in Moline, Illinois, on August 7, 1926. She now resides in New Hampshire, and is associate professor of music at New England College in Henniker, New Hampshire. Her major composition teachers were Alexander Tcherepnin and Karl Ahrendt.

She belongs to ASCAP, Sigma Alpha Iota, and other professional organizations; and she has won several composition prizes including the 1972 Delius Composition Competition. In addition to composing, she is working on a biography of Carl Ruggles.

ELLEN TAAFFE ZWILICH

(BMI)

Ellen Taaffe Zwilich, born in Miami, Florida, on April 30, 1939, studied at Florida State University and the Juilliard School, where her principal teachers were Roger Sessions and Elliott Carter. She has the distinction of being the first woman to receive the doctorate in composition from Juilliard.

Her *Symposium for Orchestra,* which was premiered by Pierre Boulez, was recently performed in Carnegie Hall by the American Symphony Orchestra under Kazuyoshi Akiyama. Her *Chamber Symphony* was premiered in Boston on November 30, 1979, by the Boston Musica Viva, Richard Pittman, conductor. Another new work, *Emlékezet,* on poems by Sándor Petöfi, was recently recorded by Magyar Radio in Budapest, Hungary.

Zwilich's music has been heard at major festivals, including the Festival of Contemporary Music at Tanglewood, the Aspen Music Festival, and the International Society for Contemporary Music "World Music Days." Her work has been performed on National Public Radio and radio in Sweden and Hungary, as well as in concert in Holland, Italy, Switzerland, and Scotland. She has received a Guggenheim Fellowship and grants from the Martha Baird Rockefeller Fund for Music, the National Endowment for the Arts, CAPS (New York State Council on the Arts) and ASCAP; among many awards are a gold medal in the 26th Annual International Composition Competition "G.B. Viotti" in Vercelli, Italy, and the Elizabeth Sprague Coolidge Chamber Music Prize.

Other Musicians' Biographies

KAREN McNERNEY FAMERA

c/o American Music Center
250 West 54th Street, Room 300
New York, New York 10019

Karen McNerney Famera is a performer and music librarian. She studied horn, theory, and composition at the Eastman School of Music, where she earned a Bachelor of Music degree in 1964, and at the Yale School of Music, where she earned a Master of Music degree in 1967. She furthered her studies with Marcel Moyse, participating in his wind chamber music seminars in Vermont from 1970 to 1975. In addition to solo and chamber recitals, Ms. Famera has performed in orchestras, bands, opera/music theater, the circus, and the Ice Capades. Recently, she formed a horn quartet, Cornucopia.

In 1973, Ms. Famera earned the Master of Library Science degree from Queens College, and has since been active as a music librarian, first at City College of New York, and since 1977 at the American Music Center. She is currently the Project Director of the American Music Center/New York Public Library Cataloging Project, funded by a grant from the National Endowment for the Humanities.

She is the author of *Mutes, flutters, and trills: a guide to composing for the horn* (Yale School of Music, thesis 1967), the editor/compiler of the *National Endowment for the Arts Composer/Librettist Program Collection at the American Music Center* (1979), and the *Catalog of the American Music Center Library*, volumes 2 - 3, and *Supplements* 1 - 4.

DIANE GOLD

1226 South Garner Street
State College, Pennsylvania 16801

Diane Gold is a member of the music faculties of Bucknell University, Juniata College, and the State College Music Academy. She received the Bachelor of Music degree from the Eastman School of Music, University of Rochester, and the Master of Arts degree from Columbia University Teachers College. She has studied flute with Joseph Mariano, Albert Tipton, and Julius Baker.

Ms. Gold has recently recorded "Music for flute and strings" for Leonarda Productions with the Alard String Quartet, featuring works by Mrs. H.H.A. Beach, Katherine Hoover, and Arthur Foote.

with them at the National Gallery, Washington, D.C., in New York on the American Landmark Festival Series, at Lincoln Center Library and at many colleges in the eastern United States. They have appeared on WQXR, WGMS, and WHUY radio and have recently commissioned works by Vivian Fine, Margaret Griebling, Will Gay Bottje, and John Bavicchi. The trio consists of flute, oboe, cello, and the combination of flute, piano, and cello.

Ms. Gold is principal flutist of the Nittany Valley Orchestra and a member of the Juniata Wind Quintet. She belongs to Sigma Alpha Iota, the National Flute Association and the League of Women Composers. She has performed at the Philadelphia Art Alliance and in New York at the Guggenheim Museum, A.I.R. Gallery, and the Donnell Library. Ms. Gold is also a performer on the baroque flute.

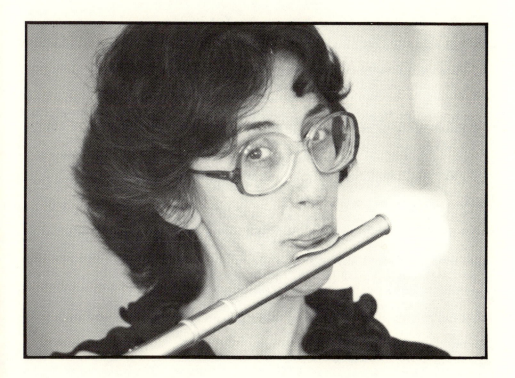

MARNIE HALL

c/o Leonarda Productions, Inc.
Post Office Box 124
Radio City Station
New York, New York 10101

Born June 5, 1942 in Clay Center, Kansas, Marnie Hall began violin studies at age nine. She entered the University of Kansas in 1960, joined the Kansas City Philharmonic in 1962, and completed her undergraduate studies in 1966. That September Ms. Hall entered the Manhattan School of Music in New York City, obtaining a Master of Music in violin in 1968. A free-lance violinist since 1966, Ms. Hall has performed with various orchestras, ballets, road shows, and Broadway shows. In 1972 she founded the Vieuxtemps String Quartet which concertized throughout the eastern United States and the Midwest until 1976.

In 1975 Ms. Hall researched and produced a two-disc anthology "Woman's Work" on her own label, Gemini Hall Records. This album introduces the music of eighteen European women composers who lived from 1587 to the present.

Following that release, Ms. Hall went on to found Leonarda Productions, a nonprofit tax-exempt corporation which is devoted to recording contemporary music in general and historical music by women composers. Leonarda's first six releases, which date from late 1979 through 1980, include the music of a number of women composers: Judith Lang Zaimont, Katherine Hoover, Rebecca Clarke, Louise Farrenc, Lili Boulanger, Germaine Tailleferre, Ludmila Ulehla and Ruth Schonthal. Other releases are being planned, and Leonarda is also in the process of publishing facsimile editions of some of its recorded music.

JANE WEINER LePAGE

c/o Music Department
North Adams State College
North Adams, Massachusetts 02147

Jane Weiner LePage was born in 1931, one of four children of Rose Metz and Robert George Allen. She graduated from Boston University with a Bachelor of Music degree with a minor in trombone, and received the Master of Science degree from the University of Massachusetts. She served also as a graduate fellow of the Learned Society of America, the Fred Waring School of Music, and the Eastman School of Music.

Ms. LePage is currently the chairperson and associate professor of music at North Adams State College. She cofounded the Berkshire Chorale, a semiprofessional vocal group, and has often been guest speaker and clinician for the Massachusetts State Music Educators Association. In 1978, she addressed the National Association of Music Educators convention on "The Future of Graduate Music Schools in the U.S."

Ms. LePage is past president of the American Association of University Women in Berkshire County, and she served a five-year gubernatorial appointment on the Advisory Board of Berkshire Community College. She has also served on the Williamstown Public School Committee, and presently holds a five-year appointment to the town's sign commission.

Her biographical note appears in *International Who's Who in Music and Musicians Directory; The World of Women; Who's Who in America,* and *Who's Who in the East.* She has published many articles on general music subjects, and her book, *Women Composers, Conductors and Musicians of the Twentieth Century,* volume 1, was published in 1980 by Scarecrow Press, Inc.

151

ROSEMARY PLATT

c/o School of Music
Ohio State University
1899 North College Road
Columbus, Ohio 43210

Rosemary Platt, pianist, has an active career as a soloist and chamber musician. Since receiving the Doctor of Music degree from the Florida State University, where she studied with noted Hungarian pianist Edward Kilenyi, she has concertized extensively in the United States and Canada and performed frequently on public radio and television. At the invitation of Antonio Janigro, Dr. Platt studied chamber music at the Mozarteum in Salzburg, Austria, for several summers. Recent activities of the Davis/Platt Duo, with Michael Davis, violinist, have included a concert at the Phillips Collection in Washington, D.C., major recital series including the *Ten Sonatas for Violin and Piano* by Beethoven, and two critically acclaimed recordings of contemporary British compositions.

Ms. Platt is a noted exponent of music by women composers and her performances of their music have been aired on radio throughout the eastern and midwestern United States and on Australian Radio. Her recording, "Music by Women Composers," features works by Jane Brockman, Ann Callaway, Emma Lou Diemer, Nancy Van de Vate, and Elizabeth Vercoe.

JEANNIE G. POOL

Post Office Box 436
Ansonia Station
New York, New York 10023

Jeannie G. Pool, born November 6, 1951, in Springfield, Ohio, is a music historian, writer, and critic who specializes in music by women composers. She is the author of *Women in Music History: A Research Guide* and lectures throughout the United States on the history of women in classical music. She is founder of the First National Congress on Women in Music held in March 1981 at Barnard College. She has published numerous articles on women in music including a major feature in the January 1979 issue of the *Music Educators Journal* entitled, "American Women Composers: Up From the Footnotes," which surveys the contributions of women composers in the United States from 1776 to the present. Her book, *Women Composers of Classical Music* was published in 1980 by G. K. Hall of Boston. She has done numerous radio programs on women composers and their works and was codirector of the Conference/Workshop on 20th-Century String Quartets by Women Composers held March 8, 1980, at Trinity School in New York City.

She studied flute at the Hartford Conservatory of Music from 1973 to 1974; received a B.A. in music from Hunter College of the City University of New York in 1977; and did graduate work in historical musicology at Columbia University. In 1976 she was a student at the University of Vienna on a scholarship from the Austrian government.

LIST OF MUSIC

GUIDE TO USE OF THE LIST OF MUSIC

The classified list of works by genre/medium, sub-arranged alphabetically by composer/title, has been designed primarily for use by performers, with the objective of stimulating more performances of music by women and assisting research of contemporary music of all types. Only original works by members of the International League of Women Composers are included. The table of contents details the arrangement within each genre by medium. Composers were asked to submit the information provided with each entry: title, instrumentation, author of text (in parentheses), composition date, duration, level of difficulty, and source of availability. Texts are in English unless otherwise noted. Six levels of difficulty have been coded on a scale of 1 to 3 (easy to difficult), incorporating plus signs after the number to indicate a more subtle distinction in some entries. Thus, 1+ is a work of very moderate difficulty, suitable for all but raw beginners. Titles preceded by a dagger (†) indicate a prize-winning work, and titles preceded by a circle (⊕) indicate a recorded work. Additional information, such as performance history, could be obtained directly from the composer, or, for American works, from the American Music Center.

To assist in obtaining copies of the music, either for purchase or on loan, a publisher/archive/composer list with addresses has been provided immediately following the complete bibliography. Users interested in the scope of one woman's output will welcome the inclusion of an alphabetical composer index at the end of this volume.

Note that compositions available only through the composer have been assigned the locator code "C".

TABLE OF ABBREVIATIONS

A	alto	hpsd	harpsichord
acap	a cappella	*Hung*	Hungarian
accord	accordion		
al-clar	alto clarinet	*Ind*	Indian
al-fl	alto flute	instr	instruments
al-rec	alto recorder	*It*	Italian
al-sax	alto saxophone		
arr.	arranged	kybd	keyboard
B	bass	*Lat*	Latin
b dm	bass drum	liturg	liturgical
Bar	baritone		
B-Bar	bass-baritone	mand	mandolin
bar hn	baritone horn	marmb	marimba
bar-sax	baritone saxophone	med	medium
bcl	bass clarinet	Mez	Mezzo-soprano
bfl	bass flute	mx chor	mixed chorus
bsn	bassoon	mot	motet
b-tbn	bass trombone		
		narr	narrator
cant	cantata	No.	number
cbsn	contrabassoon	Nos.	numbers
cel	celesta		
Chin	Chinese	ob	oboe
cl	clarinet	obblig	obbligato
cbcl	contrabass clarinet	Op.	Opus
chor	chorus	opt	optional, ad lib.
cond	conductor	ora	oratorio
contr	contralto	orch	orchestra
cym	cymbal(s)	org	organ
db	double bass	perc	percussion
dbl chor	double chorus	pic	piccolo
desc	descant	pic-tpt	piccolo trumpet
dm	drum	pno	pianoforte
		pno red	piano reduction
educ	educational material	pno-voc sc	piano-vocal score
elect.	electronic	pub	published
Eng	English		
Enghn	English horn	qnt	quintet
eq voices	equal voices	qt	quartet
fl	flute	rec	recorder
Fr	French	*Russ*	Russian
fr-hnd	four-hands		
Ger	German	S	soprano
glock	glockenspiel	sac	sacred
gr	grade(s)	sax	saxophone
gtr	guitar	sc	score
		sec	secular
harmca	harmonica	sn dm	snare drum
Heb	Hebrew	sop-cl	soprano clarinet
hndbl	handbells	sop-sax	soprano saxophone
hn	French horn	speak chor	speaking chorus
hrp	harp	stgs	strings

stg qt	string quartet	unis	unison
T	tenor	var	various
tamb	tambourine	vcl	violoncello
Tam-T	Tam-Tam	vibe	vibraphone
temp blks	temple blocks	vla	viola
ten-sax	tenor saxophone	vln	violin
timp	timpani		
treb	treble	ww	woodwinds
tbn	trombone		
tpt	trumpet	xylo	xylophone
trans	translated by		

SOLO VOCAL MUSIC — UNACCOMPANIED

ANDERSON, BETH

Crackers and Checkers (1977)	1:00	2+	C
I Can't Stand It (1976)	3:00	2+	C
If I Were a Poet (1975)	2:00	2+	T-ST
I Wish I Were Single Again (1977)	1:00	2+	C
Kitchy Kichin (1979)	3:00	3	C
Nongovernmental Process (1976)	1:00	2+	Poet
Poem to Michael, John, and Alison (1975)	3:00	2+	C
Sally's Success (1979)		3	C
Six Stories in Series (1979)		3	C
Swatches (1966) (5-song cycle for solo S)	5:00	2+	ACA
Yes sir ree (1978) (solo voice and opt perc)	3:00	2+	C

BEATH

Seawatcher: A Song for Solo Voice (David Cox) (1974)		JAS

HSU

Allelujah (1960) (S)	6:00	W-Y
At a Glance (Chin) (1960) (S)	3:00	W-Y
The Founders (Ruth Murray Jones) (S)	2:00	W-Y
Let Me Serve (Isabelle Carter Young) (S)	3:00	W-Y
Regret (1955) (S)	3:00	W-Y
Song of Ching Hai (Chin) (1956) (S)	3:00	W-Y

LACKMAN

Cadenza for Solo Voice   3:00   2   C

PIZER

When to the Sessions of Sweet Silent Thought, Op. 47
    (Shakespeare) (1978)
    (med-high voice)   5:00   3   AMC

SOLO VOCAL MUSIC — WITH
KEYBOARD ACCOMPANIMENT

ALLEN

Night Blooms (1978)
    (S and pno)   4:00   2   ACA

ANDERSON, BETH

Beauty Runs Faster (1978)   1:00 - 3:00   2+   Jsh

A Day (1967)   1:00   2+   ACA

In Six (1979)   1:00 - 2:00   3   C

Paranoia (1969)
    (voice and pno or voice and 2 fl)   1:00   2+   ACA

A Postcard (1967)   1:00   2+   ACA

Time Stands Still (1978)   3:00   2+   Jsh

Twinkle Tonight (1978)   3:00   2+   Jsh

Womanrite (1972)   4:00+   2+   Jsh

ANDERSON, JAY

Among the Leaves (1954)   1:45   2   C

Bird in the Willow Tree (1953)   2:00   2   C

Bye Bye Good Friend (1960)   2:30   2   C

Christ My Refuge (M.B. Eddy) (1943)   2   Dom

Down by the River (1950)   2:15   2   C

Evening Star (1951)	2:00	2	C
Farewell Dear Voyager (1966)	2:00	2	C
A Flower (1966)	2:00	2	C
Little Grey Dove (1963)	2:10	2	C
Loneliness Walks Beside Me (1951)	2:00	2	C
Love Must Be As A Summer's Day (1951)	2:00	2	C
Man Sleep'n By My Side (1951)	2:05	2	C
My Lady (1951)	1:45	2	C
My Love, My Love (1952)	2:00	2	C
My Mother Entreats Me (1952)	1:45	2	C
Reflections (1942)	1:45	2	C
Sadness Comes at Night While Others Sleep (1955)	2:00	2	C
September (1954)	2:05	2	C
Song in the Mist (1967)	2:40	2	C
Spring (1963)	2:05	2	C
Stranger Passing By (1956)	1:45	2	C
Swallows Fly Gaily (1954)	2:00	2	C
There Was a Time (1965)	2:10	2	C
Tiger and Rabbit (1966)	2:00	2	C
Tunes Number One, Two & Three (1926)	1:45	2	C
Tunes Number Four, Five & Six (1929)	1:15	2	C
Turquoise (1953)	1:50	2	C
Wendell is Dead (1957)	1:50	2	C
Wendy (1958)	1:50	2	C
Willow Tree Wings With the Wind (1959)		2	C

BEATH

Indonesian Triptych (1977)
(solo voice and pno, also instrumental ensemble)   C

In This Garden (David Cox) (1976)
(cycle of 5 songs for med voice with pno accompaniment)   JAS

Songs from the Beast's Choir (Carmen Bernos do Gaxztold)
  (cycle of five songs) C

Three Cautionary Songs (David Cox) (1975) C

BEESON

Anita
  (T and pno) 4:00 3 C

⊕ *Far Away Love*
  (S and pno) 2:30 2 C

BOLZ

Splendor of the Sea and Splendor of the Seasons
  (2 songs for high voice and pno) 2:08 1+ C

Winds of Heaven and Winds of the Waters
  (2 songs for high voice and pno) 6:02 2 C

de BOHUN [Boone]

Beyond the Stars (1970) 2:05 2 Ars

Celestia (1954) 2:00 2 Ars

Fantasia (1954) 3:20 2 Ars

Goodnight Kiss (1955) 2:05 1 Ars

Lovely Heart (1956) 3:20 3 Ars

Mirrored Love (1961) 2:30 2 Ars

Sea Thoughts (1954) 1:50 2+ Ars

Sonnet (Shakespeare) (1957) 3:00 2 Ars

Time Cannot Claim This Hour (1955) 3:00 3 Ars

When Songs Have All Been Sung (1956) 1:30 1 Ars

Winter Song (1968) 1:40 1 Ars

BRENNER

Be Not Grieved (Baha'i writings) (1976) 2:00 2 C

The Day is Over (1971) 2:00 2 C

The Desire (1974) 2:00 2 C

Inheritance (1971) 2:00 2 C

Little Funny Things (1978)	2:00	2	C
Little Girl, You're Beginning, Not Ending (1974)	2:00	2	C
Love and Unity (Baha'i writings) (1973)	2:00	2	C
Mischakadunsky (1974)	2:00	2	C
Round and Around (1978)	2:00	2	C
Sun in the Sky (1971)	2:00	2	C

BRITAIN

All Alone on the Prairie (1945)	4:00	C
†*Baby I Can't Sleep* (1936)	3:00	C
Barcarola (1961)	4:00	Oss
Berceuse (1927)	3:00	C
Casablanca by the Sea (1967)	5:00	LC
The Chalice (1948)	4:00	UW
The Earth Does Not Wish for Beauty (1940)	8:00	C
Elegy (1937)	3:00	C
Elvira de la Luz (1967)	5:00	Hero
Eternal Cycle (1942)	4:00	C
Eternal Spirit (1964)	3:00	C
Farewell at Dawn (1949)	4:00	C
Fulfillment (1980)	4:00	C
Goddess of Inspiration (1948)	3:00	C
Had I a Cave (Robert Burns) (1926) (Bar and pno)	3:00	Hero
Half Rising Moon (Tabb) (1926)	3:00	OH
Have I Told You (1967)	4:00	C
Hush My Heart (1961)	4:00	Hero
I Found a Star (1980)	3:00	C
In Living Ecstasy (1938)	4:00	C
Lasso of Time (1940)	4:00	NK

Life's Ebb and Flow (1941)	4:00	C
Little Man (1951)	3:00	C
Lotusland (1972)	4:00	Hero
Love Me Today (1942)	4:00	C
Love Song (1978)	4:00	C
Love Still Has Something of the Sea (1952)	4:00	C
Lullaby of the Bells (1964)	4:00	Hero
My Dream (1956)	3:00	C
†*Nirvana* (1927)	3:00	Hero
Open the Door to Me (1928)	4:00	Hero
Requiem (1929)	3:00	C
Revelation (1958)	3:00	C
The Secret (1962)	3:00	C
Serenade (1942)	3:00	C
Soil Magic (1955)	3:00	C
Sunken City (1928)	4:00	C
Stillness (1940)	3:00	C
A Tribute (1967)	3:00	Hero
Twilight Moon (1938)	4:00	C
Vision of Loveliness (1948)	4:00	C
Weep Not (1979)	4:00	C
Western Testament (Sara Lee Stadelman) (1964)	60:00	C
When We Shall Part (1934)	4:00	C
† *Withered Flowers* (Friedl Schreyvogal) (1926)		ComP
You (1961)	4:00	Hero
Your Hand (1949)	3:00	C

BRUSH

And I Heard a Great Voice (sac solo with kybd)	5:00	2+	C

Atterbrand	4:00	2	C
Bartlesville, Our Town	5:00	2	Brt
Give Me the Sea (1967) (vocal solo with kybd)	5:00	3	C
God of Grace and God of Glory (hymn for solo voice and kybd)			C
Goddess of the Sun	5:00	3	C
Hill Girl's Lament (solo voice with kybd)			
Like the Shore Bird (1954) (coloratura S with kybd)	5:00	3	C
Love Divine (hymn for solo voice with kybd)			C
Meadowlarks (1953) (coloratura S with kybd)	6:00	3	C
My Life is Filled with Music (1957) (solo voice with kybd)	5:00	3	C
O Those Hills of Oklahoma	5:00	2	C
Twilight (1958) (vocal solo with kybd)	4:00	2+	C
Velvet Shoes (1957) (vocal solo with kybd)	4:00	2+	C

CECCONI-BATES

Some Cheese for Charles (1963) (narr and pno)	8:00	2	C

COHEN

Song (1955) (S and pno)	10:00	2	C

DEMBO

Song Cycle (Anna Akhmatova) (S and pno)	20:00	3	C
3 Songs (Chin) (S and pno)	5:00	2	C
3 Songs (Edna St. Vincent Millay) (S and pno)	5:00	2+	C

DIEMER

A Miscellany of Love Songs (1970-76)
(T or S and pno)   18:00   3   See

Song Cycle (1958)
(Bar and pno)   C

Song Cycle (1967)
(T and pno)   C

Song Cycle (1950)
(S and pno)   C

Song Cycle (1958)
(S and pno)   C

FORMAN

⊕ *E.E. Cummings Songs* (3)
(S and pno)   9:00   2+   C

FULLER-HALL

Sephestia's Lullaby (1978)
(S and pno)   3:50   2+   C

GLAZIER

A Woman of Valor
(S and pno)   4:00   3   C

HAYS

For Woman
(5 songs for Mez and pno)   11:00   3   Q-H

HEINRICH

Five Nocturnes, Op. 21 (Robert Frost)
(S and pno)   15:00   1+   C

Sacred Song Cycle on Isaiah Texts, Op. 12
(S and org)   15:00   2   C

HOOVER

Lullay, Lullay (1971)
(S and pno)   3:00   2   AMC

To Many a Well (1977)
(Mez or S and pno)   5:00   2   AMC

HYSON

Balou (1967)
(S and pno) .... 2:30   2+   C

Songs of Job's Daughter (1970)
(S and pno) .... 12:00   2+   C

JANKOWSKI

Cycles (1969)
(5 songs for S and pno) .... 10:00   2+   C

KENDRICK

April Whimsy
(med-high voice and pno) .... 3:00   2   Fem

Before the World Was
(med-high voice and pno) .... 3:00   2   SMus

Hear My Cry, O God
(med-high voice and pno) .... 3:00   2   SMus

Hush Little David
(med voice and pno) .... 3:00   2   Fem

In This Soft Velvet Night
(med-high voice and pno) .... 3:00   2   Fem

I Will Lift Up My Eyes Unto the Hills
(med-high voice and pno) .... 3:00   2   SMus

Jade Summer
(med-high voice and pno) .... 3:00   2   Fem

Lo! I Am With You Always, Unto the End of the World
(med-high voice and pno) .... 3:00   2   Fem

Look Unto Me, Saith Our God
(med voice and pno) .... 3:00   2   SMus

The Lord God Omnipotent Reigneth
(med-high voice and pno) .... 3:00   2   Fem

Music is Beauty
(med voice and pno) .... 3:00   2   Fem

My Sister Sang to Me
(med-high voice and pno) .... 3:00   2   Fem

Song About Sue
(med-high voice and pno) .... 3:00   2   Fem

Tribute—To My Mother
(med-high voice and pno) .... 3:00   2   Fem

Wealth of Mine (med-high voice and pno)	3:00	2	Fem
When I Was Twelve (med-high voice and pno)	3:00	2	Fem
White Sky (high S and pno)	3:00	2	Bel-M

LACKMAN

Hair (S or T and pno)	4:00	2+	C

MARCUS

† *American Song Cycle* (Robert Frost) "Good Hours" "Stopping by Woods on a Snowy Evening" "Tree At My Window"	12:00	3	C
Ask Me No More (Tennyson)	5:00	3	C
Desert Winds	3:00	2	SMP
Evening Song (Sidney Lanier)	5:00	3	C
Four Preludes on Playthings To The Wind (Carl Sandburg)	20:00	3	C
Music I Heard (Conrad Aiken)	5:00	3	C
Song Cycle (Dylan Thomas) "In the Beginning" "I Have Longed to Move Away" "Here in This Spring"	18:00	3	C

PAULL

Two Songs for Baritone (1971) "In a Silent World" "Where Shall We Go?" (Bar and pno)	10:00	3	AMC
Two Songs for Soprano (1971-74) "In a Silent World" "Who We Are" (S and pno)	6:00	2	AMC

PIZER

Five Haiku, Op. 48 (1978) (med-high voice and pno)	6:00	3	AMC
Five Haiku II, Op. 50 (1979) (Mez and pno)	8:00	3	AMC

Holy Eucharist, Rite II, Op. 46 (1978)
  (according to the Episcopal Proposed Book of Common
  Prayer)
  (voice and pno or org)   8:00   2   AMC

Look Down, Fair Moon, Op. 36 (Walt Whitman) (1976)
  (high or med voice and pno)   3:00   3   AMC

PREOBRAJENSKA

Art Songs, Op. 1 (1945)
  (voice and kybd)   45:00   AMC

Undertones of Frost (L.V. Inke) (1960)   20:00   AMC

PROCACCINI

Memory, Op. 76 (1979)
  (vocalise for S and pno)   9:00   3   C

3 Liriche, Op. 1 (1955)   8:00   2   C

REID

Five Haiku (1973)   8:00   2+   C

RICHTER

She at His Funeral (1954)   3:00   3   CF

⊕ *Transmutation* (1949)   11:00   3   CF

⊕ *Two Chinese Songs* (1953)   3:00   2   CF

ROBERTS

Class Song   4:00   2   C

In a Secret Garden   3:00   2   C

Love Unspoken   3:00   2   C

ROGERS

Calendar (Eve Merriam)
  (S or 2 S and pno)   3:00   2   C

I Shall Be Coming Back to You (Hilda, age 10)
  (S and pno)   5:00   2   C

Six Songs for Soprano and Piano (Eugène Guillevic, *Fr*) 16:00   2+   C

Three Songs for Soprano and Piano (Adrienne Rich)   12:00   2+   C

To Make a Play (May Swenson)
(S and pno)   5:00   2   C

SAMTER

Drei Lieder (R.M. Rilke)   6:00   C

Drei Lieder (Stefan George)   5:00   C

Sechs Lieder (R. Magnus)   12:00   C

Vier Lieder nach Chr. Morgenstern   5:00   C

"Winter" Zwei Lieder (W. Borchert, A. Holz)   3:00   C

Zwei Lieder (Ingerborg Bachmann)   12:00   C

Zwei Lieder (Christa Reinig)   4:00   C

Berlin-Zyklus (funf Lieder after Alcona Gustas)   10:00   C

Song of Yourself (H.J. Heise)   4:00   C

Zwei Lieder
"Herbst" (Apollinaire)
"Grimace d'Artiste" (E. Södergran)   3:00   C

Der Schaffner (J. Prévert)
(narr and pno)   3:00   C

Morgenmahlzeit (J. Prévert)
(narr and pno)   2:00   C

Die Kartenhexe (W. Mehring)
(narr and pno)   3:00   C

SCHONTHAL

By The Roadside (W. Whitman) (1975)
(S and pno)   6:30   2+   OUP

Nine Lyric-Dramatic Songs (W.B. Yeats) (1960)
(Mez and pno)   21:00   2+   C

Seven Songs of Love and Sorrow (1977)
(S and pno)   18:00   2+   C

Songs With Words by R.M. Rilke (1939-42)
(S and pno)   23:00   3   C

⊕ *Totengesänge* (Schonthal) (1963)
(S and pno)   23:00   3   C

SEMEGEN

† *Prayer of Hannah (1 Samuel 2)* (1968)
(S and pno)   6:00   2   ACA

Silent, Silent Night (William Blake) (1965)
(T and pno)   6:00   2   ACA

SIMONS

Three Songs (Hilda Morley)

"Early Ballad"
"Sleep Song"
"Aubade"
(Mez and pno)   5:00   3   ACA

SINGER

American Indian Song Suite
(4 songs based on traditional Indian songs)
(med voice and pno)   5:00   2+ C

† *Arno is Deep* (Frederika Blankner)
(med voice and pno)   3:00   2+ C

† *A Cycle of Love: A Woman's Story* (Marx, Lowell,
Singer, Mason)
(S and pno)   9:00   2+ HB

Dirge (Madeline Mason)
(med voice and pno)   4:00   2+ C

Downing the Bell Tower (Suzanne Dale)
(med voice and pno)   3:00   2+ C

Gift (Patricia Benton)
(high voice and pno)   2:00   2+ C

Hannah (Lloyd Schwartz)
(Mez and pno)   3:30   2+ C

† *Memoria* (Frederika Blankner)
(high voice and pno)   4:00   2+ C

† *Sanguinaria* (Bernard Grebanier)
(med voice and pno)   3:30   2+ C

Summons (Patricia Benton)
(med voice and pno)   3:30   2+ HB

Where Do the Wild Birds Fly? (Jeanne Singer)
(med voice and pno)   3:30   2+ C

SMELTZER

A Doctor Date with Doctor Brute (1980)
(Mez and pno)   15:00   1+ C

Come In (1960)
(S and pno)   4:00   2   C

Love (1960)
(S and pno)   3:00   1   C

Song (1977)
(S and pno)   4:00   2   C

SMITH

Three Love Songs for Solo Voice and Piano (1954-55)

"I Will Sing the Song"
"The Door That I Would Open"
"The Love I Hold"
(high voice or med voice or low voice and pno)   5:00   2   Mowb

Invocation for Solo Voice and Piano (1967)
(med-high voice or low voice and pno)   2:00   2   Mowb

SWISHER

Love's Shadow Comes Slow
(low voice and pno)   3:00   2   AMC

Rest, Love
(low voice and pno)   3:00   2   AMC

Sisters
(cycle for S and pno)   3:00   2   AMC

Sonnets: for
(cycle for S and pno)   9:00   3   C

VAN DE VATE

† *Cradlesong* (1962)
(S and pno)   3:00   1+ AMC

† *Four Somber Songs* (1970)
(cycle for Mez and pno)   11:00   3   AMC

† *The Earth Is So Lovely* (1962)
(med voice and pno)   3:00   1+ AMC

To the East and To the West (1972)
(high voice and pno)   3:00   1+ AMC

Two Songs (1960)
    "Death Is the Chilly Night"
    "Loneliness"
    (voice and pno)   4:00 2 AMC

Youthful Age (1960)
    (S and pno)   :45 2 AMC

VELLÈRE

O Blanche Fleur (Ch. Van Lerberghe, *Fr*) (1934)   4:00 2 C

Les Cloches (Apollinaire, *Fr*) (1949)   2 C

Croquis (Maurice Carème) (1948)
    six songs   2 Brg

Entre Les Biches et Les Daims (Ch. Van Lerberghe)   2 C

Faune (G. Marlow) (1933)   2 C

La Ronde (Paul Fort) (1917)   1:30 2 C

Trois Petits Poèmes (Marie Brunfaut) (1936)   2 C

Vous M'avez Dit Tel Soir (Verhaeren) (1940)   2 C

VERCOE

Eight Riddles from Symphosius (1964)
    (Mez and pno)   12:00 2+ C

WALKER

Collected Songs (1976)
    (8 songs for med-high voice and pno)   2 Walk

My Love Walks in Velvet (1978)
    (med-high voice and pno)   4:00 1 Walk

Though Love Be a Day (1979)
    (8 songs for high voice and pno)   13:00 2 Walk

Wedding Song (1976)
    (high voice and org)   4:00 2 Walk

WARREN

Dreams   C

For You with Love   GSch

King Arthur's Farewell from "The Legend of King Arthur"   C

Light the Lamps Up!		C
Melody Out of My Heart		C
More Things are Wrought by Prayer		HWG
Silent Noon		C
Singing Earth (pno-vocal version)		C
Snow Towards Evening (in *Songs by 22 Americans*)		GSch
Sonnets for Soprano (Millay) (pno-vocal version)		CF
Sweetgrass Range		C

20 SELECTED SONGS BY ELINOR REMICK WARREN
"Sailing Homeward"
"Lady Lo-Fu"
"To A Blue-Eyed Baby"
"To The Farmer"
"If You Have Forgotten"
"White Horses of the Sea"
"Lonely Roads"
"Christmas Candle"
"The Nights Remember"
"The Little Betrothed"
"God Be In My Heart"
"Heather"
"Who Loves the Rain"
"Wander Shoes"
"By A Fireside"
"We Two"
"The Wind Sings Welcome"
"Summer Stars"
"Tawny Days"
"Great Memories"
(med and high voice and pno)   CF

WEIGL

† *A Christmas Carol*   1   ACA

WYLIE

God's Grandeur, Op. 13 No. 2 (G. Manley Hopkins)
(S and pno)   3:00   2+   C

Light, Op. 16 No. 4 (Elizabeth Scott)
(S and pno)   2+   C

The Wanderer (Jeanne Torosian) (1940)   2+   C

ZAIMONT

The Ages of Love (1971)
   "Chaste Love" (Lord Byron)
   "Love's White Heat" (Edna St. Vincent Millay)
   "Disdainful, Fickle Love" (Millay)
   "An Older Love" (Millay)
   "Love's Echo" (Christina Rossetti)
   (cycle for Bar and pno)   12:30   3   ACA

⊕ *Chansons Nobles et Sentimentales (Fr)* (1974)
   "Harmonie du Soir" (Baudelaire)
   "Chanson d'Automne" (Verlaine)
   "Claire de Lune" (Verlaine)
   "Dans l'interminable ennui de la plaine" (Verlaine)
   "Départ" (Rimbaud)
   (high voice and pno)   13:00   3   ACA

† *Coronach* (Doris Kosloff, Adelaide Crapsey, J. Zaimont,
   William Jay Smith, Stephen Crane) (1970)
   (5 songs for S and pno)   11:30   2   AMC

 † *Four Songs for Mezzo-Soprano and Piano*
   (e.e. cummings) (1965)   9:00   3   AMC

⊕ *Greyed Sonnets:* Five Serious Songs (1975)
   "Soliloquy" (Millay)
   "Let It Be Forgotten" (Sara Teasdale)
   "A Season's Song" (Millay)
   "Love's Autumn" (Millay)
   "Entreaty" (Christina Rossetti)
   (cycle for S and pno)   14:00   3   ACA

High Flight (John Gillespie Magee, Jr.) (1980)
   (high voice and pno)   3:20   1+   C

PSALM 23 (1979)
   (Mez and pno)   8:15   2+   C

ZIFFRIN

Three Songs for Woman's Voice (1957)
   "Woman at the Spring Drip" (Millen Brand)
   "Song of Night" (Millen Brand)
   "The Maid Who Sells the Rose" (Carolyn Hill)
   (Mez and pno)   5:00   3   C

ZWILICH

Einsame Nacht (Herman Hesse, *Ger*)
   (song cycle for Bar and pno)   12:00   3   C

Emlékezet (Sándor Petŏfi, *Hung*)
   (S and pno)   7:00   3   C

Im Nebel (Herman Hesse, *Ger*) (contr and pno)	4:00	3	C
Trompeten (Georg Trakl, *Ger*) *Trumpets* (Eng trans composer) (S and pno)	3:00	3	C

● # SOLO VOCAL MUSIC — WITH TAPE ●

ANDERSON, BETH

The People Rumble Louder (1975) (solo voice and tape)	1:00	2+	Asm
Thus Spake Johnston (1973) (solo voice and electronics)	45:00	2+	C

COHEN

Beginning (1974) (S and tape)	10:00	2	C

GILBERT

Tracings (1977) (tape, poetry)	5:00		C

HAYS

Southern Voices (tape with/without narrative live)	18:00		Q-H

● # CHAMBER VOCAL MUSIC — SINGLE VOICE WITH ONE TO FOUR PLAYERS ●

ALLEN

Love Song (Marlowe) (1978) (Enghn and S)	8:00	1	ACA

ANDERSON, BETH

He Says He's Got (1977) (voice and gtr)	2:00	2+	C
Ocean Motion Mildew Mind (1979) (solo voice and perc)	3:00	3	C

BEATH

Askesis (Günther Grass) (1975)
(voice, hpsd, vcl, perc)   C

Poems From the Chinese (1979)
(cycle of songs for cl, vcl, pno with solo female voice)   C

BEESON

The Dead
(S, vln, fl, pno)   4:00   2   C

The Wave
(S, vln, fl, pno)   2:30   2   C

BOLZ

Invocation (1957)
(S and stg qt)   3:00   2   C

† *Such Be the Thought* (Walt Whitman) (1976)
(med voice, fl, vcl, pno)   6:03   3   C

de BOHUN [Boone]

Slumber Song (1957)
(voice and melody instrument)   2:40   2   Ars

Songs of Estrangement (1958)
(S with stg qt)   6:45   2   Ars

BRITAIN

Overtones (1970)
(fl and voice)   3:00   UCLA

CECCONI-BATES

Something Songs Unrelated (R. Wayne Archer) (1976)
(S, cl (E-flat pic cl), pno)   12:00 2   C

Three Serious Songs (W. de la Mare, Philip Agree) (1977)
(S, cl, pno)   10:00 2   C

CHANCE

Duo I (1975)
(S with finger cym and fl)   7:00   3   See

Three Rilke Songs (1966)
(S, fl, Enghn, vcl)   14:00 3   See

DEMBO

4 Poems of Emily Dickinson
(narr, fl)   6:00   2   C

Four Songs (Elinor Wylie)
(S, hn, pno)   15:00   3   C

Songs of Pan (James Joyce)
(S, fl, hrp)   8:00   2   C

DIEMER

Four Chinese Love Poems (1965)
(S, hrp or pno)   10:00   3   See

FORMAN

⊕ *Lorca Songs* (4)
(S and gtr)   9:00   2   C

Rilkelieder (3)
(S, 2 fl, Enghn, vcl)   9:00   2   C

GARDNER

⊕ *Changing* (1974)
(Mez and gtr)   4:00   2   Iris

Sea Chantress (1978)
(voice, fl, hammered dulcimer)   3:00   1   Iris

Song of Our Coming (1976)
(Mez and gtr)   3:00   2   Iris

Thirteen Songs: Collection (1974)
(Mez and gtr or autoharp)   3:00-5:00   2+   Iris
                                                         each

Three Mother Songs (1977)
(Mez and gtr)   2:00-4:00   2+   Iris
                                                         each

GILBERT

Circumflexions on Mallarmé (1977)
(S)   3:00   2   C

HEINRICH

Birches, Op. 9 (Robert Frost)
(song cycle for S and vln and vla [or pno])   23:00   3   C

Five Shakespearean Sonnets, Op. 14
(narr, vln)   14:00   2   C

HOOVER

Four Carols (1970)
(S, fl)   9:00   2   AMC

*Selima, or Ode on the Death of a Favorite Cat
Drowned in a Tub of Goldfishes* (1979)
(S, cl, pno)   6:30   3   AMC

Seven Haiku (1973)
(S, fl)   7:30   3   AMC

Wings (1974)
"Acceptance"
(S, fl, cl, vln, pno)   3:30   2+   AMC
"Proud Songsters"
(S, fl, cl, vln)   2:15   2+   AMC
"Auspex"
(S, fl, cl, vln, pno)   3:00   2+   AMC

HSU

Evening Prayer (*Chin*)
(S with vln obblig)   3:00   W-Y

Light of God (*Chin/Eng*) (1960)
(S with fl or vln obblig)   4:00   W-Y

Parting Song (*Chin*) (1956)
(S with cl obblig)   4:00   W-Y

Ring Out Liberty Bell (1976)
(vocal solo with hrp and vibe)   6:00   W-Y

Songs of Nature, cycle for Soprano with optional
percussion obblig
"Rain"
(xylo obblig)
"Moon"
(glock obblig)
"Storm"
(timp obblig)   10:00   W-Y

Songs of Sung, Poems of Sung Dynasty, for soprano
(*Chin/Eng*) (1967)
† "Waves on Sand" (Li Yu)
(fl obblig)   3:00   W-Y
"Prelude to the Water Tune" (Su Shih)
(fl and vcl obblig)   5:00   W-Y
"Ugly Six" (Chou Pang-jen)
(cl and vcl obblig)   5:00   W-Y
"Slow Sound" (Li Ch'ing-chao)
(ob and vcl obblig)   4:00   W-Y
"River of Red" (Yo Fe)   4:00   W-Y

HYSON

Gestures (1977)
(S and cl)   7:00   3   C

Memories of New England (1974)
(Mez, vln, pno, perc)   18:00   3   C

Three Love Songs From The Bengali (1975)
(Mez, fl, vcl)   10:00   3   C

View From Sandburg (1979)
(S, cl, vla, pno)   20:00   3   C

Winter Triptych (1972)
(S, fl, vln, and pno)   14:00   2+   C

A Litany of Faith, Op. 13
(S, tpt, org)   6:00   2   C

New Hampshire Poems of Robert Frost, Op. 6
(song cycle for S, fl)   2:00   2   C

JANKOWSKI

Icons: Fragments of a Poem (1971)
(S, al-fl, hrp, vcl, vibe)   9:00   3   CMP

A Naughty Boy (1979)
(S, cl, pno)   10:00   3   CMP

LACKMAN

Omen of Victory
(Mez, fl, cl, ob, vcl)   6:00   2   C

LE BARON

In the Desert (Stephen Crane) (1973)
(S, fl, marmb, temp blks)   3:00   2   AMC

I Saw a Man Pursuing the Horizon (Stephen Crane) (1972)
(Bar, pno, hrp)   2:30   2   AMC

LOMON

Five Songs on Poems of William Blake (1962)
(Mez, vla)   8:00   2+   Ars

Phase II (1975)
(S, vcl, pno)   8:00   2+   AMC

MEACHEM

Dragon-Fly—Haiku Kaleidescope (1976)
(S, vln, tpt, 2 perc)   3:00   2+ C

Three French Songs (1974)
"Le Papillon"
"La Cigale et la Fourmi"
"L'Hippopatame"
(S, fl [pic], pno)   12:00   3   C

PARKER

Of Irlaunde (*Irish*) (1979)
(Bar, pno)   15:00   3   Hin

PAULL

Lullabies (Three Lullabies) (1977)
(Mez, gtr, elect. pno or pno)   9:00   1   AMC

† *O Wind* (1972-75)
(med voice and stg qt)   12:00   3   AMC

PREOBRAJENSKA

Fingerflow (Javanese Dance) (L.V. Inke) (1960)
(med voice, fl, mand, 2 perc including timp)   20:00   AMC

PROCACCINI

Canciones, Op. 53 (1972)
(S, cl, bsn, pno)   9:00   2   C

Chanson, Op. 59 (1975)
(voice and gtr)   10:00   2   C

Elegia, Op. 44 (1970)
(Mez, fl, pno)   8:00   2   C

REED

Love Come Take My Hand
(Mez and fl)   3:30   2   AMC

ROGERS

A Collection of Chinese Songs
(S or T, vla, vcl)   7:00   2+ C

"The Man With the Blue Guitar" (Wallace Stevens)
(song cycle for S, vcl, bcl and pno)   15:00   2+ C

SAMTER

Funf Oboenlieder (Reinig, Bremer, Kaléko, Pieritz)
(voice, ob)   11:00   C

Hellbrunn-Zyklus (after R. Magnus)
(S, fl, ob, bsn)   20:00   C

Tänzerinnen, drei Lieder (nach N. Sachs,
E. Lasker-Schüller, G. V. C. Vring)
(S, fl [pic], cl [bcl], pno)   8:00   C

SCHONTHAL

The Solitary Reaper (W. Wordsworth) (1978)
(T, fl, vln, vcl, pno)   8:00   2   C

SILSBEE

A Canticle (1974)
(S, ob, hpsd)   10:00   3   C

Hymn (A. R. Ammons) (1968)
(S, ob, pno)   6:00   3   C

Leavings (1976)
(S, auxiliary perc, pno - 2 players total)   6:00   3   ACA

Mirages (without text) (1969)
(B, vcl and quarter-tone hpsd)   9:00   3   ACA

Only the Cold Bare Moon (cycle on eight *Chin* Prose
poems, in *Eng*) (1970)
(S, fl, pno)   21:00   3   ACA

SINGER

Banquet (Lloyd Schwartz)
(S, hn)   2:00   2+ C

† *From Petrarch* - On the recent deaths of his friends
(trans Schwartz)
(Mez, hn, pno; alternate version: Mez, cl, pno)   7:00   2+ Cor

The Salt Cathedral VII (James McCleod)
(T, vln, pno)   4:00   2+ C

Sonnet (Patricia Benton)
(S or Mez, cl, pno)   4:00   2+ C

To Stir A Dream (Patricia Benton)
(S, cl, pno)   3:00   2+ C

SMITH

Vocal Selections from "Daisy" - Act One
(solos and duets with pno) 1   GSC

VAN DE VATE

Letter to a Friend's Loneliness (1976)
(S and stg qt) .... 10:00   2+   AMC

VELLÈRE

Berceuse (Carco)
(voice and stg qt or stg orch)) 2   C

Les Chants de l'Ombre (Maurel)
(Mez, stg trio) 2   C

Désepoir (M. Brunfaut)
(voice, stg qt) 2   C

Vielle Chanson du Xe Siècle
(voice and stg qt or stg orch) 2   C

VERCOE

† *Herstory I: A Song Cycle for Soprano, Vibraphone and
Piano* (1975) .... 22:00   3   C

† *Herstory II: 13 Japanese Lyrics for Soprano, Piano
and Percussion* (1979) .... 20:00   3   C

WALKER

Elizabethan Songs (1975)
(Bar, ob, perc, pno) .... 12:00   2   Walk

Songs for Voice and Guitar (1976)
(high voice and gtr) .... 10:00   2   Walk

WALLACH

Amen
(solo voice and solo instr) .... 1:00   AMC

Cords
(S, 2 string basses) .... 10:00   AMC

WARREN

Sonnets for Soprano and String Quartette
(Edna St. Vincent Millay) .... 15:00   CF

WEIGL

⊕ *Dear Earth*
(Bar or Mez, hn, vln, vcl, pno) 10:00 2 ACA

⊕ *Echoes from Poems* (Patricia Benton)
(cycle for med voice, hn or vcl, vln or fl, pno) 12:00 2 ACA

⊕ *Lyrical Suite* (from "All My Youth") (Fredericka Blankner)
(med voice, fl or cl or vln, vcl, pno) 13:00 2 ACA

⊕ *Nature Moods* (from "The Green Kingdom")
(Harry Woodbourne)
(high voice, cl or fl, and vln) 10:00 2 ACA

Revelation
(med voice, stg qt) 4:30 2 ACA

⊕ *Requiem for Allison* (Peter Davies)
(S, stg qt) 8:00 2 ACA

Songs Beyond Time (F. Blankner)
(cycle for high voice, vln or fl, and pno) 12:00 2 ACA

⊕ *Songs from "Do Not Awake Me"* (Marion Edey)
(suite for med voice, fl or vln, and pno) 17:00 2 ACA

⊕ *Songs from "No Boundary"* (Lenore Marshall)
(suite for Mez, vla or cl or vln, and pno) 12:00 2 ACA

⊕ *Songs Newly Seen in the Dusk*
(med voice and vcl) 2 ACA

Songs of Concern and Along the Moving Darkness
(various American poets)
(med voice, fl or vln, pno) 2 ACA

⊕ *Songs of Remembrance* (Emily Dickinson)
(Mez, fl or cl, and pno) 12:00 2 ACA

Take My Hand (Edith Segal)
(five songs for Mez, pno, and obblig fl or vln) 12:00 2 ACA

ZAIMONT

The Magic World: Ritual Music for Three (*American Ind*) (1979-80)
(cycle for B-Bar, pno and perc: wood blocks, tamb, triangle, cym, jingle bells, tubular bells, toms, bell-tree, glock) 22:00 3 C

Psalm 23 (original version, 1978)
(Bar or Mez, fl, vln, vcl, pno) 8:15 2 C

Psalm 23 (arr, 1979)
(Mez, fl, pno) 8:15 2 C

A Woman of Valor (1977) (Mez and stg qt)	7:30	3	ACA
⊕ *Two Songs for Soprano and Harp* (1978) "At Dusk in Summer" (Adrienne Rich) "The Ruined Maid" (Thomas Hardy)	10:10	3	AMC

ZIFFRIN

Haiku (Kathryn Martin) (1971) (song cycle for S, vla, hpsd)	15:30	3	C
⊕ *Trio for Xylophone, Soprano and Tuba* (1973)	8:30	3	C

CHAMBER VOCAL MUSIC — SINGLE VOICE WITH FIVE OR MORE PLAYERS

ALLEN

† *Grave Music* (Ted Hughes) (1972) (S, vln, vla, vcl, db, perc)	10:00	2	ACA

ANDERSON, BETH

Becoming/Being (1969) (dramatic S, 2 fl, pic, cl, bcl, Enghn, bsn, al-sax, tpt, bar hn, db, tbn, perc)	7:00	2+	C

BRITAIN

† *Barcarolla* (1958) (8 vcl and vocalise)	5:00		See
The Earth Does Not Wish for Beauty (1975) (voice, 2 tpts, hn, tbn, tuba)	8:00		C

CHANCE

Edensong (1973) (S, fl, cl, vcl, hrp, perc - 3 players)	9:00	3	See

COHEN

Shir Shel Shirim (1967) (S, ob, gtr, vibe and 2 perc)	10:00	2	C

DIEMER

Four Poems by Alice Meynell (1976) (S, fl, 2 vlns, vla, vcl, pno, hpsd, hrp, perc)	12:00	3	CF

FORMAN

Three Songs for Rachel
(S, 2 fl, Enghn, vcl, perc)   10:00   2+ C

GARDNER

⊕ *The Cauldron of Cerridwyn* (1978)
(woman's voice, rec, lute, 2 vla da gamba, Baroque
vln, small perc)   3:30   2   Iris

⊕ *Moonflow* (1975)
(voice or other instr, and pno)   3:30   2   Iris

HAYS

Tunings
(for any 3 to 10 players from: S, solo vln, vln duo,
vla, vcl, db, cl, rec, perc, pno, fl, bsn)   10:00-60:00+ 2+ Q-H

HSU

Prelude To The Water Tune (1956)
(S, fl and vcl obblig, stgs, hrp, cel, Chin brass perc)   8:00   W-Y

Song of Old Fisherman (*Chin/Eng*) (1960)
(Bar, ww, stgs and hrp)   8:00   W-Y

LE BARON

Her Cardboard Bathroom (Rev. Fred Lane) (1976)
(narr, 2 fl, ob, cl, db)   8:00   2   AMC

The Sea & the Honeycomb (Antonio Machado) (1979)
(Mez, pic, fl, cl, bcl, pno, 2 perc)   7:00   3   AMC

MEACHEM

Six Gaping Beaks: Haiku Kaleidescope (1976)
(S, fl, cl, hn, tpt, bsn, 2 perc)   5:00   3   C

ORENSTEIN

Poppies in October (1970)
(S, tpt, fl, cl, vla, vcl)   6:00   2+ C

PARKER

Echoes from the Hills (Emily Dickinson) (1979)
(seven songs for S, fl, cl, hn, 2 vln, vla, vcl)   20:00   3   Hin

PIZER

Five Haiku for Medium-High Voice and Small Chamber Ensemble, Op. 48 (1978)
  (voice, 2 perc [gong, suspended cym, temp blks, triangle, whip, vibe, xylo] , 1 kybd [cel, pno] , vla, vcl)   6:00   3   AMC

PREOBRAJENSKA

Undertones of Frost (L. V. Inke) (1960)
  (Symphonic sequence in four movements for voice, fl, ob, bsn, tbn, vibe, vln, db)   20:00   AMC

REID

Note the Silence (1975)
  (voice, brass qnt, pno, perc)   14:00   3   C

SEMEGEN

† *Lieder auf der Flucht* (Ingerborg Bachmann) (1967)
  (S, fl, cl, hn, pno, vibe, wood blocks, sn dm, triangle, vln, vcl [8 players])   8:30   2+ ACA

SILSBEE

† *De Amore et Morte* (*Medieval Lat*) (1978)
  (S, cl/bcl, vln, vcl, 2 perc, pno)   22:00   3   ACA

Raft (A.R. Ammons) (1976)
  (narr, 5 perc)   7:00   3   ACA

Scroll: Five Haiku (1977)
  (S, fl, tpt, perc, vln, db, pno)   8:00   3   ACA

SIMONS

Diverse Settings (Evelyn Poussette-Dart)
  "A Fragment Afar"
  "As the Rose Becomes its Aura"
  "As Moon from Eternal Whereabouts"
  "As Departure Fell"
  "Slow, Slowly"
  "As Slowly One by One"
  "Has Gone, Has Gone"
  (S, fl, ob, cl, bsn, 2 vln, vla, vcl, db, vibe, perc) ·   13:00   ACA

⊕ *Pied Piper of Hamelin* (Robert Browning)
  (fl, pno, complete vln section divided into 3 groups, narr)   18:00   Mer

⊕ *Set of Poems for Children*
    "Night was Creeping" (James Stephens)
    "Rain" (Robert L. Stevenson)
    "Fog" (Carl Sandburg)
    "Is The Moon Tired" (Christina Rosetti)
    "My Shadow" (Robert L. Stevenson)
    (fl, ob, cl, bsn, vln, vla, vcl, db, narr)   8:00   Mer

SMELTZER

Jonathan Richards My Bicentennial Baby (1976)
    (S, pno, 2 fl, 2 tpt, dm)   10:00 2 ISWP

ZWILICH

Allison (in memory of Allison Krause, killed at Kent
    State University)
    (narr, fl/pic, cl, bcl, hn, tpt, tbn, vln, db, perc [timp,
        traps, mixed perc])   8:00 3 C

● CHAMBER VOCAL MUSIC — TWO OR MORE VOICES UNACCOMPANIED ●

PIZER

Madrigals Anon, Op. 51 (Anonymous poems, 13th-15th
    centuries) (1979)
    (SSAT, B or Bar)   5:00 2+ AMC

PROCACCINI

"La Levataccia," Op. 47 (1971)
    (4 voices SATB)   3:00 3 C

3 Canti Popolari, Op. 38 (1969)
    (2 treb voices)   6:00 2 C

SMELTZER

Two Studies (3 Part Madrigal and Motet) (1964)
    (SSA, also for SAT)   4:00 1 C

VELLÈRE

Procession Nocturne (J. Aderca) (1959)
    (SATB qt or choir)   4:00 2 C

WALLACH

Five-fold Amen
    (two solo voices)   5:00   AMC

Two Introits
(chamber choir)   2:00   AMC

WYLIE

Five Madrigals, Op. 13 no. 1 (William Blake)   10:00   2+   C

CHAMBER VOCAL MUSIC — TWO OR MORE VOICES
WITH INSTRUMENTS

ANDERSON, BETH

Alleluia (1978)
(2 T and 3 vcl or 2 tpts)   3:00   2+   C

An Argument (1969)
(trio for S, Bar, and tuba)   3:00   2+   ACA

⊕ *Torero Piece* (1973)
(2 solo voices)   7:00 - 45:00   2+   ACA

CECCONI-BATES

Five Songs From The Poetry of A. Poliziano (*It*) (1976)
(S, T, pno)   15:00   2   C

Four Early Songs (1956, 1962)
(S, T, fl, pno, vln, vcl)   7:00   2   C

Menagerie: Mythical and Musical (R. Wayne Archer)
(1978)
(solo voices [SATB], fl [pic], 2 cl [bcl], tpt,
2 tuba, vibe, pno)   18:00   3   C

Three Summer Songs (Emily Dickinson) (1979)
(S, B, pno, cl, perc)   8:00   3   C

Willie Was Different (Norman and Molly Rockwell) (1973)
(narr, Mez, ww qnt, pno)   17:00   2   C

DIEMER

Three Mystic Songs (1963)
(S, Bar, and pno)   15:00   3   See

PARKER

Songs for Eve (Archibald MacLeish) (1975)
(5 movements for 4 solo voices SATB and stg qt)   70:00   3   Hin

PROCACCINI

Evocazione, Op. 52 (1972)
(S, Mez, pno)   4:00   2   C

ROGERS

Seven Macabre Songs (Howard Nemerov)
(S, T, pno)   15:00   2   C

SAMTER

Drei "Chöre nach der Mitternach" (Nelly Sachs)
(3 voices, pno or org)   12:00   C

Ode an Singer (P. van Ostaijen)
(S, narr, pno)   4:00   C

Erfindungen (after Chr. Morgenstern)
(5 songs for 3 voices, rec, pno)   12:00   C

Die Selbstkritik (W. Busch)
(3 voices, pno)   3:00   C

Drei Duette (W. Busch)
(S, Bar, cl, perc, pno)   7:00   C

Im Atemholen, Getretener Quark (Goethe)
(4 voices, pno fr-hand)   2:00   C

Ulkiade "Der Kartoffelpuffer" (F. Lasker-Schüler)
(S or T, pno, narr)   9:00   C

Sechs Wechselgesänge (Klabund)
(Mez, Bar, perc, pno)   8:00   C

Der Schaffner (J. Prévert)
(Bar, pno, narr)   3:00   C

S'gibt Hungrige Leute (Trindade)
(male and female narr, pno)   2:00   C

SILSBEE

Bourn (1974)
(S, counter-T or A, vcl, hpsd)   10:00   3   ACA

Huit Chants en Brun (Garcia Lorca, *Fr* translation)
(S, Mez, cl, vla)   22:00   3   ACA

Icarus (William Carlos Williams) (1977)
(8 voices, recs, bongo dms)   6:00   3   ACA

Now (Cummings) (1969)
(S, Mez, fl, vcl, prepared pno)   10:00   3   C

SIMONS

Trialogue No. 1 (Dylan Thomas: "The Tombstone Told
   When She Died")
   (Mez, Bar, vla)   6:30   ACA

Trialogue No. 2 (Dylan Thomas: "Myselves Grieve,"
   "From Ceremony After a Fire Raid")
   (Mez, Bar, vla)   8:00   ACA

Trialogue No. 3 (Dylan Thomas: "Now (Say Nay)")
   (Mez, Bar, vla)   8:00   ACA

SINGER

† *L'Envoi* (Patricia Benton)
   (2 S, pno)   4:00   2+ C

SMITH

Scenes from "Daisy," Acts I and II
   (S, A, narr, pno)   1   GSC

VELLÈRE

Chansons Enfantines (M. Carème) (1958)
   (2 and 3 voices, pno)   2   JM

WALKER

A Wonder Told Shyly (1978)
   (madrigal singers, vibe, db)   17:00   2   Walk

WEIGL

⊕ *Songs of Love and Leaving*
   (Mez, Bar, cl, pno)   2   ACA

ZAIMONT

⊕† *Songs of Innocence* (William Blake) (1974)
   "Piping Down the Valley Wild"
   "Elegy: The Garden of Love"
   "I Asked a Thief"
   "How Sweet I Roam'd"
   (S, T, fl, vcl, hrp)   10:45   2   FC

CHAMBER VOCAL MUSIC — SINGLE OR MULTIPLE VOICES WITH TAPE

ANDERSON, BETH

She Wrote (1974)
(voice, 2 vln, tape)   10:00-25:00   2+   ACA

Skate Suite (1979)
(voice, vln, vcl, electric bass, tape)   23:00   3   ACA

Tulip Clause (1973)
(T, al-fl, cl, bcl, ten-sax, org, vla, vcl, db,
timp, tape or any instrs and tape)   2+   ACA

CHANCE

Bathsabe's Song (George Peele) (1971)
(speaker, "live" al-sax, 6 pre-recorded tracks of
al-sax, opt dancer)   7:00   3   See

COHEN

Finnegans Wake (1968)
(2 female voices, 2 male voices, tbn, vcl, pno,
electric gtr, 4 perc, elect. tape, cond)   10:00   2   C

GILBERT

The Orange Book (1974)
(S, sax, tape)   17:00   2   C

Paisaje con dos tumbas y un perro asiro (Lorca) (1977)
(S, tape)   10:00   2   C

LE BARON

Concerto for Active Frogs (1974)
(small SATB chor, B voice, tape collage, ob, cl,
al-sax, perc — flexible instrumentation: any mix of
ww and/or brass is acceptable)   10:00   1   AMC

MEACHEM

In Icy Moonlight (from Haiku Kaleidescope) (1976)
(S, fl, perc, pno, tape)   10:00   3   C

PIERCE

Buffalo Bill (e.e. cummings) (1978)
(voice, B-flat cl, pno, tape)   14:30   3   See

SOLO INSTRUMENTAL MUSIC — HARPSICHORD SOLO

RICHTER

Short Prelude in Baroque Style (1974)	2:00	2	CF
Soundings (1965)	9:00	3	CF

ROBERTS

⊕ *Chaconne*	7:00	3	IsH
⊕ *Charlot Suite*	12:00	3	C
Das Kleine Buch der Bilder	23:00	2	C
Fantasy after Psalm 150	4:00	2	C
Gavotte	2:00	2	C
Passacaille	5:00	3	C
⊕ *Rondo — Hommage to Couperin*	7:00	3	IsH
Three Bagatelles	5:00	2+	C
⊕ *Triptych*	7:00	3	C

SINGER

Caprice	2:00	2	C
† *Suite* "Prologue" "Jig-Frolic" "Arietta" "Epilogue"	6:00	2	HB

SMELTZER

German Chorale for Harpsichord (1961)	1:00	1	C
Study for Harpsichord (1961)	2:00	2	C
Study for Harpsichord with Romantic Touches (1961)	2:00	1	C
Two Studies for Harpsichord (1964)	4:00	1	C

SOLO INSTRUMENTAL MUSIC — ORGAN SOLO

ALLEN

Postlude for Organ (1975)	5:00	1	ACA

BOLZ

Episode for Organ (Autumn Joy) (1979)	3:00	2	Ars

BRITAIN

Pyramids of Giza (1971)	5:00		C

BRUSH

Pastorale (1954)	4:00	3	LorP
Two Expressive Pieces (1956)	10:00	2+	JF

DIEMER

Carols for Organ (1979)	12:00	2	SacM
Celebration - Seven Hymn Settings (1970)	21:00	2	APH
Contrasts (1976) (*in* Preludes and Postludes, vol 4)	2:00	2	APH
Declarations (1972)	8:00	3	See
Fantasie (1958)	7:00	3	OUP
Fantasy on "O Sacred Head" (1967)	7:00	3	B+H
He Leadeth Me —Hymn Setting for Organ (1951)	4:00	2	OUP
Hymn Preludes and Free Accompaniments 2 (1978)	12:00	1	APH
Jubilate (1976) (*in* Preludes and Postludes, vol 4)	2:00	2	APH
Little Toccata (1978) (*in* Jon Spong Collection of Organ Music)	2:30	2	Arv
St. Anne (1951)	1:30	1	HF
Seven Hymn Preludes (1965)	14:00	2	HF
Ten Hymn Preludes (1960)	20:00	2	CF
Three Fantasies on Advent-Christmas Hymns (1978)	12:00	2	APH
Toccata (1964)	8:00	3	OUP
Toccata and Fugue (1969)	7:00	3	See

GLAZIER

   Prayers of a Dreamer   C

HAYS

   For My Brother's Wedding   4:30   2   Q-H

HEINRICH

Four Chorale Preludes on Hymns of Praise, Op. 5	20:00	2+	C
Three Partitas on American Hymn Tunes, Op. 7	25:00	1+	C
Variations and Toccata on a Theme of Mendelssohn, Op. 10	8:00	2+	C

MAGEAU

   Three Pieces for Organ (1969)   8:00   2   WLSM

PROCACCINI

Andante Elegiaco, Op. 48 (1971)	5:00	1	C
Improvviso E Toccata, Op. 33 (1968)	6:00	3	C

RICHTER

   Variations on a Theme by Neithart von Reuenthal (1974)   13:00   3   CF

SAMTER

   Prisma   10:00   C

SMELTZER

   Piece for Organ (1961)
      "Introduction"
      "Sostenuto"
      "Dance"   4:00   1   C

SMITH

   Prelude in D Flat (1932, rev. 1968)   2:30   2   Mowb

WALKER

   Passacaglia and Fugue (1976)   3   Walk

Song for Organ (1968)	5:00	1	Walk

WARREN

Processional March	GSch

ZIFFRIN

Toccata and Fugue for Organ (1955-56)	6:00	3	C

SOLO INSTRUMENTAL MUSIC — PIANO SOLO

ANDERSON, BETH

Eighth Ancestor: Second Movement (1979)		3	C
Skate Suite (1979)	23:00	3	C

BEESON

The Bold Chevalier	3:30	3	C
The Fantastic Suite	5:00	3	C
In Green Meadows	3:00	3	C
Journey Through the Darkness	3:00	3	C
A Land of Fortune	2:30	3	C
The New Birth	5:00	3	C
Tear Drops of a Flower	2:30	3	C
A Time to Remember	2:30	3	C
The Utopian Road	2:30	3	C
Why Did You Leave Me?	4:00	3	C

BOLZ

Floret (1965) (a mood caprice for piano)	3:07	2+	Sis
Two Profiles for Piano (1972)	3:04	2	Sis

de BOHUN [Boone]

Annunciation of Spring (1952) (suite for piano)	9:00	3	Ars

BRITAIN

Adoration (1955)	4:00		UCLA
Alaskan Trail (1967)	7:00		UCLA
Angel Chimes (1951)	3:00		AME
Barcarola (1948)	4:00		C
Cactus Rhapsody (1956)			UCLA
The Chateau (1938)	4:00		C
Covered Wagon (1925)			NK
Dance Grotesque (1929)	3:00		C
Drouth (1939)			C
Egyptian Suite (1969)	12:00		UCLA
Enchantment (1949)	4:00		UCLA
Ensenada (1956)	3:00	1	Ric
Epiphyllum (1966)	4:00		Hero
Escape (1949)	4:00		UCLA
The Famous 12 (1965)	5:00		LC
Four Sarabandes (1963)	10:00		C
Goddess of Inspiration (1948)	3:00		UCLA
Hawaiian Pianorama (1971)			C
Heel and Toe (1949)	3:00	1	UCLA
Infant Suite (1935)	8:00		C
Joy (1953)			C
Kuilimi (1977)	4:00		UCLA
Lakalani (1970)	4:00		C
Lei of Love (1978)	4:00		UCLA
Mexican Weaver (1954)	3:00		AMC
Prelude (1925)	4:00		NK
Radiation (1953)	4:00		UCLA
Riding Herd in Texas (1966) (ten pieces for piano)		1	Hero

Saint Francis of Assisi (1941)	6:00		C
San Luis Rey (1941)	6:00		C
Serenada del Coronado (1940)	5:00		UCLA
Serenata Sorrentina (1946)	3:00		C
† *Sonata,* Op. 17 (1958)	10:00		C
Song of the Joshua (1956)			C
Torillo (1949)	4:00	1	Hero
Western Suite (1925)	10:00		OH
Wings of Silver (1951)	3:00	1	WilM

BRUSH

American Circle (1979)	6:00	3	C
The Night Lights (1953)	6:00	3	C
† *Osage Hills Suite* (1972)	15:00	3	C
Rhapsody	20:00	3	C
Sarabande	5:00	2	C
Suite for Piano (1952)	7:00	3	C

CECCONI-BATES

Four Preludes (1962)	9:00	3	C
Three Pieces about Piano (1978)	12:00	3	C

DANFORTH

Karelian Light (1977)	10:00	2	C
† *Suite for Piano* (1971)	10:00	3+	C

DEMBO

Dance No. 1	4:00	2+	C
Haiku No. 1 & 2	2:00	2+	C
† *Metamorphosis* (three pieces)	15:00	3	C

DIEMER

Four on a Row (1972)	5:00	1+	NSM
Seven Etudes (1965)	18:00	3	CF
Sound Pictures (1971)	10:00	1+	B&H
⊕ *Toccata* (1979)	7:00	3	Ars

FRASIER

Piano Sonata I (1980)	13:00	3+	Ars

FULLER-HALL

Jazz Impromptu (1978)	4:00	2	C

GARDNER

Seven Modal Improvisation Studies (1978) (pno, or any bass instr with any treb instr)	5:00 each	2	Iris
Song Studies for Piano (1979)	1:00-6:00 each	2+	Iris

HAYS

Chartres Red	3:00	3	Q-H
Etude Bass Bases	4:00	3	Q-H
Past Present	7:00	3	Q-H
Saturday Evenings	5:00	2	Q-H
⊕ *Sunday Nights*	5:15	3	ABI

HOOVER

Piano Book			
"Chase" (1977)	2:30	3	AMC
"Lament" (1977)	4:30	3	AMC
"Three Plus Three" (1977)	2:00	3	AMC
"Allegro Molto" (1978)	2:30	3	AMC
"Forest Bird" (1980)	2:30	3	AMC

HSU

Etude (1952)	4:00	2	W-Y
† *Impromptu* (1980)	5:00	3	W-Y

Jade Fountain (1958)	3:00	2	W-Y
† *Perpetual Momentum* (1974)	5:00	3	W-Y
Piano Sonata (1958)	10:00	3	W-Y
† *Piano Suite* (1964)	8:00	3	W-Y
Running Water (1962)	3:00	2	W-Y
Sound of Autumn (1958) (suite for piano)	7:00	2	W-Y
Swaying Willow (1958)	3:00	2	W-Y
Variations (1956)	6:00	3	W-Y

LACKMAN

Fits	(variable: aleatoric)		C
Rondo for Piano Solo	5:00	2	C
Three Little Pieces for Piano	4:00	1	C

LOMON

Five Masks (1980)	17:00	3	AMC
Rondo (1959)	4:00	2+	AMC
Toccata (1961)	6:00	3	AMC

MAGEAU

Cityscapes (1978)			C
Cycles and Series (1970)	10:00	3	C
Ragtime (1977)	8:00	2+	AMC

MARCUS

A Child's Day (Suite)	10:00	2+	HB
A Day in New York City (Suite)	20:00	2+	C
Etude Erotique	3:00	2+	HB
Look! No Fingers!	3:00	2+	C
Monologue	10:00	2+	C

Paratones	5:00	2+	C
Piano Sonata, No. 1	20:00	2+	C
Piano Sonata, No. 2	17:00	2+	AMC
Refractions Through a Prism (Suite)	15:00	2+	C
Sound Score	15:00	2+	C
Theme and Variations	7:00	2+	HB
Three Modules	10:00	2+	C
Two Preludes	10:00	2+	C
Youth In Orbit (Suite)	20:00	2+	C

ORENSTEIN

Three Easy Pieces (1979)	7:00	2	C

PAULL

† *The Man Alone* (1970-74)	11:00	1	AMC

PIERCE

Blending Stumps (1976) (prepared pno)	11:00	3	See
Coming to Standing (1975)	8:00	2+	See
Dry Rot (1977) (prepared pno)	15:30	3	See
Greycastle (1974) (prepared pno)	8:30	2+	See
The Lost River, Sevier (1978)	11:00	3	See
Offering to Birdfeather (1974)	5:00	2+	See
Orb (1976) (prepared pno)	9:00	3	See
Serenade, On Zander's Cobweb Photo (1979)	12:00	2	C
Six Waltzes for Prepared Piano (1980)	10:00	2	C
Song in Licia For Salvonarola (1974)	8:00	2+	See

Soundings (1978)	11:00	2+	See
Spectres: 5 Easy Eraser Preparations (1975)	8:00	2+	See
Transverse Process (1977)	11:00	2+	See
Variations 7 (1978) (prepared pno)	7:00	3	See

PIZER

A Mon Père, Pour Mon Père, Op. 40 (1977)	4:00	3	AMC
Expressions Intime, Op. 14-18 (1974-75)	11:00	2+	AMC
Jimnobody No. 1, Op. 22 (1976)	1:30	2	AMC
Jimnobody No. 2, Op. 24 (1976)	2:00	2	AMC
Piano Sonata No. 2, in One Movement, Op. 10 (1974)	8:00	3	AMC
2 Brief Pieces, Op. 12-13 (1975)	3:30	2+	AMC

PROCACCINI

Sonata in Tricromia, Op. 2 (1955)	15:00	2	Bng
Sonata, Op. 3 (1956)	15:00	2	C
Fantasia, Op. 4 (1956)	13:00	3	C
Sonatina, Op. 18 (1958)	8:00	2	C
Un Cavallino Avventuroso, Op. 22 (1960) (musical fairytale for pno, opt narr)	15:00	2	C
Nove Preludi, Op. 29 (1966)	16:00	2	C
Sonatina No. 2, Op. 43 (1970)	7:00	2	C

REID

Three Bagatelles (1969)	5:00	2	C

RICHTER

Bird of Yearning (1976)	16:00	3	CF
Eight Pieces for Piano (1961)	6:30	3	CF
Exequy (1980)	2:20	2	C

Fragments (1963)	5:00	3	CF
Remembrances (1977)	3:30	2	E–V
Requiem (1978)	21:00	3	CF
Short Prelude in Baroque Style (1974)	2:00	2	CF
⊕ *Sonata for Piano* (1954)	21:00	3	CF

ROBERTS

Landler	1:00	1	C
Three Bagatelles	5:00	2+	C
⊕ *Twelve Time-Gardens*	25:00	3	HoE

SAMTER

Drei Aphorismen	5:00		C
Drei Klavierstücke zu Plastiken von Jos. Magnus	5:00		C
Drei Phasen	5:00		C
⊕ *Eskapaden*	7:00		C
Match	4:00		C
Prisma	10:00		C
Varianten	8:00		C

SCHONTHAL

Eleven Pieces for Piano (1978)	8:00	2	C
Fiestas y Danzas (1961)	13:00	3	C
In Homage of . . . (1978) (24 Preludes)	18:00	3	C
Reverberations for Piano with Added Timbres (1974)	16:00	3	C
Sonata Breve (1973)	7:00	3	OUP
Sonata in E-Flat (1947)	16:00	3	C
Sonata quasi un'improvisazione (1964)	16:00	3	C
Sonatensatz (1973)	7:00	3	C
Sonatina (1938)	10:00	2	AMC
Variations In Search of A Theme (1976)	16:00	3	OUP

SEMEGEN

    Three Pieces for Piano (1966)   8:00   2   ACA

SILSBEE

    Bagatelle (1963)   4:00   2   ACA

⊕† *Doors* (1976)   11:00   3   ACA

SIMONS

    Night Sounds
        "The Evening Haze"
        "Thinking of Past Things"
        "The Stars on the Pond"
        "The Rain Beats on the Rain"   2:00   1+ Mer

    Piano Work   10:40   3   ACA

    Time Groups No. 1
        No. 1—No. 84, or   45:00
        In groups of 28   15:00   ACA

    Windfall (aleatoric)   8:00   ACA

SINGER

    † *Four Pieces*
        "Toccatina"
        "Baroque Frolic"
        "Petit Etude"
        "Remembrance"   10:00   2   C

    † *Introduction and Caprice*   3:30   2   C

    † *Ricky's Rondo*   4:30   2   C

    † *Suite in Harpsichord Style*
        "Prologue"
        "Jig-Frolic"
        "Arietta"
        "Epilogue"   6:00   2   HB

    Sweet Stacy Suite   5:00   2   C

SMELTZER

    A Russian Theme and Variations (1961)   4:00   2   C

    Kaleidescope (1962-68)
        (9 pieces for piano)   10:00 2+ C

    Piece (1961)   2:00   1   C

Reverie (1962)   3:00   2   C

Twelve Mood Pictures: Variatons for Piano on the
      Theme of Yankee Doodle and the Interval Sets
      1-9-7-6:1-7-7-6 (1975)
      "Fanfare"
      "March of the Feathered Hats"
      "Agitations"
      "The Capricious Roadrunner"
      "Anticipation"
      "Triumphal March at Yorktown"
      "Waltz"
      "Dance of the Fireflies"
      "Lament"
      "Chimes at Noon"
      "Chimes in the Evening"
      "Alleluia" (A Jazz Toccata)   25:00   3   ISWP

SMITH

Characteristic Suite (1949)
      "Canon"
      "Waltz"
      "Passacaglia"
      "March"
      "Toccata"   12:00   3   Mowb

Episodic Suite (1935)
      "Yellow and Blue"
      "Nocturne"
      "Waltz"
      "March"
      "Toccata"   8:00   2   Mowb

Prelude (Recital Piece) (1949)   1:15   2   TPres

Sonatine in C (1943-44)   10:00   3   Mowb

Variations Humoresque (1949)   8:40   2   Mowb

SWISHER

Variations on an Original Theme   5:00   3   AMC

VAN DE VATE

Nine Preludes for Piano (1978)   13:30   3   AMC

⊕ *Sonata for Piano* (1978)   10:00   3   AMC

VELLÈRE

Capriccio (1959)   8:00   2   C

Deux Danses (1930)	7:00	2	C
Deuxième Sonatine (1965)	12:00	2	JM
Divertissement (1953)		2	C
Du Lac (1950) (6 pieces)		2	C
Feuillets Epars (10 pieces)	25:00	2	CBD
Promenade Au Bord	10:00	2	JM
Sonatine (1960)		2	C

VERCOE

⊕ *Fantasy* (1975)	10:00	3	Ars
Six Gratitudes (1978)	9:00	2+	C
Sonaria for Piano (1980)	12:00	3	C
Three Studies (1973)	3:00	1+	Ars

WALKER

April, Rag and Fantasy (1977)	8:00	1	Walk
Five Pieces for Piano (1972)	10:00	2	Walk
Four Light and Lively Pieces (1979)	10:00	1	Walk
Preludes (1974)	11:00	2	Walk
Sonata for Piano (1979)	8:00	3	Walk
Suite for Piano (1969)	10:00	2	Walk

WALLACH

Piano Study in Open-Ended Form	6:00		AMC
Three Piano Pieces (1967)	6:00		AMC
Wisps (1978)	12:00		AMC

WYLIE

† *Five Preludes,* Op. 12	12:00	2	Cor
Mandala, Op. 33 no. 2	(varies)	3	C

⊕† *Psychogram,* Op. 25	11:00	3	Gal
Soliloquy for Left Hand(alone), Op. 23	5:00	3	HB
Sonata No. I, Op. 7	10:00	1+	C
Sonata No. II, Op. 16 no. 1	15:00	2	C
Sonatina, Op. 10	3:00	1+	C

ZAIMONT

Calendar Collection (1977) (12 descriptive preludes for the developing pianist)	14:30	2	Alf
⊕ *A Calendar Set: 12 Virtuosic Preludes* (1974-78)	26:40	3	LPl
"Deceit" (1979)	2:40	1+	C
Judy's Rag (1974)	4:30	2	Tetr
⊕ *Nocturne: La Fin de Siècle* (1978)	7:10	3	Gal
† *Piano Variations* (1965)	6:00	3	C
† *Portrait of a City* (1961) (suite in 5 mvts)	5:45	2	C
Reflective Rag (1974)	4:00	2	Tetr
Scherzo (1969)	7:00	3	C
Stone (1980) (pno: kybd and stgs)	11:00	3	C
"Sweet Daniel" (1979)	4:00	2	AMC
Toccata (1968)	3:50	3	C
White-key Waltz (1966)	1:00	2	C

ZIFFRIN

Suite for Piano (1955)	8:00	2	C
Theme and Variations for Piano (1949)	4:00	2	C

● SOLO INSTRUMENTAL MUSIC — WOODWIND/BRASS SOLO ●

ALLEN

Limericks for Flute (1972, rev. 1980)	12:00	2	ACA

DEMBO

Suite
(fl)   2:30   1+   C

FRASIER

Three Short Sketches
(cl)   3:30   3   C

GILBERT

Solo for Clarinet (1972)   6:00   2   C

HAYS

Breathless
(bfl)   3:00   3   Q-H

Winded
(C fl)   2:00   2   Q-H

HEINRICH

The Humours of Harlequin, Op. 15 (Based on four paintings
of Claude Gillot)
(fl)   7:00   2   C

Rondo-Variations on "B-A-C-H", Op. 8
(fl)   5:00   1+   C

HOOVER

Set for Clarinet (1978)   5:00   2   AMC

HSU

† *Capriccio* (1976)
(fl)   3:00   W-Y

Impromptu (1956)
(cl)   4:00   W-Y

HYSON

Lyric Interlude for Unaccompanied Flute (1979)   2:30   2+   C

ORENSTEIN

For Carlos, In Memoriam (1969)
(fl)   3:00   2+   C

Piece for Solo Flute (1975)	1:00	2+	C
Piece I for Solo Clarinet (1971)	3:00	3	C
Three Pieces for Solo Clarinet (1971)	8:00	3	C

PIERCE

Prelude and Fugue (1974) (fl)	6:00	2+	See

PREOBRAJENSKA

Two Short Works for A-Flat Saxophone (1971) "Caprice" "Fantasy"	4:00		AMC

PROCACCINI

Andante e Rondo, Op. 50 (1971) (fl)	5:00	2	C

REED

Obtude, Two Etudes for Solo Oboe	4:00	3	AMC
Two Autumn Moods (tuba)	4:30	3	AMC

ROGERS

Suite of Short Pieces for Alto Recorder		1	C

SEMEGEN

Music for Clarinet Solo (1979)	7:00	2+	ACA

SILSBEE

3 Chants (1975) (fl)	11:00	3	ACA

SWISHER

Theme and Variations (fl)	2:00	2	AMC

WALLACH

Contemplations
(bcl)   10:00   AMC

Moment
(ob)   6:00   AMC

WEIGL

Oiseau de la Vie (Bird of Life)
(fl or cl)   10:00   2   ACA

ZAIMONT

† *Capriccio* (1971)
(fl)   4:30   3   AMC

Valse Romantique (1972)
(fl)   4:40   2   AMC

ZIFFRIN

⊕ *Four Pieces for Tuba* (1973)   11:20   3   Msg

SOLO INSTRUMENTAL MUSIC — WOODWIND/BRASS
WITH KEYBOARD

ANDERSON, BETH

Eighth Ancester: Second Movement (re-orchestrated 1979)
(fl with pno or hrp)   1+   C

The Preying Mantis and the Bluebird (1979)
(fl with pno or hrp)   1+   Jsh

BARNETT, CAROL

Romanza (1974)
(fl and pno)   3:20   2   C

Sonata for Horn and Piano (1973)   8:30   2   C

BOLZ

Duo Scherzando (1978)
(tpt and pno)   2:05   2   HB

Polychrome Patterns (1965)
(a sonatina for cl and pno)   7:07   3   C

BRITAIN

Pastorale (1975) (fl and pno)	7:00		C
Casa del Sogno (1958) (ob and pno)	4:00		C
† *Phantasy* (1970) (fl and pno)	8:00		C
† *Phantasy* (1942) (ob and pno)	8:00		See

BRUSH

The Old Trail (fl and pno)	5:00	2	C

CECCONI-BATES

Sonata for French Horn and Piano (1978)	9:00	3	C

DEMBO

Dance (cl and pno)	2:30	1+	C
Hebraic Reflections: Fantasy for Flute and Piano	5:00	3	C
Humoresque (fl and pno)	2:00	2+	C
Humoresque (ob and pno)	3:00	2+	C
Pastorale (treb rec and pno)	2:00	1+	C
Three Pieces (bsn and pno)	4:30	2+	C
Two Twelve Tone Sketches (cl and pno)	5:00	2+	C

DIEMER

Serenade for Flute and Piano (1954)	5:00	3	Arm
Sonata for Flute and Piano or Harpsichord (1958)	12:00	3	SMP
Suite for Flute and Piano (1947)	9:00	2+	Arm

FULLER-HALL

Trumpet Concertino (1979)
(tpt and pno)   6:30   2+   C

HAYS

For A. B.
(cl and pno)   3:00   2   Q-H

HEINRICH

Sonata in F Major for Flute and Harpsichord, Op. 18
(four movements)   11:00   2   C

HOOVER

Medieval Suite (1979-80)
"Overture: de Coucy"
⊕ "On the Betrothal of Princess Isabelle of France,
Aged 6"
"The Black Knight"
"The Drunken Friar"
"Demon's Dance"
(fl and pno)   16:00   3   AMC

JANKOWSKI

Sonata for B-Flat Trumpet and Piano (1970)   10:00   2+   C

MARCUS

Nocturne
(fl and pno)   15:00   3   C

PAULL

Two Songs for Trumpet (1970-74)
(tpt and pno or electric pno)   6:00   2   AMC

PIERCE

Echo (And Narcissus) (1980)
(fl and pno)   6:00   2   C

Sargasso, Norwich Chorale,
Arabesque (1976-77)
(B-flat cl and pno)   20:00   3   See

PIZER

Qulisoly, Op. 38 (1976)
(fl and pno)   3:00   2+   AMC

PROCACCINI

Introduzione e Allegro, Op. 39 (1969)
(fl and pno)   6:00   2   C

Lied No. 2, Op. 71 (1978)
(ob and pno)   4:00   2   C

Meditazione, Op. 69 bis (1978)
(hn and pno)   5:00   2   C

Sonata, Op. 63 (1976)
(fl and pno)   13:00   3   C

Sonata, Op. 32 (1968)
(bsn and pno)   10:00   2   C

Tre Pezzi, Op. 30 (1966)
(bsn and pno)   7:00   3   Ledc

REID

Air for Horn (1973)
(hn and org or pno)   5:00   2   C

RICHTER

Sonata for Clarinet and Piano (1948)   11:00   3   CF

SAMTER

Aspekte
(fl and pno)   9:00   C

Drei Tanzminiaturen
(cl and pno)   5:00   C

Facetten
(fl and pno)   8:00   C

SCHONTHAL

Music for Horn and Piano (1978)   12:00   2   C

Sonata (1975)
(cl and pno)   13:00   2   C

Sonata Concertante (1976)
(cl and pno)   13:00   2   C

SEMEGEN

† Quattro (1967)
(fl and pno)   4:30   2+   ACA

† Three Pieces for Clarinet and Piano (1968)   5:30   2+   ACA

SILSBEE

Phantasy (1972-73)
(ob and hpsd)   9:00   3   ACA

SIMONS

Facets No. 3
(ob and pno, or vla and pno)   7:00   Mer

SINGER

† Legend
(fl and pno)   5:00   2   C

† Nocturne
(cl and pno)   5:00   2   Cor

STANLEY

Sonata for Trombone and Piano   4:30   3   C

SWISHER

Sonata for Clarinet and Piano   9:00   3   AMC

VAN DE VATE

Sonata for Oboe and Piano (1970)   13:00   3   AMC

VELLÈRE

Arlequinade (1959)
(tpt and pno)   1:00   2   JM

Dialogue (1960)
(ob and pno)   3:00   2   JM

Intermède (1960) (fl and pno)		2	JM
Sérénité (1959) (cl and pno)	2:00	2	JM

WALKER

Etude for Flute and Piano (1979)	12:00	2	Walk
Sonata for Flute and Piano (1978)	12:00	2	Walk

WYLIE

Sonata for Flute and Piano, Op. 20	20:00	3	AMC
Song and Dance, Op. 9 (cl and pno)		2	C
Wistful Piece, Op. 16, no. 2 (fl or ob or vln and pno)	4:00	1+	C

ZAIMONT

† *Flute and Piano Sonata* (1962)	8:30	2	C
Trumpet and Piano Sonata (1971)	12:00	2+	C

● SOLO INSTRUMENTAL MUSIC — UNACCOMPANIED SOLO STRING ●

ALLEN

Passages for Solo Viola (1973)	17:00	3	ACA

BRITAIN

† *Barcarola* (1948) (vln)	4:00		C
Casa del Sogno (1955) (vln)	4:00		C
† *The Chateau* (1938) (vln)	4:00		C
Dance Grotesque (1929) (vln)	3:00		C
† *Legend* (1928) (vln)	5:00		C

Prison (1935)
  (vln)   4:00   NK

† *Serenade* (1944)
  (vln)   3:00   C

HSU

Air on G String (1956)
  (vln)   2:00   W-Y

Happy Valley (1956)
  (vln)   2:00   W-Y

† *Impromptu No. 1* (1956)
  (vln)   5:00   W-Y

Longing (1951)
  (vln)   3:00   W-Y

† *Violin Suite* (1964)   8:00   W-Y

MAGEAU

Contrasts (1976)
  (vcl)   8:00   3 JAS

Statement and Variations (1979)
  (vla)   8:00   3 AMC

PROCACCINI

Sonatina, Op. 28 (1965)
  (vcl)   6:00   3 C

RICHTER

Darkening of the Light (1961)
  (vla)   9:00   3 CF

Darkening of the Light (1976)
  (vcl)   9:00   3 CF

ROGERS

"Relays"
  (vln)   7:00   3 C

SAMTER

Monolog-Einer Geige
  (vln)   6:00   C

Monolog (vcl)	4:00		C

SCHONTHAL

Four Epiphanies for Unaccompanied Viola (1975)	10:00	3	OUP

SEMEGEN

⊕† *Music for Violin Solo* (1973)	8:30	3	ColU

SILSBEE

Runemusic (1979) (vcl)	12:00	3	ACA

SIMONS

Circle of Attitudes - (Dance Suite: with or without dancer)
"Bereavement"
"Awareness"
"Fear"
"Dauntlessness"

"Abandonment"	17:00	3	ACA

VAN DE VATE

Six Etudes for Solo Viola (1969)	7:30	3	Sis
Six Etudes for Solo Violin (1979)	7:30	3	AMC
Suite for Solo Viola (1975)	9:00	3	AMC
Suite for Solo Violin (1975)	9:00	3	Sis

VELLÈRE

Soliloqué (1961) (vln)	5:00	2	C

VERCOE

Sonaria for Cello Alone (1980)	6:00	2+	C

SOLO INSTRUMENTAL MUSIC — SOLO STRING WITH KEYBOARD

ALLEN

Nightshades (1977, rev. 1979)
(vcl and pno)   15:00   3   ACA

BARNETT

Memoriam (1975)
(vla and pno)   4:45   2   C

BEESON

In Green Meadows
(vln and pno)   3:00   2   C

BOLZ

Sonata for Violoncello and Piano (1957)   7:00   2+   C

BRITAIN

Translunar Cycle (1980)
(vcl and pno)   10:00   UCLA

BRUSH

Romance sans Paroles (1950)
(vln and pno)   8:00   3   C

Sketches (1967)
(vln or fl and pno)   12:00   3   C

† *Valse joyeuse* (1959)
(vln and pno)   6:00   2   ComP

CECCONI-BATES

Sonata No. 1: Two Rhapsodic Movements (1975)
(vln and pno)   7:00   3   C

Sonata No. 2: Una cosa per violino (1978)
(vln and pno)   15:00   3   C

COHEN

City Dances (1976)
(vln and pno)   10:00   2   C

DIEMER

Sonata for Violin and Piano (1949)   12:00   3   See

FULLER-HALL

Adagio (1974)
(vln and pno)   3:15   2   C

LE BARON

Spicebox of Strings (1972)
(vln and pno)   1:50   2   AMC

LOMON

Phase I (1969)
(vcl and pno)   7:00   2+   AMC

MAGEAU

Fantasy Music (1972)
(vln and pno)   8:00   3   AMC

MARCUS

Sonata
(vln and pno)   17:00   3   AMC

PIZER

Qulisoly, Op. 38 (1976)
(vln and pno)   3:00   2+   AMC

PREOBRAJENSKA

Sonata No. 2 in D Major for Violin and Piano (1958)   15:00   AMC

PROCACCINI

Dialogo, Op. 34 (1968)
(vla and pno)   5:00   2   C

Fantasia, Op. 10 (1957)
(vln and pno)   13:00   2   C

Mystère, Op. 62 (1976)
(db and pno)   5:00   2   C

Sonata, Op. 40 (1969)
  (vla and pno)   14:00   3   C

Sonata Rapsodica, Op. 8 (1957)
  (vcl and pno)   12:00   2   C

RICHTER

Aria and Toccata (1957)
  (vla and pno)   10:00   3   Bel-M

Landscapes of the Mind II (1971)
  (vln and pno)   15:00   3   CF

Suite for Violin and Piano (1964)   9:00   3   CF

Three Violin Pieces (1961)
  (vln and pno)   2   CF

SAMSON

Blue Territory I (1975)
  (vln and pno)   6:30   2   C

Blue Territory II (1975)
  (vln and pno)   7:10   2+ C

Experimental Shorts (1969)
  (vln and pno)   4:00   2   C

SAMTER

⊕ *Dialog*
  (vln and pno)   7:00   C

Fraternité
  (vcl and pno)   8:00   C

Metamorphosen
  (vln and pno)   10:00   C

Mini-Trilogie
  (vln and pno)   7:00   ECG

Mosaik
  (db and pno)   7:00   C

Permutation
  (vcl and pno)   9:00   C

SCHONTHAL

Sonata for Violin and Piano (1962)   13:00   3   C

Sonata Concertante for Cello and Piano (1973)	13:00	3	C
Sonata Concertante for Viola and Piano (1975)	13:00	3	C

SILSBEE

Pharos (1977) (vcl and pno)	7:00	3	C

SINGER

Dialogue (vln and pno)	4:00	2	C
Romance (vln and pno)	4:00	2	C

SMITH

Two Pieces for Viola and Piano (1944) "Nocturne" "Festival Piece"	8:00	3	Mowb

VAN DE VATE

Sonata for Viola and Piano (1964)	14:00	3	TPres

VELLÈRE

Divertissement (1962) (vln and pno)	10:00	2	C
Nocturne (1954) (vcl and pno)	7:00	2	C
Sonate (1952) (vln and pno)	15:00	2	CBD

VERCOE

Balance: Duo for Violin and Cello (1974)	20:00	3	Ars
Pasticcio: Pattern and Imagery from Paul Klee (1965) (vcl and pno)	10:00	2+	C

WALLACH

Little Duet (1966) (vln and pno)	3:00		AMC

WEIGL

Burlesque
(vcl or tbn and pno)   4:00   1   ACA

WYLIE

Sonata for Viola and Piano, Op. 16, No. 3   20:00   2   AMC

ZAIMONT

† *Grand Tarantella* (1970)
(vln and pno)   5:00   2   AMC

ZIFFRIN

Sonata for Organ and Cello (1973)   12:00   3   C

Sono
(vcl and pno)   16:00   3   C

ZWILICH

⊕ *Sonata in Three Movements* (1973 - 74)
(vln and pno)   12:00   3   E-V

SOLO INSTRUMENTAL MUSIC —
UNACCOMPANIED PERCUSSION

BARNETT, CAROL

Suite Vibes in F (1978)
(solo vibe)   7:15   3   C

COHEN

A Mazement (1974)
(perc)   10:00   2   C

DIEMER

Three Pieces for Carillon (1972)   10:00   3   GoC

Toccata (1955)
(marmb)   5:00   3   MfP

PIERCE

Fool's Gold (1978)
(vibe)   14:00   3   See

The Great Horned Owl (1977)
(kelon marmb)   11:30   3   C

Popo Agie (1979)
(vibe)   14:00   3   See

SIMONS

⊕ *Design Groups #1*
(perc: 1 to 3 players)   5:00 - 7:00   Mer

She's Down The Road By Miss Winnie
(solo perc ensemble of 12 perc)   15:00   Mer

SOLO INSTRUMENTAL MUSIC — SOLO PERCUSSION WITH KEYBOARD

LOMON

Dialogue (1964)
(vibe and hpsd)   8:00   3   AMC

PROCACCINI

Dialoghi, Op. 75 (1979)
(pno and perc)   16:00   2   C

REID

Braxton (1974)
(pno and perc)   13:00   3   C

SOLO INSTRUMENTAL MUSIC — UNACCOMPANIED PLECTRAL

ALLEN

Partials for Harp (1976)   14:00   2   ACA

BOLZ

Narrative Impromptu (Street of Dreams) (1979)
(hrp)   5:05   2+   Ars

BRITAIN

Anima divina (1966) (hrp)	8:00		See
The Chateau (1965) (hrp)			C
Love Song of the Taj Mahal (Alma Halff) (1947) (hrp and narr)			UCLA
Reflection (1965) (hrp)	4:00		Hero
Western Suite (1965) (hrp)			C

LOMON

Dust Devils (1976)	8:00	2+	Ars

PIERCE

Maola (1977) (hrp)	12:00	3	See
Serenade, On Zander's Cobweb Photo (1979) (gtr)	12:00	1	C

PROCACCINI

5 Pezzi Incaici, Op. 60 (1975) (gtr)	12:00	2	Zan
6 Studi, Op. 61 (1975) (gtr)	12:00	1	C

SCHONTHAL

Fantasia In A Nostalgic Mood (1978) (gtr)	8:00	2	C

WALKER

Fantasy for Lute (1979)	6:00	3	Walk
Four Pieces for Lute (1977)	10:00	2	Walk

ZIFFRIN

Rhapsody for Guitar (1958)	6:00	3	C

● **SOLO INSTRUMENTAL MUSIC — SOLO PLECTRAL WITH KEYBOARD** ●

SILSBEE

Gylphs (1979) (gtr and hpsd)	16:00	3	C

● **SOLO INSTRUMENTAL MUSIC — OTHER INSTRUMENTAL MUSIC (INSTRUMENTATION SPECIFIED)** ●

ANDERSON, BETH

Preparation for the Dominant: Outrunning the Inevitable (1979) (ocarina or other treble instrument in C)	4:00	3	Jsh

BARNETT, CAROL

Alma del Payaso (1979) (accord)	8:30	3	C

PIERCE

Concord Bridge (1976) (carillon)	5:00	2+	C

● **SOLO INSTRUMENTAL MUSIC — SOLO INSTRUMENT WITH TAPE** ●

ANDERSON, BETH

Good-bye Bridget Bardot or Hello Charlotte Moorman (1974) (vcl and tape)	10:00-45:00	2+	ACA
Promised Church Beautiful River (1977) (tbn and tape)	15:00-25:00	2+	C
They Did It (1975-76) (pno and tape)	10:00	2+	ACA
Tower of Power (1973) (org and tape)	10:00-30:00	2+	ACA

COHEN

Changes (1974) (vln and tape)	10:00	2	C

Chess Set (1971)
(perc and tape)   10:00   2   C

Zodiac Cast (1969)
(fl and tape)   10:00   2   C

DANFORTH

Into the Vortex (1980)
(four timp and tape)   C

HAYS

City Cedar
(Buchla and pno)   2:00–3:00   C

Fire Pink
(Buchla and pno)   2:00–3:00   C

Pamp
(pno, tape, and bird whistles)   7:00   3   Q-H

Pink Turtlehead
(Buchla and pno)   2:00–3:00   C

Pipsissewa
(Buchla and pno)   2:00–3:00   C

Trailing Arbutus
(Buchla and pno)   2:00–3:00   C

Wildflowers
(Buchla and pno)   2:00–3:00   C

MAGEAU

Interaction (1969)
(cl and tape)   C

MARCUS

Three Modules
(pno and Moog synthesizer)   10:00   3   C

PAULL

† *Antifon* (1974)
(pno and tape)   10:00   3   AMC

SEMEGEN

Music for Cello and Tape (1980)   10:00   2+   ACA

† *Music for Viola and Tape* (1980)   12:00   2+   AMC

STANLEY

Duo-Sonata for Tape Recorder and Piano (1970)
(pre-recorded tape and pno)   9:00   3   C

WALLACH

Prelude and Toccata
(pno and tape)   7:00   AMC

CHAMBER INSTRUMENTAL MUSIC — KEYBOARD(S)
WITH MULTIPLE PLAYERS

BOLZ

Capitol Pageant
(pno, 4-hands)   4:00   2+   Sis

BRITAIN

Angel Chimes (1951)
(2 pnos)   UCLA

Cactus Rhapsody (1965)
(2 pnos)   UCLA

Minha Terra (Barrozo Netto) (1956)
(2 pnos)   Ric

† *Pastorale* (1939)
(2 pnos)   UCLA

Le Petit Concerto (1957)
(2 pnos)   Hero

Rhapsodic Rhapsody (1956)
(for pno and orch; arr for 2 pnos)   LC

BRUSH

American Circle (1979)
(2 pnos)   6:00   3   C

DEMBO

Triptych
(pno, 4-hands)   12:00   3   C

DIEMER

Pianoharpsichordorgan (1974)
(live or may be taped separately)
(pno, hpsd, org)   7:00   3   See

HSU

† *Fantasia for Two Pianos* (1955)   10:00   3   W-Y

HYSON

Eight Light-Hearted Variations on The Jolly Miller (1971)
(pno duet)   5:00   2   NK

Fantasy on Three English Folk Songs (1970)
(pno duet)   2:30   2   NK

The Legend of St. Katherine (1972)
(pno duet)   14:00   2+   C

Our British Cousins (1976)
(pno duet)   6:00   2   NK

Partita (1970)
(pno duet)   14:00   2+   C

A Western Summer (1976)
(pno duet)   6:00   2   NK

LOMON

Soundings (1975)
(pno, 4-hands)   7:00   2+   Ars

Triptych (1978)
(2 pnos)   8:00   2+   AMC

MAGEAU

Pacific Ports (1979)
(pno, 4-hands)   5:00   2+   C

PIERCE

Antares (1974)
(pno, 4-hands)   6:00   3   C

Danse Micawber
Sweeney Among the Nightingales (1974)
(pno, 4-hands)   10:00   2+   See

Loure and Rondeau (1974)
(pno, 4-hands)   3:00   2   C

Variations in 4/4
(pno, 4-hands)   3:00   2   C

PROCACCINI

Little Horse's Story, Op. 40 (1978)
(pno, 4-hands)   15:00   2   C

Marionette, Op. 51 (1972)
(pno, 4-hands)   10:00   3   C

Sensazioni Sonore, Op. 35 (1968)
(four pieces for 2 pnos)   13:00   3   Sonz

RICHTER

Melodrama (1958)
(2 pnos)   16:00   3   CF

Variations on a Theme by Latimer (1964)
(pno, 4-hands)   9:00   3   CF

SAMTER

Duo Ritmico
(pno, 4-hands)   7:00   C

Gemini
(pno, 4-hands)   7:00   C

SILSBEE

Letter from a Field Biologist (1979)
(2 pnos)   17:00   3   C

SIMONS

Illuminations for Two Pianos
(aleatoric)
"Snow Water"
"Drops of Laughter"
"One Flower Two Gardeners"
"Five Sprays of the Snow Foundatain"   40:00   ACA

Two Dots
(graphic sc)
(2 pnos)   14:00   ACA

SINGER

American Short Subjects
(2 pnos)   4:00   2   C

SMELTZER

Piece in 12-tone Style (1960)
(2 pnos)   3:00   1   C

Theme and Variations for 2 Pianos (1961)   8:00   2+   C

SMITH

American Dance Suite (1935; revised 1966)
"One Morning in May"
"Lost My Partner"
"Negro Lullaby"
"Chicken Reel"
(2 pnos)   10:00   2   Mowb

Concerto for Piano and Orchestra (1938-39: revised 1971)
(reduction for 2 pnos)   22:00   3   Mowb

ZAIMONT

† *Snazzy Sonata* (1972)
"Moderate Two-Step"
"Lazy Beguine"
"Be-Bop Scherzo"
"Valse Brilliant"
(pno: 4-hands)   18:00   3   C

CHAMBER INSTRUMENTAL MUSIC —
PIANO TRIOS/PIANO QUARTETS

ANDERSON, BETH

The Eighth Ancestor (1980)
(2 vln, vcl, pno, or baroque fl, alto rec, vcl, hpsd)   3   Jsh

Skater's Suite (1980)
(2 vln, vcl, pno, or baroque fl, alto rec, vcl, hpsd) 23:00   3   Jsh

DEMBO

† *Trio No. 1*
(vln, vcl, pno)   15:00   3   C

DIEMER

    Quartet for Piano, Violin, Viola, and Cello (1954)   12:00   3   See

HOOVER

  ⊕ *Trio* (1978)
     (vln, vcl, pno)   18:00   3   AMC

HSU

  † *Trio for Violin, Cello and Piano* (1955)   10:00   W-Y

PROCACCINI

  Trio, Op. 5 (1956)
     (vln, vcl, pno)   15:00   2   C

RICHTER

  Landscapes of the Mind III (1979)
     (vln, vcl, pno)   25:00   3   CF

SAMTER

  Klaviertrio
     (vln, vcl, pno)   8:00   C

  Metamorphosen
     (vln and cembalo)   10:00   C

  Nelly-Sachs-Trio
     (vln, vcl, pno)   9:00   C

SMITH

  Trio — Cornwall (1955)
     (vln, vcl, pno)   14:40   3   Mowb

VELLÈRE

  Trio (1947)
     (vln, vcl, pno)   25:00   2   C

ZIFFRIN

  Trio for Violin, Cello and Piano (1975)   18:00   3   C

CHAMBER INSTRUMENTAL MUSIC — WIND QUINTETS
(OR SUBDIVISIONS THEREOF)

ALLEN

Wind Songs (1975)
(ww qnt)   13:00   2+   ACA

BOLZ

Pageant (1976)
(ww qnt)   10:00   3   HB

BRITAIN

Four Sarabandes (1965)
(ww qnt)   8:00   See

DANFORTH

Theme and Variations (1973)
(fl, cl, bsn)   15:00   3   C

DEMBO

Trio
(fl, ob, bsn)   14:00   3   C

† *Woodwind Quintet*
(fl, ob, cl, bsn, hn)   9:00   3   C

DIEMER

Music for Woodwind Quartet (1972)
(fl, ob, cl, bsn)   10:00   2+   OUP

Woodwind Quintet, No. 1 (1960)   8:00   2   B&H

FRASIER

60 Second Trio
(ob, cl, bsn)   1:00   2+   C

Woodwind Trio I
(ob, cl, bsn)   2:45   3   C

Woodwind Trio II
(fl, ob, bsn)   12:00   3+   C

Woodwind Quintet II   10:00   3+   C

GARDNER

Sailing Song (1978)
(ww qnt or fl (pic), vln, vla, 2 vcl)   5:00   2   Iris

GLAZIER

Prayers of a Dreamer
(arr. for ww qnt)   C

HOOVER

Homage to Bartok (1975)
(ww qnt)   14:00   3   AMC

HSU

Theme and Variations for Woodwind Trio (1964)
(fl, cl, bsn)   10:00   W-Y

LACKMAN

Woodwind Quintet   12:00   2   C

MEACHEM

Trio for Winds (1971)
"Invention"
"Andante"
"Rondo"
(fl, cl, bsn)   10:00   2   C

PROCACCINI

† *Clown Music* - Four Pieces for Wind Quintet, Op. 36 (1968)   11:00   3   Zan

SAMTER

Mobile
(ob and bsn)   7:00   C

Sketch
(fl, cl, bsn)   8:00   C

Sketch für drei Holzbläser
(ob, cl, bsn)   8:00   EdC

Sketch II
(fl, cl, bsn)   8:00   C

SMELTZER

Kaleidescope (1979)
"Dialogue"
"Lazy Practice Room at Noon on the Moon"
"Folk Dance"
"Little Song"
"Fanfare"
"Bach's Nightmare"
"Train Whistle"
"Rat-Race Toccata"
(ww qnt)   10:00   2   C

STANLEY

Woodwind Quintet (1951)   2   C

VAN DE VATE

Woodwind Quartet (1964)
(fl, ob, cl, bsn)   7:30   2+ SMP

VELLÈRE

Prelude (1961)
(ob, cl, bsn, hn)   3:00   3   JM

Quartetto (1964)
(fl, ob, cl, bsn)   13:00   2   JM

WEIGL

⊕† *Brief Encounters*
(ww qt)   14:00   2   ACA

Mood Sketches
(ww qt)   12:00   2   ACA

WYLIE

Five Occurrences, Op. 27
(ww qnt)   12:00   3   C

ZAIMONT

† *Two Movements for Wind Quartet*
(fl, ob, bsn, hn)   4:30   2   C

CHAMBER INSTRUMENTAL MUSIC — BRASS QUINTETS
(OR SUBDIVISIONS THEREOF)

BRITAIN

Adoration (1976)
(2 tpts, hn, tbn)   6:00   UCLA

† *Awake to Life* (1968)
(brass qnt)   6:00   UCLA

FULLER-HALL

Jazz Impromptu (1979)
(brass qnt)   4:00   2   C

LE BARON

† *Three Motion Atmospheres for Brass Quintet* (1974)
(2 tpts, hn, ten-tbn, b-tbn or tuba)   5:00   1   AMC

LOMON

Equinox (1978)
(brass qt: 2 tpts, 2 tbns)   4:00   2+   AMC

Solstice (1978)
(brass qt: 2 tpts, 2 tbns)   4:00   2+   AMC

REED

Brass Quartet No. 1
(2 tpts, hn, tbn)   5:00   3   AMC

RICHTER

One for Two and *Two for Three* (1947, rev. 74)
(tbn duet and trio)   5:00   3   CF

Ricercare (1958)
(brass qt)   4:00   2   CF

STANLEY

Quartet for Brass (1950)   2   C

VAN DE VATE

Diversion for Brass (1964)
(2 tpts, hn, tbn or euph)   3:30   2   AMC

Short Suite for Brass Quartet (1960)
(2 tpts, tbn, b-tbn)   6:00   2+   TPres

† Quintet for Brass (1974, rev. 1979)
(2 tpts, hn, tbn, tuba)   12:00   3   AMC

VELLÈRE

Deux Essais (1965)
(tpt, hn, tbn)   7:00   2   JM

CHAMBER INSTRUMENTAL MUSIC —
STRING TRIOS/STRING QUARTETS

ALLEN

Constellations (1979)
(stg qt)   20:00   2+   ACA

ANDERSON, BETH

Music for Charlemagne Palestine (1973)
(stg qt or vln, vcl, harmonium)   5:00-15:00   2+   C

BRITAIN

† Epic Poem (Musical Portrait of Thomas Jefferson) (1927)
(stg qt)   8:00   UCLA

Prison (Lament) (1935)
(stg qt)   4:00   UCLA

† String Quartet (4 Movements) (1934)   18:00   UCLA

CECCONI-BATES

Quartet brevis (1976)
(stg qt)   10:00   3   C

DANFORTH

String Quartet (1967)   10:00   2   C

HAYS

Tunings
(stg qt)   13:00   3   Q-H

HSU

String Quartet No. 1 (1958)	8:00		W-Y
String Quartet No. II (1968)	6:00		W-Y

LACKMAN

String Trio (vln, vla, vcl)	3:00	1	C
String Quartet No. 1	9:00	2	C
String Quartet No. 2	10:00	2+	C

MARCUS

String Quartet No. 1	20:00	3	C
String Quartet No. 2	20:00	3	C

PIZER

Interfuguelude, Op. 43 (1977) (stg qt)	4:00	2+	AMC

PROCACCINI

Improvvisazioni, Op. 37 (1968) (vln, vla, vcl)	7:00	2	C
Quartetto, Op. 42 (1969) (stgs)	7:00	2	C

RICHTER

Ricercare (1958) (stg qt)	4:00	2	CF
String Quartet No. 2 (1958)	16:00	3	CF

SAMTER

Episoden (vln, vla)	7:00		C

SCHONTHAL

† *String Quartet* (1962)	14:00	3	C

SEMEGEN

Compositions for String Quartet (1965)	8:00	2	ACA
String Quartet No. 1 (1963)	8:00		C
String Quartet No. 2 (1964)	16:00		C

SILSBEE

Quest (1977) (stg qt)	15:00	3	ACA

SIMONS

Duo for Violin and Cello	12:00		ACA
Facets No. 4 (stg qt)	10:30		Mer
String Quartet	12:00		ACA
Two Violin Sonate (2 vln)	18:00		ACA

SMITH

⊕ *Quartet for Strings* (1964)	15:00	3	Mowb

STANLEY

String Quartet (1951)		2	C

VAN DE VATE

Music for Student String Quartet (1977)	6:00	2	AMC
† *String Quartet No. 1* (1969)	13:00	3	AMC
† *Trio for Strings* (1974)	14:00	2	Ars

VELLÈRE

Prelude and Scherzo (1949) (stg trio)		2	C
Quatrième Quatuor (1962) (stg qt)	14:00	2	C
Troisième Quatuor (1951) (stg qt)	15:00	2	C

WALLACH

String Quartet (1968) — 8:00   AMC

WEIGL

Adagio for Strings
(stg qt, or stg orch) — 4:00   1   ACA

† *Andante for Strings*
(stg qt, or stg orch) — 5:00   1   ACA

WYLIE

String Quartet No. I, Op. 1 — 15:00   2   C

String Quartet No. II, Op. 8 — 20:00   2   C

String Quartet No. III, Op. 17 — 22:00   2+   Cor

ZAIMONT

De Caeleste Infinitate (Of the Celestial Infinite) (1980-82)
(stg qt) — 42:00   3   C

ZIFFRIN

String Quartet (1970) — 15:00   2+   C

ZWILICH

⊕ *String Quartet 1974* — 15:00   3   Mrg

CHAMBER INSTRUMENTAL MUSIC — ENSEMBLES:
ONE TO FOUR PLAYERS

ALLEN

Legends (1972)
(fl, ob, vcl, perc) — 18:00   2+   ACA

Lost Angels (1979)
(tpt, bsn, pno) — 15:00   2+   ACA

† *Quatrain* (1975)
(vln, vla, cl, bcl) — 7:00   2+   ACA

Rhymes
(tpt, tbn, perc) — 8:00   1+   ACA

When the Moon of Wild Flowers is Full (1973)
(fl and vcl)   6:00   1   ACA

ANDERSON, BETH

Dactylology (1967)
(fl, cl, Enghn, bsn)   10:00   2+   C

BARNETT

Suite for Two Flutes (1977)   5:30   2   C

BOLZ

Linear Trilogy
(ww trio, fl, cl, bsn)   4:00   2   C

de BOHUN [Boone]

The Americas Trio (1960)
(fl, cl, bsn)   4:30   2   Ars

BRITAIN

† *Cactus Rhapsody* (1977)
(cl, vcl, pno)   8:00   UCLA

† *Chipmunks* (1940)
(ww, hrp, perc)   5:00   C

Dance Grotesque (1960)
(2 fl)   4:00   See

† *In the Beginning* (1962)
(4 hn)   6:00   See

Les Femeux Douze (1966)
(vln, vcl)   5:00   C

Pastorale (1967)
(rec, ob, hpsd, hrp)   7:00   UCLA

† *Phantasy* (1942)
(ob, hrp, pno)   8:00   UCLA

Phantasy (1974)
(ww-trio: cl, ob, bsn)   8:00   UCLA

Processional (1969)
(4 tbn)   3:00   HB

Recessional (1969)
(4 tbn)   3:00   HB

The World Does Not Wish for Beauty (1977)
  (4 tubas)   8:00   HML

BRUSH

Duets for Flute and Bassoon   C

CECCONI-BATES

From the Tug Hill Plateau (1979)
  (stg trio and fl or ob)   10:00   3   C

Seven Variations on "Terra Tremuit" (1977)
  (fl, ob, cl, bsn)   12:00   3   C

Two Movements for Flute, Oboe, Clarinet, Bassoon (1977) 8:00   2   C

Two Movements for Two Trumpets and Piano (1977)   7:00   2   C

CHANCE

Ceremonial (1976)
  (4 players: 32 instr)
  (perc qt)   15:00   3   See

⊕ *Daysongs* (1974)
  (al-fl and 2 perc players)   10:00   3   See

Declamation and Song (1977)
  (vln, vcl, vibe, pno)   15:00   3   See

Duo II (1978)
  (ob and Enghn)   8:00   3   See

Duo III (1980)
  (vln and vcl)   7:00   3   C

Duo IV (1980)
  (al-sax and timp)   3   C

COHEN

Trio (1956)
  (hn, cl, bsn)   10:00   2   C

DANFORTH

Cloistered Walls (1980)
  (vcl, hpsd, perc)   C

Four Miniatures (1979)
  (pno, vibes bells)   1   C

Rain Forest (1978)
(solo marmb with 3 perc)   10:00   2   C

DEMBO

Suite
(2 T-rec, B-rec, vla da gamba)   5:00   2   C

† Trio
(fl, cl, pno)   3:00   3   C

DIEMER

Movement for Flute, Oboe and Organ (1974)   10:00   3   CF

Movement for Flute, Oboe, Clarinet, and Piano (1976)   10:00   3   See

FRASIER

Flute Quartet I   10:00   2+   C

Trio
(fl, vibes, vcl)   6:45   3+   C

FULLER-HALL

Abbreviated Duet (1976)
(2 cl)   1:35   2   C

Bravura (1978)
(tpt duet)   1:45   2   C

Controversy (1978)
(hn trio)   3:00   2   C

6 Movements (1979)
(4 tubas, or 2 tubas and 2 euphoniums)   6:30   2+   C

GARDNER

⊕ Crystal Bells (1976)
(fl, gtr, vcl, and others at random)   6:30   3   Iris

Energies (1973)
(fl, ob, vla)   7:00   3   Iris

⊕ Innermoods (1975)
(fl [al-fl], gtr)   3:00   2   Iris

⊕ Romance (1975)
(fl or al-fl, vla or vcl, gtr)   3:30   2   Iris

⊕ Touching Souls (1975)
(al-fl, gtr, small perc)   6:00   3   Iris

GLAZIER

Currents
(fl, vcl, pno)   C

HAYS

Lullaby
(fl, vln, pno)   3:00   2   Q-H

Segments/Junctures
(cl, vla, pno)   11:00   3   Q-H

Tommy's Trumpet
(tpt duo)   4:00   2   Q-H

Tunings
(vln duo)   3:30   3   Q-H

HOOVER

⊕ *Divertimento* (1975)
(fl, vln, vla, vcl)   13:00   2+   AMC

Duets (1977, 1979)
(2 fl)   6:00   3   AMC

Saxophone Quartet
"Going to London"
"Count Off"
"Ira's Tune"
"Honk"
(sop-sax, al-sax, ten-sax, bar-sax)   12:00   3   AMC

⊕ *Sinfonia* (1976)
(4 bsn)   12:00   3   AMC

Trio for Flutes (1974)
(3 fl)   8:00   2   AMC

Two Dances (1976)
(fl, ob, gtr)   6:00   2   AMC

HSU

Evening Prayer (1951)
(arr. from vocal solo with obblig vln)
(fl duet)   3:00   W-Y

Parting Song (1956)
(arr. from vocal solo with obblig cl)
(fl duet)   4:00   W-Y

Light of God (1960)
(arr. from vocal solo with obblig vln)
(fl duet)   4:00   W-Y

HYSON

Three Night Pieces (1976)
(fl, cl, vcl)   10:00   3   C

JANKOWSKI

Daguerreotypes (1979)
(cl, perc)   8:00   3   C

Declarations (1972)
(vcl, 3 perc players)   11:00   3   C

Four Haiku (1980)
(tpt, marmb)   12:00   3   C

No Time to Mourn (1975)
(vln, 2 cl)   7:00   3   C

LACKMAN

Fragments
(fl, vcl, pno)   6:00   1+   C

LE BARON

Fertility Dance (1971)
(fl, marmb, 2 bongos, db)   1:00   2   AMC

The Moonbeam Wishbook (1980)
(music for film)
(org, pno, hrp)   3:00   AMC

Music for Peyote Cactus (1973)
(vla, ob, ten-sax, perc [large gong, temp blks,
    tamb, wind chimes])   7:00-12:00   1   AMC

Resonances (1971)
(pno, hrp, timp)   4:00   2   AMC

Rite of the Black Sun (based on a text by Antonin
Artaud) (1980)
(perc qt and 7 dances - dancers optional)   15:00   3   AMC

LOMON

Celebrations: Nimbus and the Sun God (1978)
(2 hrps)   18:00   3   AMC

Furies (Erinnyes) (1977)
(ob, ob d'amore, Enghn)   8:00   3   AMC

MAGEAU

Dialogues (1977)
(SATB rec qt)   8:00   3   C

Dialogues (1979)
  (cl, vcl, pno)   12:00   3   AMC

Doubles (1977)
  (SATB rec qt)   6:00   2   AMC

Sonata Concertate (1980)
  (fl, vcl, hpsd)   10:00   3   AMC

MEACHEM

Variations for Two Flutes (1970)   3:00   2   C

ORENSTEIN

Dialogue (1975)
  (cl and vcl)   1:00   2+ C

Music for Flute, Viola and Percussion (1971)
  (fl [pic, al-fl], vla, marmb, vibe, timp, Tam-T,
   suspended cym, guiro, claves, triangle)   7:00   2+ C

October 31 (1975)
  (ob and vla)   1:00   3   C

Trio (1975)
  (2 cl, vcl)   2:00   2+ C

PAULL

Interplay (1972-77)
  (fl and 3 pnos)   12:00   2   AMC

Requiem (1975)
  (2 perc)   12:00   3   AMC

PIERCE

A Common Chase (1979)
  (rec and marmb)   9:00   2+ C

After Dubuffet's "Limbour As A Crustacean" (1979)
  (cl, sn dm, 3 tom-toms, marmb)   14:00   3   C

Job 22:28 (1978)
  (cl duo)   15:00   3   See

Quartet, Music for Dance (1979)
  (prepared pno, cl, hn, marmb)   18:30   3   C

PIZER

Interfuguelude, Op. 43 (1977)
(fl, Enghn, hn, bsn)   4:00   2+   AMC

PREOBRAJENSKA

Trio (1976)
(fl, vln, vla)   3:00   AMC

PROCACCINI

Invenzione, Op. 9 (1957)
(fl, ob, cl [or bsn], pno)   7:00   2   Cari

Lied, Op. 65 (1977)
(fl and hrp)   5:00   2   C

Quartetto, Op. 27 (1965)
(fl, ob, bsn, pno)   14:00   2   C

Serenata Notturna, Op. 67 (1977)
(hn and hrp)   5:00   2   C

REED

Chromasia
(al-sax and 2 perc)   6:00   3   See

Three Short Dialogues
(3 B-flat cl)   4:45   2+   Shaw

REID

Sketches (1971)
(2 ob and Enghn)   7:00   2+   C

RICHTER

Pastorale (1975)
(2 ob)   3:00   2   CF

ROGERS

Five Duos for Clarinet and Cello   12:00   2   C

*"Threads" - A Study in Percussion Sonorities for
Two Players*
(marmb, xylopipes, cym, dms, timp, triangles,
wood blocks, pno)   20:00   2+   C

Trio for Flute, Viola and Bassoon (3 movements)	14:00	2	C

SAMSON

Mousterian Meander (1976) (rec, vcl and pno)	6:20	1+	C
Oboe Duet (1972) (2 ob)	4:20	2	C
Quartet for Flute, Clarinet, Viola and Cello (1973)	6:40	2	C

SAMTER

Essay (vln and cym)	5:00	C
Les extrêmes se touchent (cl, vcl, pno)	9:00	C
Kaleidoskop (fl and vln)	7:00	C
⊕ *Kontrapost* (fl, al-rec, pno)	10:00	C
Rivalités (fl, cl, vcl, pno)	10:00	C
Rotation (fl and cym)	5:00	C
Trialog (vln, db, pno)	8:00	C

SEMEGEN

⊕ *Jeux des Quatres* (1970) (B-flat cl, tbn, pno, vcl)	12:30	2	ACA
Suite for Flute and Violin (1965)	11:00	2	C

SILSBEE

Pharos II (1979) (vcl, perc, pno)	12:00	3	ACA
Quartet (1980) (cl, vln, vcl, pno)	15:00	3	ACA
Trialogue (1976) (cl, vln, pno)	9:00	3	ACA

SIMONS

Facets No. 1
  (hn, vln, pno)   6:00   Mer

Facets No. 2
  (fl [pic] , cl, db)   7:00   Mer

The Great Stream Silent Moves
  (pno, hrp, perc: small Tam-T, tom-toms,
      cym, b dm, thundersheet, xylo)   10:00   Mer

Quartet for Flute and Strings
  (fl, vln, vla, vcl)   8:00   ACA

SINGER

† *From the Green Mountains*
  "Winter Identity"
  "Yankee Springtime"
  (vln, cl, pno)   7:00   2   HB

Grandmother's Attic (1980)
  (fl, ob, vln, vcl)   12:00   2   C

† *Rhapsody*
  (vln, cl, pno)   3:30   2   C

Suite for Horn and Harp (four movements)   12:00   2   Cor

† *Sweet Stacy Suite*
  "Sephardic Dance"
  "Echoes from Spain"
  "American Tune"
  (vln, cl, pno)   6:00   2   C

† *Then and Now* - Theme and Variations
  (vln, cl, pno)   7:30   2   C

SWISHER

Suite for Three Alto Saxophones and Piano   10:00   3   C

Theater Trio
  (tpt, al-sax, pno)   9:00   3   AMC

VAN DE VATE

Incidental Piece for Three Saxes (1976)
  (3 E-flat al-sax)   5:00   2   AMC

⊕ *Music for Viola, Percussion and Piano* (1976)   16:00   3   AMC

VELLÈRE

Pirouettes (1964)
(2 vln)   6:00   2   CBD

Quatuor (1963)
(4 cl)   14:00   2   JM

Sonate (1961)
(vln and vla)   12:00   2   C

Bagatelles (1960)
(3 cl)   12:00   2   JM

WALLACH

Coalescence (1980)
(sax qt)   12:00   AMC

Quartet
(ww and stgs)   7:00   AMC

Trio (1968)
(3 reed instr)   6:00   AMC

WEIGL

Dialogues
(fl and vln, or vln and cl)   9:00   2   ACA

⊕ New England Suite
   "Vermont Nocturne"
   "Maine Interlude"
   "Berkshire Pastorale"
   "Connecticut Country Fair"
   (cl or fl, vcl, pno)   12:00   2   ACA

Three Discourses
(fl or vln, and vcl)   14:00   2   ACA

Trialogue
(fl, vla, hrp or pno)   14:00   2   ACA

ZIFFRIN

The Little Prince (1953)
(suite)
(B-flat cl and bsn)   7:00   2   C

Movements for B-Flat Clarinet and Percussion (1972)   12:00 3   MfP

ZWILICH

Clarino Quartet (1977)
(4 tpt: first part, pic-tpt)   12:00   3   Mrg

CHAMBER INSTRUMENTAL MUSIC — ENSEMBLES:
FIVE TO TWELVE PLAYERS

ALLEN

Tombeaux des Morts (1973)
(vla, vcl, db, hrp, pno)   9:00   2+   ACA

ANDERSON, BETH

Skate Suite's Water-Strider Courrente (re-orchestrated 1979)
(fl, cl, pno, org, db, perc)   3   C

Eighth Ancestor (1979)
(fl, cl, org, pno, db, perc)   3   C

BOLZ

† *Lyric Sonata*
(2 vln, vla, vcl, fl, cl, bsn)   8:06   2+   C

CHANCE

⊕ *Ritual Sounds* (1975)
(brass qnt and perc: 3 players)   7:00   3   See

DEMBO

Sextet
(fl, ob, cl, bsn, hn, pno)   8:00   3   C

DIEMER

Sextet (1963)
(ww qnt, pno)   18:00   3   See

⊕ *Toccata for Flute Chorus* (1968)
(pic, 4 fl [in E-flat, C, G and bfl])   8:00   3   CF

FORMAN

Goya Fanfare
(tpt, tbn, db, perc)   4:00   2+   C

FULLER-HALL

Overture of Hymns (1979)
(brass qnt, org, timp)   5:00   2+   C

GARDNER

Sailing Song (1978)
(fl [pic], vln, vla, 2 vcl [or ww qnt])   5:00   2   Iris

Winter Night, Gibbons Moon (1980)
(11 fl: 3 pic, 3 fl, 3 al-fl, 2 bfl)   13:00   3   Iris

HAYS

Characters
(pno or hpsd, stg qnt, 2 cl, ob)   17:00   3   Q-H

Tunings
(stg qnt)   Q-H

Windpipes
(5 fl)   10:00   3   Q-H

HSU

† *Song of Old Fisherman* (1978)
(vcl solo with ww, stgs, hrp)   5:00   W-Y

JANKOWSKI

Flute Sextet (1972)
(2 pic, 2 fl, al-fl, bfl)   6:00   2+   C

LE BARON

*Extensions: Three Movements for Large Percussion
Ensemble and Harp* (1975)
(xylo, marmb, vibes, glock, tubular bells, rototoms,
large Tam-T, med & large gongs, med cym, antique
cym, med suspended cym, tamb, b dm, temp
blks, glass & bamboo wind chimes, wood blks,
triangle, sn dm, 2 bongos, 2 med maracas, slapstick,
timp, pno, hrp)   12:00   2   AMC

Giuoco Piano (1971)
(pic, fl, 2 tpt, 2 tbn, db)   2:00   2   AMC

Memnon (1976)
(6 hrp)   5:00   2   Hen

† *Metamorphosis* (1977)

(pic, fl, ob, cl, hn, tem-tbn, hrp, marmb, glock,
  xylo, large Tam-T, cowbell, temp blks, 3 wood
  blocks, slapstick, tamb, 3 suspended cym, siz
  cym, small gong, 5 rototoms, 3 tomtoms, b dm)
  (cond and 7 players required)   17:00   3   APR

Passacaglia (1971)
  (vln, fl, ob, cl, bsn, vcl)   2:30   2   AMC

MAGEAU

Forensis (1973)
  (fl, ob, cl, bsn, 2 perc)   C

MARCUS

A Setting to Seasons
  (fl, ob, cl, vln I and II, vla, vcl, db, pno)   25:00   3   C

Textures
  (fl, stg qt, pno)   15:00   3   C

ORENSTEIN

Quintet for Strings (1974)
  (2 vln, vla, vcl, db, cond)   9:00 2+   C

PIZER

Nocturne, Op. 28 (1976)
  (hrp, cel, ob, vla, vcl)   5:00 2+   AMC

Piece of Eight: Octet for Winds, Op. 42 (1977)
  (2 ob, 2 cl, 2 hn, 2 bsn)   4:00   3   AMC

PREOBRAJENSKA

Mazurka, Op. 2 No. 1 (1947)
  (fl, 2 cl, hn, 2 vln, vla, vcl)   4:00   AMC

PROCACCINI

Divertimento, Op. 6 (1956)
  (pno, tpt, vibe, musical saw, timp)   10:00   2   C

Divertissement, Op. 79 (1980)
  (4 tpt, tbn)   11:00   3   C

Concertino for Bassoon and 9 Instruments, Op. 66
  (1977)
  (fl, ob, cl, hn, vibe, vln, vla, vcl, db, with bsn solo)   7:00   3   C

Marionette for Piano and 10 Instruments Op. 58
  (1975)
  (fl, ob, cl, bsn, hn, vibe, vln, vla, vcl, db, with pno solo)   10:00 3 C

Meditazione, Op. 69 (1978)
  (hn, stg qt)   5:00 2 C

Preludio e Marcia for Horn and 8 Instruments, Op. 68
  (1977)
  (fl, ob, cl, bsn, vln, vla, vcl, db, with hn solo)   10:00 2 C

Quintetto for Horn and String Quartet, Op. 46 (1971)   12:00 2 C

Serenata, Op. 31 (1967)
  (2 vln, vcl, fl, hpsd)   12:00 2 C

REID

Escape Wheel for Five (1976)
  (pno, db, 3 cl)   12:00 3 C

ROGERS

A Christmas Overture: Festival of Carols
  (pic-tpt solo with B-flat tpt, fleugelhorn,
    brass qnt, org, 2 perc)   14:00 2 C

"Fortune Cookies" for An Odd Quintet (Eve Merriam)
  (players are required to read text)
  (3 vln, vla, vcl, opt dm)   10:00 2 C

*Octet for the Eight Instruments of the New Violin
Family* (as developed by C. M. Hutchins)   11:00 2 C

Wedding March: Processional, Recessional
  (org, 9 perc)   6:00-7:00 2 C

SILSBEE

Spirals (1975)
  (stg qt and pno)   19:00 3 ACA

SIMONS

Quintet for Winds and String Bass
  (fl, ob, cl, bsn, db)   8:00   ACA

Time Groups No. 2
  (cl, hn, bsn, 2 vln, vla, vcl, db)   15:00   Mer

STANLEY

Overture
(3 tpt, 3 tbn, tuba or bar hn, timp)   3:00   2+   C

VAN DE VATE

† *Quintet* (1975)
(fl, ob, cl, vcl, pno)   10:00   3   AMC

WYLIE

Airs Above the Ground, Op. 32 no. 2
(fl, cl, vln, 4 or 8 vcl)   8:00   3   C

Imagi, Op. 29
(fl, cl, vln, ob, vcl, perc)   varies   2+   C

† *Incubus,* Op. 28
(fl, cl, perc and vcl ensemble)   10:00   3   ASUC

† *Nova,* Op. 30 no. 1
(fl, cl, vcl, perc, with marmb solo)   9:00   3   AMC

Terrae Incognitae, Op. 34
(fl, vla, gtr, pno, perc)   20:00   3   C

Three Inscapes, Op. 26
(fl, vla, gtr, pno, perc)   22:00   3   C

† *Toward Sirius,* Op. 31
(fl, ob, vln, vcl, pno, hpsd)   10:00   3   C

ZIFFRIN

Concerto for Viola and Woodwind Quintet (1977-78)
(vla, fl, ob, cl, bsn, hn)   29:00   3   C

In the Beginning . . . (1968)
(4 perc [1: sn dm; 2: b dm, suspended cym; 3: tom-tom,
triangle; 4: glock, cowbell, field dm] , pno)   4:00   1+   MfP

"Make a Joyful Noise . . ." — *Quintet for
Recorders* (1966)   5:00   3   C

Quintet for Oboe and String Quartet (1976)
(ob, 2 vln, vla, vcl)   17:00   3   C

ZWILICH

⊕ *Chamber Symphony* (1979)
(fl [pic] , cl [bcl] , vln, bla, vcl, pno)   17:00   3   Mer

CHAMBER INSTRUMENTAL MUSIC — ENSEMBLES:
THIRTEEN OR MORE PLAYERS

CHANCE

Darksong (1972)
(2 fl, 2 cl, 2 hn, hrp, gtr, pno, perc: 5 players)   8:00   3   See

HAYS

Pieces From Last Year
(3 al-rec or fl, al-fl, 2 ocarinas, 3 vln,
3 vla, 3 vcl, pno)   9:00   3   Q-H

Pieces From Last Year
(ww, brass, stgs)   9:00   3   Q-H

MARCUS

Anecdotes
(2 or 4 pno, 8 or 16 vln, 4 or 8 vcl, cond)   15:00   3   C

MEACHEM

Moon Shadows (1979)
(2 pic, 12 fl, 2 al-fl)   5:00   3   C

Sunbursts (1979)
(pno solo with 2 pic, 12 fl)   3:00   3   C

PROCACCINI

Piccolo Concerto for 15 Instruments, Op. 19 (1959)
(2 fl, 2 ob, 2 cl, 2 bsn, 2 hn, 2 tpt, xylo, vibe, timp)   16:00   2   C

ROGERS

Dyadiastasis
(fl, ob, 2 cl, bsn, 3 tpt, 2 tbn, timp, 2 perc)   8:00   2+   C

Proclamation! Piece: A Processional
(fl, ob, 2 cl, bsn, 3 tpt, 2 tbn, timp, 2 perc)   7:00   2+   C

VAN DE VATE

Three Sound Pieces for Brass and Percussion (1973)
(2 tpt, 2 hn, 2 tbn, tuba, 6 perc players)   10:00   3   AMC

ZIFFRIN

XIII for Chamber Ensemble (1969)
(2 fl, cl, 2 bsn, 2 hn, tbn, timp, wood block, stg qt)   12:00   2+ C

● CHAMBER INSTRUMENTAL MUSIC — UNSPECIFIED INSTRUMENTS ●

ANDERSON, BETH

Valid for Life (1973)
(for large strung things and large soft instr
and tape)   10:00 - 20:00   2+ Asm

BOLZ

Form, Fantasy and Fugue
(qt of like instr [stgs or ww etc.])   6:03   2+ C

DIEMER

Declamation (1960)
(brass and perc)   4:00   2   EV

FULLER-HALL

Round Trip Ticket (1977)
(jazz band)   5:00   2   C

GARDNER

⊕ *Prayer to Aphrodite* (1975)
(al-fl and stgs)   5:00   2   Iris

A Rainbow Path (1980)
(fls, stgs, ww, small perc, and hrp in
chamber-size combinations)   40:00   2   Iris

Seven Modal Improvisation Studies (1978)
(pno or any bass instr with any treble instr)   5:00   2   Iris
                                                    each

HSU

† *Percussions East and West* (1966)
(perc ensemble)   6:00   W-Y

† *Sonorities of Chinese Percussions with Tune of Three
Variations of Plum Blossoms* (1968)
(perc ensemble)   5:00   W-Y

† *Traveler's Suite* (1960)
(stgs and pno)   10:00   W-Y

SILSBEE

River (1974)
(guided improvisation piece)
(2 groups of players; instrumentation opt)   8:00 - 20:00   3   ACA

ʼ

SIMONS

⊕ *Design Groups No. 1*
(perc: 1 to 3 players)   5:00-7:00   Mer

⊕ *Design Groups No. 2*
(duo for any combination of high and low
pitched instr)   8:00-10:00   Mer

⊕ *Silver Thaw*
(any combination of 1 to 8 players)   10:00   Mer

Variables
(any 5 instr)   23:00   Mer

ZAIMONT

† *Music for Two* (1971)
(suite in 5 movements)
(any 2 ww or stg instr)   9:00   2   AMC

CHAMBER INSTRUMENTAL MUSIC —
MULTIPLE INSTRUMENTS WITH TAPE

COHEN

Music for My Sister (1975)
(fl, ob, tape)   10:00   2   C

DIEMER

Quartet (1974)
(fl, vla, vcl, hpsd, tape [performer-prepared])   13:00   3   See

Trio (1973)
(fl, ob, hpsd, tape [performer-prepared])   10:00   3   See

GARDNER

⊕ *Atlantis Rising* (1978)
    (fl (al-fl), vln (vla), vcl, prepared pno,
        wood chimes, elect. tape)   9:00   2   Iris

⊕ *Lunamuse* (1975)
    (fl, gtr, vcl, small perc, tape loop or audience drone)   9:00   2+   Iris

HAYS

Glub
    (bfl, pic, tape)   10:00   3   Q-H

Only
    (multiple pno, and 2 or 4 tapes)   8:00   3   Q-H

SEMEGEN

Six Plus (1965)
    (tape, fl, hn, vcl, hrp, vln, cond)   14:00   2   ACA

ELECTRONIC MUSIC

ANDERSON, BETH

Joan (1977)
    (15 track tape)   12:00   C

Ode (1976)
    (tape)   20:00   C

Tulip Clause and Buchla Bird Hiss
Down the Road of Life (1973)
    (solo tape)   12:00   C

COHEN

A*R*P (1972)
    (elect. tape)   10:00   C

Devonshire Air (1973)
    (3 cassette tapes)   10:00   C

Santa Rosa Sound (1978)
    (elect. tape)   10:00   2   C

DIEMER

Harpsichord Quartet
    (polyphonic synthesizer and sequencer [tape])   6:00   C

Patchworks (1978) (synthesizer and sequencer [tape])	15:00	C
Presto Canon (polyphonic synthesizer and sequencer [tape])	2:30	C
Scherzo (polyphonic synthesizer and sequencer [tape])	6:00	C

HAYS

Awakening (tapeized poem by Paul Ramsey) (tape)	2:00	Q-H
In the Saddle (cowboy movie)	40:00	Q-H
Only (2 or more tapes, or with 2 or more pno)	8:00	Q-H
Pamp (tape alone; or pno, tape and bird whistles)	7:00	Q-H
Park People's Dream (from *Uni Suite*) (tape solo)	6:00	ABI
⊕ *13th Street Beat, Syn-Rock, Arabella Rag* (and 15 other short electronic musics on tape and disc)	00:40-2:00 each	P-S

JANKOWSKI

Strephenade (1973) (2-channel stereo)	6:00	C

LE BARON

† *Quadratura Circuli* (1978) (tape)	7:00	AMC

MEACHEM

Kilogram Meters Per Second Squared *(A Study in Acceleration)* (1977) (tape)	3:00	C

PIZER

In the Land of Nod (realized 1979, Pizer Studio)
    (Multi-track tape, grand pno, double-manual hpsd,
    ARP Pro-soloist kybd synthesizer, TEAC 2340
    4-track reel-to-reel tape-deck)   11:35   C

Sunken Flutes (realized 1979, Pizer Studio)
    (Multi-track tape, ARP Pro-soloist kybd synthesizer,
    TEAC 2340 4-track reel-to-reel tape-deck)   12:52   C

REED

Untitled for Tape   8:00   AMC

REID

Gyro-Space I (1979)   7:30   C

Electronic Sketch No. 1   3:00   C

Electronic Sketch Band on a Schumann Romance   4:00   C

SEMEGEN

⊕† *Arc: Music for Dancer* (realized 1977, Electronic
    Music Studios, SUNY Stony Brook)   13:40   ACA

⊕† *Electronic Composition No. 1* (realized 1972,
    Columbia-Princeton E.M.C.)   5:47   ACA

† *Electronic Composition No. 2: Spectra* (realized 1979,
    Electronic Music Studios, SUNY Stony Brook)   10:40   ACA

Out of Into (film score: film by Irving Kreisberg)
    (realized 1971, Columbia-Princeton E.M.C.)   16:00   ACA

⊕† *Spectra Studies* (realized 1974-76, SUNY Stony Brook,
    Electronic Music Studios and Columbia-Princeton E.M.C.)
    (experimental studies in timbral combinatorialities using
    Buchla 100, 200 units, Synthi 1000 [London E.M.S.],
    Steiner-Parker Units)   120:00   ACA

Trill Study (realized 1971, Columbia-Princeton E.M.C.)   3:00   ACA

STANLEY

Electronic Prelude (1967)   C

ORCHESTRAL MUSIC

The orchestral instrumental code used below is based on abbreviations for the standard instrumentation, listing the orchestral choirs in order:

> wind: flute, oboe, clarinet, bassoon; brass: French horn, trumpet, trombone, tuba;
> percussion; strings.

Auxiliary instruments requiring an *additional* player are placed after the related principal instrument, separated by a slash; instrumental doubling for a single player is indicated by placing the secondary instrument in parentheses. Wind and brass instruments not called for are noted as 0.

> Example: 3(pic)2/Eng hn 22 422(bs tbn)0 timp, 3 perc, pno, hrp, stgs

This translates to: 3 flutes (with one double on piccolo), 2 oboes, 1 English horn, 2 clarients, 2 bassoons; 4 French horns, 2 trumpets, 2 trombones (with one double on bass trombone), no tuba; timpani, 3 percussion players, piano, harp, violins I and II, violas, celli and basses.

● ## ORCHESTRAL MUSIC — CHAMBER ORCHESTRA ●

BARNETT

Overture to the Midnight Spectacle (1973-78)	5:00	2	C

BRITAIN

Angel Chimes (1954) (1111 1100 cym, cel or pno, stgs)	3:00		AMC
Infant Suite for Small Orchestra (1935) (1111 1100 timp, perc, stgs)	7:00		FC
Lament: Prison (1940) (2121 1200 timp, stgs)	3:00		See
Nocturn for Small Orchestra (1934) (2221 2220 timp, perc, stgs)	8:00		C
Serenata Sorrentina (1946) (2112 2220 timp, perc, stgs)	3:00		UCLA

COHEN

Prism (1967)	10:00	2	C

GARDNER

Rain Forest (1977) (1221 1000 glock, hrp, stgs)	7:00	2+	Iris

JANKOWSKI

OR (1976)	13:00	2	C

LE BARON

Three Movements for Strings & Percussion (1973)
   (stg orch and 5 perc players [xylo, marmb, vibe,
     glock, tubular bells, timp, triangle, susp cym])   11:00 2 AMC

PROCACCINI

Sinfonietta for Small Orchestra, Op. 7 (1956)
   (2222 2220 timp, stgs)   25:00 2 Cari

Musica Barbara for Chamber Orchestra and
Piano Concertante, Op. 20 (1959)
   (2220 2222 timp, perc, pno, stgs)   12:00 2 C

Tre Danze for 2 Trumpets and String Orchestra,
   Op. 24 (1961)   11:00 2 C

Un Cavallino Avventuroso for Orchestra, Op. 23 (1960)
   (2222 2200 timp, perc, vibe, cel, stgs)   15:00 2 C

RICHTER

Bird of Yearning (1967)
   (concert suite for reduced orch)
   (2121 2110 timp, perc, cel, hrp, pno, solo pno, stgs)   15:00 3 CF

Fragments (1976)
   (2222 2111 timp, perc, cel, hrp, stgs)   6:00 3 CF

ROGERS

Bridges
   (402/bcl/1 0000 pno fr-hnd, stgs)   10:00 2 C

Fanfare for Chamber Orchestra
   (ww, tpt, stgs)   2 C

SAMSON

Encounter (1973)
   (1111 2110 3 perc, hrp, stgs)   7:35 2+ C

Night Visits (1976)
   (1111 1110 vln, vcl, db)   10:30 2 C

SILSBEE

Pathways (1979)
   (1111 1110 timp, perc, stgs)   3 C

SIMONS

Piece for Orchestra
(1111 2000 pno, stgs)   10:00   ACA

SMITH

American Dance Suite (1935-36, revised 1963)
(theater orch)
(1121 2210 timp, perc, pno or hrp, stgs)   10:00   TPres

Folkways Symphony (1948)
Based on Western Themes:
"Day's A-Breakin'"
"Night Herding Song"
"Cowboy's Waltz"
"Stomping Leather"
(2222 2210 timp, perc, hrp, pno fr-hnd, stgs)   14:00   TPres

Liza Jane (1940)
(1121 2210 timp, perc, stgs)   4:00   TPres

Overture and Mexican Dances (from *"The Stranger
of Manzano"*) (1943-45)
"Overture"
"El Jarabe"
"La Botella (Valse)"
"Le Virgen y Las Fieras"
(1121 2210 timp, perc, xylo, vibe, cel, hrp, stgs)   20:00   TPres

VAN DE VATE

Variations for Chamber Orchestra (1958)
(fl, ob, B-flat cl, bsn, stgs)   10:00   2 C

VELLÈRE

La Route Ascendante (1962)   17:00   2 CBD

WALKER

Fanfare (1978)   2:00   1 Walk

WYLIE

Concerto Grosso, Op. 15
(7 solo ww and stgs)   20:00 2+ AMC

Suite for Chamber Orchestra, Op. 3   1+ C

ORCHESTRAL MUSIC – STRING ORCHESTRA

BRITAIN

† *Suite for Strings* (1940)   16:00   FC

BRUSH

Suite for Strings
(stg orch or stg sextet)   16:00   3   C

HYSON

Partita for String Orchestra (1970)   15:00   2   C

PROCACCINI

Divagazioni, Op. 21 (1959)   10:00   3   C

Musica Per Archi, Op. 49 (1971)   14:00   2   C

RICHTER

⊕ *Lament* (1956)   10:00   3   BrB

VELLÈRE

Nuits: Suite for Strings (1946)   2   C

† *Petite Symphonie* (1956)   20:00   3   C

WYLIE

Suite for String Orchestra (1941)   1+   C

ORCHESTRAL MUSIC – FULL ORCHESTRA

ALLEN

A Toutes les Heures (1974)   8:00   3   ACA

Chrysalis (1973)   12:00   2   ACA

BARNETT

Adon Olam Variations (1976)	9:00	2	C
Allusions (1978)	12:30	2	C

BARTHELSON

Overture to "Feathertop" (1961) (college or community orch)	8:00	2	CF Rental
Weather Report (1973) (college or community orch)	15:00	2	CF Rental

de BOHUN [Boone]

Annunciation of Spring (1955) (3132 4220 stgs)	11:00	2	Ars
Motive and Chorale (1962) (2222 2220 stgs)	4:00	2	Ars

BRITAIN

The Builders (1970) (2222 4221 timp, perc, stgs)	4:00	UCLA
Cactus Rhapsody (1953) (3322 4331 timp, perc, stgs)	8:00	FC
Canyon (1939) (3333 4331 timp, perc, stgs)	5:00	C
† *Cosmic Mist Symphony* (1962) (3222 4331 timp, perc, stgs)	24:00	FC
Cowboy Rhapsody (1956) (3222 4331 timp, perc, stgs)	13:00	FC
Dròuth (1939) (3222 4331 timp, perc, stgs)	6:00	FC
† *Heroic Poem* (1929) (3222 4331 timp, perc, stgs)	8:00	FC
Jewels of Lake Tahoe (1945) (2112 2221 timp, perc, stgs)	5:00	UCLA
Kambu (1963) (2222 4331 timp, perc, stgs)	8:00	C
† *Light* (1935) (3333 4331 timp, perc, stgs)	8:00	FC

Minha Terra (Barbaroso Netto) (1958)
(2222 3221 timp, perc, stgs)   5:00   Ric

† Ontonagon Sketches (1939)
(3333 4331 timp, perc, stgs)   20:00   See

Paint Horse and Saddle (1947)
(2222 4331 timp, perc, stgs)   7:00   C

Pastorale (1939)
(2322 2200 timp, perc, stgs)   7:00   FC

Prelude to a Drama (1928)
(3222 4331 timp, perc, stgs)   6:00   See

† Pyramids of Giza (1973)
(2222 4331 timp, perc, stgs)   8:00   C

Radiation (1955)
(3222 4331 timp, perc, stgs)   4:00   C

Red Clay (1946)
(3223 4331 timp, perc, stgs)   7:00   C

Saint Francis of Assisi (1941)
(2222 4331 timp, perc, stgs)   7:00   FC

San Luis Rey (1941)
(3222 4331 timp, perc, stgs)   4:00   FC

Saturnale (1939)
(3333 4331 timp, perc, stgs)   9:00   FC

Southern Symphony (1935)
(3333 4331 timp, perc, stgs)   23:00   FC

Symphonic Intermezzo (1928)
(3222 4331 timp, perc, stgs)   7:00   C

This is the Place (1958)
(2222 4331 timp, perc, stgs)   5:00   C

Umpqua Forest (1946)
(3223 4331 timp, perc, stgs)   8:00   C

† We Believe (1942)
(3323 4331 timp, perc, stgs)   6:00   C

BRUSH

Freedom Suite   10:00   3   C

River Moons   7:00   3   C

CHANCE

Liturgy (1979)
(2333 4321 hrp, cel, 4 perc, stgs)   18:00   3   See

DIEMER

Fairfax Festival Overture (1967)
(college/community orch and important pno part)   7:00   3   See

Festival Overture (1961)
(college/community orch)   7:00   2+   E-V

Suite for Orchestra (1954)   C

Symphony (1952)   C

Symphony (1959)   C

HAYS

Southern Voices
(4232 4331 perc, pno, stgs)   14:00   2+   Q-H

HSU

Concerto for Orchestra (1962)
(2222 2221 timp, perc, stgs)   10:00   W-Y

† *Sky Maiden's Dance Suite* (1966)
(2222 0000 perc, hrp, cel, stgs)   10:00   W-Y

JANKOWSKI

Demeanour (1974)
(symphony orch)   14:00   2+   C

† *Lustrations* (1978)
(symphony orch)   18:00   3   CMP

MAGEAU

Montage (1970)
(3111 2121 timp, 2 perc, hrp, cel, stgs)   6:00   C

Variegations (1968)
(symphony orch)   C

MARCUS

Fantasias No. 1 and No. 2
(symphony orch)   20:00   3   C
each

Fantasy
(symphony orch) 15:00 3 C

Garden of the Gods
(symphony orch) 12:00 3 C

Symphony of the Spheres
"Depicting the Sounds in the Universe"
"Depicting the Search for Life"
"Depicting the Vastness of the Universe"
(symphony orch) 20:00 3 AMC

PIERCE

Behemoth (1976)
(2111 2110 timp, perc, hrp, stgs) 15:00 3 See

PREOBRAJENSKA

† *American Tone Poem*
(symphony orch - 3 movements) C

PROCACCINI

Fantasia per Orchestra, Op. 16 (1958)
(322/bcl/2 4331 timp, xylo, cel, perc, stgs) 13:00 2 Cari

Sensazioni Sonore: Four Pieces for Orchestra, Op. 41
(1969)
(322/bcl/2 4331 timp, perc, xylo, stgs) 13:00 2 Sonz

RICHTER

Abyss (1964)
(2121 4(or 2)110 timp, perc, cel, hrp, pno, stgs) 20:00 3 Bel-M

Bird of Yearning (1967)
(concert suite)
(2222 3220 timp, perc, cel, hrp, pno, stgs) 15:00 3 CF

Blackberry Vines and Winter Fruit (1976)
(3222 4321 timp, perc, cel, hrp, stgs) 13:00 3 CF

Eight Pieces for Orchestra (1961)
(3333 4331 timp, perc, hrp (opt), pno, stgs) 7:00 3 CF

Variations on a Sarabande (1959)
(2222 4221 timp, perc, hrp (opt), pno, stgs) 8:00 2 CF

ROBERTS

Elegy for President John F. Kennedy 20:00 2 C

ROGERS

Ostinatia
(10 ww, 4 brass, 6 perc, pno, hpsd, vln,
solo vcl, 20-40 stgs)   12:00   2   C

SEMEGEN

Fantasia for Orchestra (1963)
(2222 4320 2 perc, vln solo, stgs)   12:00   C

† *Triptych for Orchestra* (1966)
(2/pic/222/cbsn 4331 perc, xylo, stgs)   17:00   2+   ACA

SILSBEE

Seven Rituals (1978)
(3333 4331 timp, 2 perc, pno, stgs)   25:00   3   ACA

Trois Historiettes (1974)
(2222 4331 timp, 2 perc, hrp, stgs)   7:00   3   C

SIMONS

Lamentations No. 1
(3/pic/3/Enghn/2/E-flat cl, bcl/3/cbsn
    443/b-tbn/1 4 timp, perc, stgs)   8:30   Mer

Lamentations No. 2
(3/pic/3/Enghn/2/E-flat cl, bcl/3/cbsn
    443/b-tbn/1   timp, perc, vibe, stgs)   7:30   Mer

Scipio's Dream
(5 Orchestra Units:
    I - 1(pic)1(Enghn)1(E-flat cl)1
        2210 perc, Vln II, ½db section
    II - 211/bcl/1 0001 vibe, vcl
    III - amplified pno, amplified perc, chor[SATB]
    IV - 1200 221/b-tbn/0 timp, vla
    V - 0011/cbsn 0120
        piccolo timpani, perc, Vlns I, ½db section)   25:00   ACA

Variables
(2222 2221 pno, perc, vibe, marmb, bells, stgs)
(may be performed by any 5 instr or multiples of 5)   23:00   Mer

SMITH

Episodic Suite (1936)
(3222 4231 timp, perc, xylo, hrp, stgs)   8:00   TPres

Hellenic Suite (1940-41)
   "Sirtos"
   "Berceuse"
   "Saga"
   (2222 4231 timp, perc, hrp, stgs)   15:00   TPres

STANLEY

Symphony Number One (1954)
   (2/pic/222 4331 perc, hrp, stgs)   12:00   2   C

SWISHER

Two Pieces for Orchestra   5:00   2   C

VAN DE VATE

Adagio for Orchestra (1957)
   (0022 2221 timp, stgs)   7:00   2+ AMC

VERCOE

Children's Caprice (1963)
   (2222 4320 timp, 2 perc, hrp, stgs)   10:00   2   C

WARREN

Along the Western Shore
   "The Dark Hills"
   "Nocturne"
   "Sea Rhapsody"
   (2/pic/2/Enghn/22/cbsn 4231 timp, 2 perc, hrp,
     cel, stgs)   14:00   CF

The Crystal Lake
   (2/pic/2(Enghn)22 4231 timp, hrp, 2 perc, stgs)   9:30   CF

The Fountain
   (2222 3230 timp, cel, 2 perc, hrp, stgs)   4:00   FC

Intermezzo (from "The Legend of King Arthur")
   (22(Enghn)2(bcl)2 4331 timp, hrp, perc, stgs)   4:30   Bel-M

Scherzo
   (2222 3230 timp, cel, perc, 2 hrp, stgs)   2:00   FC

⊕ *Suite for Orchestra*
   (2/pic/222 4341 timp, 3 perc, cel, hrp, stgs)   17:00   CF

Symphony in One Movement
   (2/pic/2/Enghn/22 4231 timp, 2 perc, cel, hrp, stgs)   17:00   CF

WYLIE

Holiday Overture, Op. 14	8:00	2	C
Involution, Op. 24 No. 2 (2122 0220 perc, stgs)	11:00	3	AMC
The Long Look Home, Op. 30 No. 2 (with poetry and slides) "Moon" "Clouds" "Snow" "Desert" "Nuclear Energy" (2(pic)2(Enghn)22 0321 perc, stgs)	36:00	3	AMC
Memories of Birds, Op. 32 No. 1 (2(pic)222/cbsn 4331 perc, stgs)	12:00	3	AMC
Suite for Orchestra, Op. 2		2	C
Symphony No. I, Op. 6	30:00	2	C
Symphony No. II, Op. 11	30:00	2+	C
† *Views from Beyond,* Op. 33 No. 1 "Ancient Wisdom" "False Fire" "Laments for Tomorrow" "Memories of Birds"	36:00	3	C

ZIFFRIN

Orchestra Piece (1976-77, revised 1979) (2222 2220 timp, b dm, cym, stgs)	8:30	2+	C
Waltz for Orchestra (revised version 1957) (2222 4231 timp, cym, triangle, sn dm, b dm, stgs)	8:00	2	C

ZWILICH

Symposium for Orchestra (1973) (3334 4331 timp, perc, 2 hrp, stgs)	12:00	3	Mer

● ORCHESTRAL MUSIC — CONCERTOS WITH ORCHESTRA ●

ALLEN

† *Arche* (1976) (vla and orch)	20:00	3	ACA

BEATH

Riddles (1974)
(cycle of 4 songs)
(T and orch)   C

BRENNER

Exhortation (1976)
(pno and orch)   10:00   2   C

BRITAIN

† *Phantasy for Oboe and Orchestra* (1942)
(ob and 2222 2221 timp, perc, stgs)   8:00   C

Rhapsody for Piano and Orchestra (1933)
(2222 3331 timp, perc, stgs)   16:00   LC

DIEMER

Concert Piece (1977)
(org solo and orch)   10:00   3   See

Concerto for Flute
(fl/pno score)   25:00   3   Arm

Concerto for Harpsichord and Chamber Orchestra (1958)   12:00   2   See

Concerto for Piano (1954)   C

FULLER-HALL

Trumpet Concertino (1979)
(tpt and orch)   6:30   2+   C

HEINRICH

Concerto for Organ and Orchestra, Op. 20   15:00   2   C

HOOVER

Concerto (1980)
(fl solo, stgs, perc)   18:00   3   AMC

Nocturne (middle movement of *Concerto*) (1977)
(fl solo, stgs, perc)   6:00   3   AMC

HSU

Cello Concerto (1963)
(vcl solo, 2222 2110 timp, perc, hrp, cel, stgs)   20:00   W-Y

LOMON

Bassoon Concerto (1979)
(3 movements)
(bsn solo with (pic)22(bcl)0 2221 timp, perc,
hrp, stgs)   20:00   3   AMC

MARCUS

Piano Concertino
(pno solo with 1122 2100 timp)   25:00   3   C

Violin Concerto
(vln solo with stg chamber orch and hrp)   30:00   3   C

PROCACCINI

Dannazione E Preghiera, Op. 13 (1958)
(Mez and stg orch)   13:00   2   Cari

Tre Liriche, Op. 57 (1974)
(S and stg orch)   8:00   2   C

Concertino, Op. 64 (1976)
(fl solo and orch)   13:00   3   C

Concerto, Op. 78 (1980)
(hrp solo and chamber orch: 1111 1000 stgs)   20:00   2   C

Concerto, Op. 12 (1957)
(org solo and orch: 3222 4300 timp, stgs)   27:00   2   Cari

Concerto for Trio and Orchestra "I Folletti", Op. 14
(1958)
(solo trio: vln, vcl, pno; 322/bcl/2 4300 timp, stgs)   27:00   2   Cari

Sonata in Tricromia for Orchestra and Piano Concertante,
Op. 11 (1957)
(321/bcl/2 4331 timp, perc, cel, xylo, vibe, hrp, pno, stgs) 15:00 2 Bng

RICHTER

Aria and Toccata (1957)
(vla and stgs)   10:00   3   Bel-M

Concerto for Piano and Violas, Cellos and Basses
(pno solo with stg orch)   20:00   3   CF

*Landscapes of the Mind I: Concerto for Piano with
   Orchestra* (1974)
   (pno solo and orch: 3333 4400 timp, perc, cel, hrp, opt
   electric gtr, opt electric bass, orch pno, stgs)   29:00   3   CF

Music for Three Quintets and Orchestra (1980)
   (ww qnt: fl, ob, cl, hn, bsn; brass qnt: 2 tpts, hn,
   tbn, tuba; stg qnt: 2 vlns, vla, vcl, db; orch:
   2222 2220 timp, perc, hrp, stgs)   25:00   3   CF

ROBERTS

Double Concerto
   (2 hpsds (1 hpsd, 1 pno) and orch)   25:00   3   C

ROGERS

Concerto for Tenor Violin and Large Orchestra
   (3344 532 euphonium, tuba; timp, 4 perc, 2 hrps
   pno-cel, stgs)   35:00   3   C

Concerto for Viola and Orchestra   2+   C

SAMTER

Konzertstück für Klavier und Orchester
   (pno and orch)   10:00   C

SCHONTHAL

Concerto No. 2 (1977)
   (pno and orch)   26:00   3   C

Concerto Romantico (1942)
   (pno and orch)   27:00   2   C

Music for Horn and Chamber Orchestra (1978)   12:00   2   C

Nine Lyric-Dramatic Songs (W.B. Yeats) (1960)
   (Mez and chamber orch)   21:00   2+   C

SEMEGEN

† *Poème 1er: Dans la Nuit* (Henri Michaux) (1969)
   (Bar solo with orch: 1(pic)11(bcl)0 0100 4 perc,
   pno, cel, hrp, stgs)   7:00   2+   ACA

SIMONS

Illuminations in Space
(vla and orch)
I: (solo vla; 2(pic, al-fl)1(Enghn)2(E-flat cl, bcl)3/cbsn
   423/b-tbn timp, vibe, bells, antique cym, perc)
II: (solo vla; 2 tps, timp, xylo, vibe, amplified perc,
    12 vcl, 4 db)
III: (solo vla; 2(pic)2/Enghn2/bcl2 2221 marmb, xylo,
     bells, chimes, perc (amplified), 12 vcl, 4 db)   12:00   Mer

SMITH

Concerto for Piano and Orchestra (1938-39, rev. 1971)
(solo pno; 2232 4331 timp, perc, stgs)   22:00   3   TPres

SWISHER

Cancion
(solo fl and chamber orch)   5:00   1   AMC

Concerto for Clarinet and Orchestra   19:00   3   AMC

Yuki no Niigata
(koto and orch)   7:00   2   C

VAN DE VATE

Concertpiece for Cello and Small Orchestra (1976)
(solo vcl, 8 vlns, 4 vlas 4 vcl, 2 contrabass,
 pno, 2 cel, 5 perc players)   7:00   2+ AMC

Concerto for Piano and Orchestra (1968)
(pno solo, 2/pic222 4231 timp, triangle, cym,   21:00   3   AMC
 bdm, stgs)

VELLÈRE

O Blanche Fleur Des Airs (Van Lerberghe)
(voice and stg orch)   2   C

Vous M'Avez Dit Tel Soir (Verhaeren)
(voice and stg orch)   2   C

Epitaphe pour un ami (1964)
(vla solo, chamber orch)   7:00   3   CBD

Fantaisie (1958)
(vln and orch)   18:00   2   C

Ophélie (Marsalleau) (1941)
(women's chor and chamber orch)   2   C

VERCOE

Concerto for Violin and Orchestra (1977)
(solo vln, 2222 4231 timp, 2 perc, hrp, stgs) 30:00 3 C

WALKER

Upon Her Leaving (1977)
(Bar and chamber orch) 15:00 2 Walk

WALLACH

Concerto for Four Winds and Orchestra (1969) 15:00   AMC

WARREN

Singing Earth (Carl Sandburg) (revised 1978)
(S or T solo, 2(pic)2(Enghn)22 4230 timp, 2 perc,
cel, hrp, stgs) 16:00   FC

Sonnets for Soprano and String Orchestra
(Edna St. Vincent Millay)
(S solo, vlns I-II, vlas, vcls, db) 15:00   CF

WYLIE

Clarinet Concertino, Op. 24 no. 1 13:00 2 C

ZAIMONT

Concerto for Piano and Orchestra (1972)
(pno solo, 3333 4231 timp, perc, stgs) 32:00 3 FC

ZWILICH

Concerto for Violin and Orchestra
(vln solo, 2222 3221 timp, perc, hrp, stgs) 22:00 3 C

ORCHESTRAL MUSIC WITH TAPE

STANLEY

† *Rhapsody for Electronic Tape and Orchestra* (1972)
(1111 2000 perc, stgs, tape player) 9:30 3 C

BAND MUSIC

The code used for band instruments is an expansion of the orchestral code already described (see page 262). Instrumental doubles (i.e., piccolo; English horn) are placed in parentheses immediately following the principal instrument (i.e., flute; oboe). Instruments usually found in bands but not provided for in the basic code—saxophones, cornets, baritones, euphoniums—are placed after the appropriate choir, separated by a comma.

Example: 5(pic, al-fl)3(Eng hn)53/cbsn, 3 sax 4321, 3 cornet, euphonium timp, 4 perc, pno, db

This translates to: 5 flutes (with doubles on piccolo and alto flute), 3 oboes (with a double on English horn), 5 clarinets (assorted), 3 bassoons, 1 contrabassoon; 4 French horns, 3 trumpets, 2 trombones, 1 tuba, 3 cornets, 1 euphonium; timpani, 4 percussion players, piano, double bass.

BAND MUSIC — WIND ENSEMBLES

BRITAIN

Rhumbando (1975)   4:00   C

CECCONI-BATES

Pasticcio (1977)   8:00   3   C

Piano Pasticcio   4:00   3   C

FULLER-HALL

Minor Distraction March (1979)
(wind ensemble and perc)   4:30   3   C

ROGERS

Wind Octet
(2122 1000)   10:00   2   C

SMELTZER

Christmas Fantasy (1960)
(0000 3311, bar hn)   10:00   2   C

BAND MUSIC — SYMPHONIC BAND

BARNETT

Arabesques (1976)   12:15   2   C

FRASIER

Introduction and Fantasy — 5:00 3+ C

Resolution — 6:00 3+ C

FULLER-HALL

Scherzo (1975) — 4:00 2 C

GARDNER

The Victoria Woodhull March (1974)
(concert or marching band) — 4:00 2 Iris

HSU

March of Chinese Cadets (1967)
(military band) — 10:00 W-Y

JANKOWSKI

† *Todesband* (1973) — 13:00 2+ C

MAGEAU

Celebration Music (1971) — C

MARCUS

Outward Bound — 10:00 2 C

PIZER

*Under and Overture, for Symphonic Band and
Antiphonal Tympani,* Op. 37 (1977/79)
(2 pic/2 al-fl/4224 2300 2 sets of timp: 5 dm per
set, perc: glock, suspended bym, crash cyms, large gong,
triangle, b dm) — 8:00 3 C

REID

New Manchester Suite (1969) — 11:00 2 C

Wasatch Symphony (1970) — 16:00 3 C

SMELTZER

The Bald Eagle March (1976) — 10:00 2 C

SMITH

Fanfare for Alma Mater (1970) (3252, 4 sax 4233, 3 cornets, bar hn, timp, perc, vibe)	4:00	2	Mowb
Sails Aloft—Overture (with Cecile Vashaw) (1966) (3273, 5 sax 4232, 3 cornets timp, perc, vibe, xylo, opt db, hrp or pno)	7:00	2	Mowb

SWISHER

Dance for Tomorrow	5:00	3	C
Lincoln Memorial	8:00	3	C
The Mountain and the Island	10:00	2	AMC
Processions	8:00	2	AMC
Thanksgiving I for Symphonic Band	8:00	2	C

ZIFFRIN

Overture for Concert Band (1958) (pic/113/bcl2, 4 sax [2 al-sax, ten-sax, bar-sax] 4231, 2 cornets, bar hn timp, b dm, cym, sn dm)	3:00	1	C

●   **BAND MUSIC — CONCERTOS WITH BAND**   ●

SWISHER

Suite for Wind Sinfonietta and Piano	9:00	2	C
Three Pieces for Band and Piano	8:00	3	C

● **CHORAL MUSIC — UNACCOMPANIED MEN'S OR WOMEN'S CHORUS** ●

ANDERSON, BETH

Incline Thine Ear To Me (1975) (chant for any group of musicians/audience)	3:00 - 10:00	2+	C

ANDERSON, JAY

Echo Below (1959) (SSA)	3:00	2	JF

BARTHELSON

Christmas, 1620
(SSA)   2   HF

BOLZ

Two Madrigals for Christmas (1968)
(SA)   2:04   2+   SF

BRITAIN

Barcarola (1949)
(SSAA chor - vocalise)   4:00   C

Drums of Africa (Jenkins) (1934)
(TTBB or SATB chor)   4:00   Wit

BRUSH

The Harp Weaver (1968)
(SSA)   C

Praise to the Holiest (hymn)   C

Praise the Lord, Ye Heavens Adore Him (hymn)   C

† Star Shined Pathetique (1952)
(SSA)   6:00   C

A Thing of Beauty (1965)
(SSA)   12:00   3   C

DIEMER

Away, Delights (1979)
(TTBB chor)   2   ABI

Four Carols (1960)
(SSA chor)   6:00   2   E-V

Fragments from the Mass (1960)
(women's chor)   8:00   2   EBM

Love is a Sickness Full of Woes (1974)
(SAB chor)   1   ChorAS

The Prophecy (1968)
(women's chor)   8:00   3   B&H

Weep No More (1979)
(SSA chor)   2   ABI

Weep You No More, Sad Fountains (1974)
(SA or TB chor)   1   ChorAS

FORMAN

Ave Beata Dea
(SSAA)   3:00   2+   C

HOOVER

Canons (1972-73)
(voices and lengths variable)   2   AMC

GLAZIER

V'Shomru
(S and SA chor)   3:00 - 4:00   2+   C

V'Shomru
(cantor and SA chor)   3:00 - 4:00   2+   C

HSU

Song and Sound (1966)
(S solo and male chor)   6:00   W-Y

HYSON

Becoming (1968)
(S and Mez soli with SSA chor)   7:00   3   C

PARKER

An English Mass (1974)
(2-part choir)   1+   C

Games (from the Opera, The Family Reunion) (1975)
(SSA)   4:00   1+   CF

Let Brotherly Love Continue (1972)
(round for 2-5 parts)   1+   ECS

Sunday Rounds (1974)
(2-6 voices, opt accompaniment)   1+   Hin

PIERCE

Dendid (African folk text)(1975)
(TTBB)   7:00   2+   C

ROGERS

Amen in 6 Parts
(chor or individual voices: SSSAAA or SSAATT)   1:30   2   C

Chapel Service for Iva Dee Hiatt
  "Call to Worship"
  "Two Anthems"
  "Amen"
  (chor SSAA or double chor)   9:30   2+   C

SIMONS

For All Blasphemers (Stephen Vincent Benet)
  (TTBBBB)   6:00   ACA

SMITH

Glory to the Green and White (1966)
  (TTBB)   2:30   1   Mowb

VELLÈRE

† Air de Syrinx (Claudel)(1956)
  (SSAA)   4:00   2   JM

La Belle Chanson que Voilà (Ph. Delaby)(1965)
  (SSA)   4:30   2   C

WALLACH

3 Short Sacred Anthems (1980)
  (treb choir)   8:30   AMC

WEIGL

Along the Way (American Women Poets)
  (suite for SSA chor)   2   ACA

Let There Be Music
  (SSA)   3:00   2   ACA

Shepherdess Moon
  (SSA)   2   ACA

Two Lyrical Poems for Women's Voices   2   Gal

CHORAL MUSIC — UNACCOMPANIED MIXED CHORUS

ANDERSON, BETH

Black/White (1976)
  (chant for audience or chor: SATB)   varies   2+   C

ANDERSON, JAY

Psalm 23 (1949) (SATB)	3:15	2	C
Psalm 91 (1939) (SATB)	2:00	2	C
Softly, Softly Fell The Snow (1942) (SATB)	2:10	2	SHMC

BARNETT

Adonai, Adonai (1979) (synagogue choir: SATB)	2:20	1	C
Ma Tovu (1973) (synagogue choir: SATB)	2:00	1	C
Silent Amidah (1974) (synagogue choir: SATB)	1:35	1	C

BARTHELSON

Choral Series (Nancy Byrd Turner and Virginia Hoff) (SATB)	2	Bos
The Pilgrims (SATB)	2	Rem

de BOHUN [Boone]

Alleluia (1957) (SATB sacred)	2:10	3	Ars
Meditation (1956) (SATB sacred)	2:10	2	Ars
Thou Shalt Light My Lamp (1955) (Bar solo, SSATB)	3:30	2	Ars

BRITAIN

Drums of Africa (Jenkins)(1934) (chor SATB or TTBB)	4:00	Wit
Immortality (Francesca Falk Miller)(1937) (SATB)	4:00	APS

BRUSH

Christmas Lullaby (SATB)	4:00	2	C
Christmas Story (SATB)	5:00	2	C
Keep America Singing (SATB)	7:00	2	C
The Lord is My Shepard (SATB)	5:00	2+	Brt
† *Star Shined Pathetique* (1952) (SATB)	6:00	2	C
This Same Jesus (SATB)	5:00	2	Brt

CHANCE

Domine Dominus (1964) (mot for dbl chor: SATB-SATB)	11:00	3	See

DEMBO

Gems (Wilfred Owen) (SSAATB)	3:30	3	C

DIEMER

At a Solemn Musick (1960)	8:00	2	B&H
I Stand Beside the Manger Stall (1959)		2	CF
Men are Fools that Wish to Die (1974)		2	ChorAS
O to Praise God Again (1972)		2	CF
Praise the Lord (1957)		2	HWG
Psalm 134 (1973)	4:00	3	See
Sing, O Heavens (1974)	4:00	2	CF
So I Have Seen a Silver Swan (1974)		2	ChorAS
Tell Me Dearest, What is Love? (1979)		2	ABI
Verses from the Rubaiyat (1967)	10:00	3	B&H
Why So Pale and Wan? (in *Choral Art*) (1971)		2	ChorAP

FULLER-HALL

Sephestia's Lullaby (1978)
(SATB)   3:50   2+   C

HSU

3 Anthems (*Chin*)
"Pray Our Lord" (1951)   2:00   C
"Jesus Our Savior" (1958)   2:00   C
"Good News for Christmas" (1965)   6:00   C

HYSON

Song to the Soul of a Child (1978)
(S solo and chor SATB)   8:00   2+   C

PARKER

Blessings (Psalm 134) (1965)
(SATB)   2   L-G

Come, Let Us Join
(SATB)   1+   L-G

O Sing the Glories (Watts) (1978)
(SATB)   4:00   2   Hin

Psalm 136 (1962)
(Bar solo, SATB)   2   L-G

Prayer (Watts) (1971)
(SATB, SATB - dbl chor)   5:00   2   L-G

Six Hymns to Doctor Watts (1975)
(SATB)   1+   ECS

PIZER

Alleluia #2, Op. 25 (1976)
(2 S soli, chor SSAATTBB)   3:30   3   AMC

Kyrie, Op. 39 (1976)
(SSAATTBB)   3:00   2+   AMC

Madrigals Anon (13th-15th century texts), Op. 51 (1979)
(SSATB)   5:00   2+   AMC

RICHTER

† *Psalm 91* (1963)
(SATB)   3:30   3   E-V

Seek Him (1965)
  (SATB)   4:30   3   CF

Three Songs of Madness and Death (1955)
  (SATB)   6:00   3   CF

ROGERS

Four Choral Amens
  (chor SATB - org opt)   8:00   2   C

SEMEGEN

Poem; For: (Robert Sward) (1967)
  (SATB)   4:00   2   ACA

Psalm 43: O Send Out Thy Light (1967)
  (SATB)   4:00   2   ACA

SIMONS

Sing O Daughter of Zion (Bible)
  (solo ATB, chor SSAATTBB)   5:00   ACA

SINGER

Ave Maria
  (SAT)   2   C

† *Madrigal* (16th century anon)
  (SATB)   2   C

The Seaman's Wife (Jeanne Singer)
  (S solo, men's chor)   6:00   2   C

SWISHER

Death Be Not Proud
  (SATB)   3:00   2   C

God Be Merciful Unto Us
  (SAATB)   3:00   2   AMC

Thanksgiving II
  (SATB)   4:00   2   C

VAN DE VATE

Psalm 121 (1958)
  (SATB)   4:00   1+   C

† *The Pond* (Annette Von Droste-Hülshoff, trans Herman Salinger) (1959)
(SATB)   3:30   2   AMC

VELLÈRE

Deux Poèmes (Fr) (Charles Van Lerberghe) (1957)
(SATB)   2   C

Mon Ame, Elle est Là-bas (Verhaeren) (1959)
(SATB)   5:00   2   C

Pastels (various, *Fr*) (1959)
(SAB)   2   C

Trois Poèmes d'Apollinaire (1957)
(SAB)   3:30   2   CBD

WALLACH

Look Down Fair Moon   2:30   AMC

† *On the Beach at Night Alone*   7:00   CFP

Tears   4:00   AMC

30 Ecumenical Responses (1977-78)
(SATB)   1:00   AMC
                                                         each

Three Whitman Visions
(SATB)   14:00   AMC

WARREN

More Things Are Wrought By Prayer
(SATB)   HWG

Rolling Rivers, Dreaming Forests
(SATB)   CF

To My Native Land
(SATB)   ECS

WEIGL

† *Bold Heart*
(SATB)   2   ACA

A Christmas Legend
(SATB)   3:00   2   ACA

Fear No More (Shakespeare)
(SATB)   4:00   2   TPres

Heart's Content
(SATB)   3:00   2   ACA

The Nightwind (R.L. Stevenson)
(SATB)   3:00   2   ACA

Ode to the Westwind
(SATB)   4:30   2   ACA

This is the Day of Light
(SATB)   2   ACA

Three Choral Songs of the Southwest (P. Benton)
(SATB)   8:00   2   TPres

WYLIE

Toward Nowhere (1953)
(SATB)   2   C

ZAIMONT

⊕ *Sunny Airs and Sober* (1974)
   "A Question Answered" (Shakespeare)
   "Winter Mourning" (Shelley)
   "Sigh No More Ladies" (Shakespeare)
   "Come Away, Death" (Shakespeare)
   "Life *Is* a Jest" (John Gay, Robert Herrick)
   (5 madrigals for chamber chor SSATB)   14:30   3   Walt

⊕† *Three Ayres* (1969)
   "O Mistress Mine" (Shakespeare)
   "Slow, Slow, Fresh Fount" (Ben Jonson)
   "How Sweet I Roam'd" (Blake)
   (S[S]ATB)   6:00   2   BrB

ZIFFRIN

Jewish Prayer (1950)
(SATB)   4:00   2   C

Prayer (1966)
(SATB)   5:00   3   C

CHORAL MUSIC — MEN'S OR WOMEN'S CHORUS WITH KEYBOARD ACCOMPANIMENT

ANDERSON, BETH

If You Have a Thought (1978)
(round for voices, composer/audience or chor, and pno)   2+   C

BOLZ

Carol of the Flowers (1967) (SSA and pno or org)	2:01	1+	ChorAP
Flower of Love, Anthem for Easter (SSA and pno or org)	2:03	2	C
Joy to All Our Hearts, Anthem for Easter (SA and pno or org)	1:05	1	C
Nowness and *Who am I* (Harold Bolz)(1970) (SA and pno)	2:00	1+	HC
That I May Sing! (Michelangelo) (1970) (SSA or opt SA and pno or org)	3:05	2+	SF

BRITAIN

Brothers of the Clouds (Kate Hammond) (1964) (TTBB)	8:00	Hero
Dickey Donkey (Lester Luther) (1935) (chor SSAA or SATB)	3:00	CF
The Earth Does Not Wish for Beauty (Lester Luther) (1966) (TTBB)	8:00	UCLA
Fairy of Spring (Butterfield) (1935) (SSA)	3:00	Hero
Holy Lullaby (Halff) (1975) (SSA)	3:00	UCLA
Hush My Heart (Halff) (1970) (chor SSAA or SATB)	4:00	UCLA
Lasso of Time (Alice McKenzie) (1940) (TTBB)	4:00	NK
Little Man (Wilton) (1965) (SSA)	3:00	UCLA
† *Noontide* (Nietzche) (1935) (SSAA)	4:00	Hero
Rain (Lester Luther) (1935) (SSA)	3:00	Hero
The Star and the Child (John Lancaster) (1956) (chor SSA or SATB)	3:00	C
Twilight Moon (Eberhart) (1938) (SSA)	4:00	C

Venete, Felii Audite Me (Father Fred Consol) (1957)
(SSAA)   3:00   C

BRUSH

† *Cradled in a Manger*
(SSA and kybd)   C

DEMBO

The Little Ghost (Edna St. Vincent Millay)
(SSAA and pno)   3:00   2+ C

DIEMER

Alleluia (1959)
(SSA and pno)   1   CF

A Christmas Carol (1959)
(SSA and pno)   1   CF

How Majestic is Thy Name (1957)
(unison chor and kybd)   1   HWG

A Little Song of Life (1964)
(SA and kybd)   1   ChorAS

The Magnificat (1959)
(SA and pno)   1   EBM

Mary's Lullaby (1959)
(SSA and pno)   1   B&H

A Musical Instrument (1979)
(women's chor and 2 pnos)   15:00   3   Hin

O Come, Let Us Sing unto the Lord (1960)
(men's chor and pno or org)   4:00   2   CF

Thine, O Lord (1961)
(2-part chor and kybd)   1   HF

Three Poems of Ogden Nash (1960)
(TTB and pno)   2   HF

Two Madrigals (1974)
(2-part chor and kybd)   1   ChorAS

Winds of Spring (1966)
(unison chor and kybd)   1   HF

Your Friends Shall be the Tall Wind (1960)
(SSA and kybd)   1   ChorAS

FRASIER

Christmas Story
(cant: unis chor, narr, pno)   10:00   1   C

GARDNER

When We Made the Music (1977)
(SSAA and pno)   8:00   3   Iris

GLAZIER

Sh'ma
(high and low voices and pno)   2:00   1+   C

Kedushah
(cantor, chor SA, org)   3:00-4:00 2   C

Come to Us in Peace (Boachem Sholom)
(SATB and pno)   1   C

HYSON

A Hymn to the Virgin (1967)
(S solo, chor SSA, pno)   2:30   2+   C

HSU

† *Merciful Father* (1974)
(women's chor and pno)   5:00   W-Y

KENDRICK

From My Window
(S solo, SSA, pno)   3:00   2   SF

Green is the Willow
(Mez solo, SSA, pno)   3:00   2   JF

Little Goody Two Shoes
(SA and pno)   3:00   2   SF

Little Miss "Whuffit"
(SSA and pno)   3:00   2   JF

PARKER

Angels, Supposedly (Pyle)(1974)
(SA and pno)   3:00   1+   Hin

Hellos and Goodbyes (1975)
(double rounds for 2-7 voices and pno)   1+   CF

A Play on Numbers (1972)
(3 movements)
(SA and pno)   10:00   2   ECS

Songs for Sunday (collections)
(SA and kybd)   1+   L-G

PAULL

America, You Touch Me to My Soul (1978)
(chor and pno)   6:00   1+   C

Christmas Go Round (1977)
(chor and pno)   6:00   1+   C

Ev'ry Merry Christmas (1977)
(chor and pno)   6:00   1+   C

Happy to be Me (1979)
(chor and pno)   6:00   1+   C

I Love the Lord Singing His Song (1979)
(chor and pno)   6:00   1+   C

My Song to Sing (1979)
(chor and pno)   6:00   1+   C

O Easter Mornin' (1979)
(chor and pno)   6:00   1+   C

Peace and Joy and Love (1977)
(chor and pno)   6:00   1+   C

Sweet Benjamin, The Easter Pig (1978)
(chor and pno)   6:00   1+   C

SINGER

† *Carol of the Bells* (Jeanne Singer)
(SSA and pno or org)   4:00   2   C

Choral Art (or Antics) (Edna Boyd)
(SSA and pno)   2:00   2   C

† *Come Greet the Spring* (Edna Boyd)
(SSA and pno)   5:00   2   C

† *Composer's Prayer* (Ora Pate Stewart)
(SSA and pno)   6:00   2   Fern

For the Night of Christmas (Bernard Greganier)
(SSA and pno, or a cappella)   3:30   2   C

SMITH

Enrich Your Life with Music (1969)
(SSAA and pno)   3:00   2   Mowb

Invocation (1967)
(SSA and pno)   2:00   2   Mowb

To All Who Love a Song (1949)
(SSA and pno)   2:20   1   Mowb

VAN DE VATE

How Fares the Night? (anonymous *Chin* from
The Book of Odes, c. 500 B.C., trans Mimi Tsoi)
(SSA and pno)   4:00   2   Mont

WARREN

From This Summer Garden
(SSA and pno)   CF

Little Choral Suite
"Rain Slippers"
"Sleep Walks Over the Hill"
"A Little Song of Life"
(SSA and pno)   CF

The Night Will Never Stay
(SSA and pno)   L-G

Songs for Young Voices
"Sing a Song of Seasons"
"Who Has Seen The Wind"
"Boats Sail on the Rivers"
"Song of the Clock"
"The Swing"
"The Falling Star"
"The Little Plant"
(SA and pno)   L-G

Windy Weather
(SSA and pno)   ECS

WEIGL

A Christmas Folksong
(SSA and pno)   3:00   2   ECS

CHORAL MUSIC — MIXED CHORUS WITH KEYBOARD
ACCOMPANIMENT

ALLEN

Psalm XIII (1978)
(chor SATB and org)   4:00   2   ACA

BEESON

A Tribute
  (chor SATB and pno)   3:00   3   C

BOLZ

Four Christmas Songs (1967)
  (chor SATB or children SA, and pno or org)   5:00   1   ChorAP

How Shall We Speak?
  (chor SATB and org or pno)   2:02   2   C

Sweet Jesus (1974)
  (chor SAB and pno or org)   3:00   2   Sis

To Love and Serve
  (chor SAB and org or pno)   2:05   1+ C

BRITAIN

Awake to Life (Lerae Britain) (1963)
  (SATB)   4:00   UCLA

† *Baby I Can't Sleep* (1936)   4:00   C

The Builders (Lerae Britain) (1965)
  (SATB)   4:00   Hero

The Chalice (Alice Halff) (1951)
  (SATB)   4:00   C

Cherokee Blessing (1977)
  (SATB)   2:00   C

Dickey Donkey (Lester Luther) (1935)
  (chor SATB or SSAA)   3:00   CF

The Earth Does Not Wish for Beauty (Lester Luther)
  (1940)
  (SATB)   8:00   APS

Earth Mother (1975)
  (SATB)   3:00   C

Eternal Spirit (Lerae Britain) (1964)
  (SATB)   3:00   Hero

Forest Procession (Lerae Britain) (1970)
  (SATB)   8:00   UCLA

† *Harvest Heritage* (Lerae Britain) (1963) (SATB)	5:00	C
Haunted (Griffin) (1935) (SATB)	3:00	C
Humble Me (Lester Luther) (1941) (SATB)	3:00	UCLA
Hush My Heart (Halff) (1970) (chor SATB or SSAA)	4:00	UCLA
In the Silence of the Temple (Collander) (1965) (SATB)	3:00	UCLA
I'se Comin' Lord to You (Alice McKenzie) (1940) (SATB)	4:00	CFSum
Lord God Within Me (Holmes) (1977) (SATB)	3:00	UCLA
Lord Have Mercy (1976) (Mass: chor SATB)	15:00	UCLA
Love Still has Something of the Sea (1971) (SATB)	4:00	UCLA
Nature Ushers in the Dawn (Harold Skeath) (1939) (SATB)	4:00	Hero
† *Noontide* (Nietzche) (1935) (SATB)	4:00	Hero
Prayer (Quarry) (1934) (SATB)	3:00	Ric
The Star and the Child (John Lancaster) (1956) (chor SATB or SSA)	3:00	C
Stillness (Lester Luther) (1941) (SATB)	3:00	UCLA
Ten Commandments (1970) (SATB)	10:00	UCLA

CECCONI-BATES

Two Latin Masses (mixed chor with org)	1	C
Two English Masses (mixed chor with org)	1	C

DEMBO

Concord Hymn (Ralph Waldo Emerson)
(SATB and org)   12:00   3   C

DIEMER

The Angel Gabriel (1959)
(mixed chor, and pno or org)   1   CF

Anthem of Faith (1966)
(mixed chor, and pno or org)   2   GSch

Before the Paling of the Stars (1957)
(mixed chor, and pno or org)   E-V

The Bells (1959)
(mixed chor, and pno fr-hnd)   2   B&H

California Madrigals (1976)
(mixed chor, and pno or org)   7:00   2   CF

For the Fruit of All Creation (hymn in *Lutheran
Book of Worship*) (1978)   APH

For Ye Shall Go Out with Joy (1968)
(mixed chor, and pno or org)   4:00   2   CF

Honor to Thee (1957)
(mixed chor and pno or org)   5:00   2   HWG

I Will Give Thanks (1959)
(mixed chor and pno or org)   SacM

Joy to the World (hymn in *Ecumenical Praise*)
(1977)   Ag

Joy to the World (1976)
(mixed chor and pno or org)   1   Ag

Laughing Song (1974)
(mixed chor and pno fr-hnd)   2   Shaw

A Little Song of Life (1964)
(chor SATB and kybd)   1   ChorAS

The Lord is Mindful (1979)
(mixed chor and pno or org)   1   Hin

The Lord is My Light (1977)
(mixed chor and pno or org)   2   Hin

⊕ *Madrigals Three* (1972)
(mixed chor and pno or org)   7:00   2   CF

Noel: Rejoice and Be Merry (1959)
(mixed chor and pno or org)   CF

Now the Spring Has Come Again (1961) (mixed chor and pno or org)	5:00	3	B&H
⊕ *O Come, Let Us Sing Unto the Lord* (1960) (mixed chor and pno or org)	4:00	2	CF
O Give Thanks to the Lord (1959) (mixed chor and pno or org)		2	BelM
O to Make the Most Jubilant Song (1970) (mixed chor and pno or org)	6:00	3	CF
Outburst of Praise (1961) (mixed chor and pno or org)		2	TPres
Praise of Created Things (1959) (mixed chor and pno or org)		1	BelM
Praise the Savior (1976) (mixed chor and pno or org)		1	Ag
Praise Ye the Lord (1960) (mixed chor and pno fr-hnd)		1	HF
Romance (1974) (mixed chor and pno)		2	CF
Spring (1965) (mixed chor and pno)		2	HerM
A Spring Carol (1960) (mixed chor and pno)		2	CF
Strong Son of God (1976) (mixed chor and pno or org)		1	Ag
Three Madrigals (1960) (mixed chor and pno or org)	5:00	2	B&H
Your Friends Shall Be the Tall Wind (1960)		1	ChorAS
When in Man's Music (1976) (mixed chor and pno or org)		1	APH
⊕ *Wild Nights! Wild Nights!* (1978) (mixed chor and pno)		2	Hin

FORMAN

The Skipper and the Witch (female narr, Bar, chor, pno)	15:00	2+	C

FRASIER

Your Eyes (chor SATB and pno)	3:00	3	C

GLAZIER

In Freedom Rejoice
(chor SATB and pno)   2 C

In Freedom Rejoice (chor SATB and pno)		2	C
Kedushah (S, chor SATB, pno)	3:00-4:00	2	C
† *Kedushah* (chor SATB and org)	3:00-4:00	2	C
A New Song unto the Lord (2 part male and female chor, pno)		1	C
A New Song unto the Lord (chor SATB and org)	4:00	1	C
Screaming Eagle (chor SATB and pno)	4:00	2+	C
Screaming Eagle (chor SATB and pno)	5:00	3	C
V'shomru (chor SATB and org)	5:00-6:00	2+	C

HOOVER

Lake Isle of Innisfree (1973) (chor SATB and pno)	4:30	2	AMC

LACKMAN

Chanson des Escargots (chor SATB and pno)	8:00	2+	C

MAGEAU

A Community Mass (1978) (chor SATB, congregation, org)		2	C

MARCUS

The House By the Side of the Road (Sam Walter Foss) (chor SATB, and pno or stg qt)	10:00	2	C
A Shakespearean Duo "A Consolation" (sonnet) "The Seven Ages of Man" (chor SATB and pno)	15:00	2	C

PARKER

I Will Sing and Give Praise (1977)
(S solo, chor SATB, org or pno) — 5:00 2 Hin

Love Songs (1978)
(chor SATB and pno) — 8:00 2 Hin

Now Glad of Heart (1959)
(Bar solo, chor SATB, pno or orch) — 2 L-G

The Time of Ingathering (1970)
(4 movements)
(contr solo, chor SATB, org) — 20:00 2 CF

The True Use of Magic (Wesley) (1976)
(chor SATB and pno) — 5:00 2 Hin

PAULL

Sheer Silver Sheen Flower Sky (1971-74)
(chor SATB and pno) — 9:00 2 AMC

PIERCE

Report to God (Milton Miller) (1978)
(chor SATB and pno) — 4:30 3 See

Take My Hands and Let Them Move (Francis R. Havergal)
(1973)
(chor SATB and org) — 3:30 2+ C

This Bread is Torn (Roger Pierce) (1975)
(hymn for the Eucharist)
(chor SATB and org) — 2:00 2+ C

PIZER

Holy Eucharist, Rite II, Op. 46 (1978)
(chor SATB or unison voices, and pno or org) — 8:00 2 C

PREOBRAJENSKA

Christmas Prayer (1962)
(chor SATB and pno) — 1:30 OPP

The Creation, Cantata (1971)
(chor SATB and pno) — 10:00 OPP

The Creed (1969)
(chor SATB and pno) — 3:30 OPP

Easter Prayer (1960)
(chor SATB and pno) — 3:00 OPP

The Lord's Prayer (1966)
(chor SATB and pno)   2:00   OPP

Prayer to Mary (1965)
(chor SATB and pno)   4:00   OPP

ROGERS

Hymn (H. O. Rogers)
(chor SATB and/or unison voices, org)   3:30   2   C

"Spaghetti": A Round (Eve Merriam)
(chor SATB or individual voices, and pno)   4:00   2   C

SINGER

American Indian Song Suite
(4 songs)
(Mez and T soli, chor SATB)   6:30   2   C

SMITH

Glory to the Green and White (1966)
(chor SATB and pno)   2:30   1   Mowb

God Bless This House (from "Daisy") (1974)
(chor SATB and pno)   2:00   2   Mowb

Our Heritage (1956)
(chor SSAATB or SSAA, and pno)   10:00   2   Mowb

SWISHER

† *God Is Gone Up With a Merry Noise*
(chor SAATB and org or pno)   3:00   2   CF

Two Faces of Love
(chor SSAATB and pno)   6:00   2   MK

Unto Thee, O Lord
(chor SATB and org)   3:00   2   C

WALKER

"The Nocturnal Nibbler" (and other Madrigals) (1979)
(chor SATB and pno)   10:00   1   Walk

WALLACH

Prayers of Steel (1977)
(chor SATB and org)   9:00   AMC

WARREN

Abram in Egypt
(pno-vocal version)
(Bar solo, chor SATB, pno)   23:00   HWG

Come to the Stable
(youth and adult choirs, opt org)   HWG

God Is My Song!
(chor SATB and org)   B&H

Good Morning, America!
(chor SATB, narr, pno)   17:00   CF

The Harp Weaver
(Bar solo, chor SSA, pno, opt hrp)   15:00   CF

Hymn of the City
(chor SATB, pno or org [also with orch accompaniment])   CF

Iris
(chor SSA and pno)   TPres

The Legend of King Arthur (revised 1974)
(Bar and T soli, chor SATB, pno)   60:00   HWG

Let the Heavens Praise Thy Wonders!
(chor SATB, opt org)   HWG

My Heart Is Ready
(chor SATB and org)   L-G

Night-Rider
(chor SATB and pno)   L-G

Our Beloved Land
(chor SATB and pno [also with orch accompaniment])   TPres

Requiem
(S and Bar soli, chor SATB, pno)   53:00   L-G

Sanctus (includes "Benedictus" and "Hosannas")
(Bar solo, chor SATB, pno [also with orch
    accompaniment])   L-G

Transcontinental
(Bar solo, chor SATB, pno)   TPres

WEIGL

A Shelter for All
(chor SATB, choral soli, pno)   10:00   2   Jel

Fairy Song (Y. Keats)   2   ACA

Four Choral Songs on Death and Man (Carl Sandburg)   2   ACA

Harbingers of Spring		2	ACA
Let My Country Awake (chor SATB, narr, choral soli, pno)	11:00	2	Jel
Madrigal (Blankner)		2	ACA
No Loveliness Is Ever Lost (Nancy Byrd Turner)		2	ACA
Ode to Beauty (H. Hesse)		2	ACA
What Once the Heart Has Loved (Dorothy Quick)		2	ACA

ZAIMONT

The Chase (J. L. Zaimont) (1972) (chor SSATB and pno)	6:00	2+	AMC
Three Choruses from the Sacred Service (1976) "Psalm: The Lord reigneth, let the Earth rejoice" "Why do we deal treacherously, brother against brother?" "Thou shalt love the Lord" (Bar solo, chor SSATB, pno)	16:30	2+	Gal
The Tragickal Ballad of Sir Patrick Spens (1980) (chor SSATB, choral soli, pno)	10:00	2+	AMC

ZIFFRIN

Death of Moses (1953-54) (cant: chor SATB, choral soli, pno)	15:00	3	C

CHORAL MUSIC — CHORAL MUSIC ACCOMPANIED BY INSTRUMENTS OTHER THAN KEYBOARD

BARNETT, CAROL

Cinco Poemas de Bécquer (1979) (SSAATTBB, gtr, S rec, wind chimes)	9:30	3	C
Three Vocalises (1976) (SSATB, vibe)	3:00	2	C

BOLZ

Grace and Love Now Mine (anthem for Easter) (SATB with tpt obblig)	3:00	2+	C
Ode to Autumn (1973) (SATB chor, vln, vla, vcl, pno)	7:04	2	C

BRENNER

Beatitudes (of Christ) (1976)
(chor and instr or acap)   2   C

Be Set Aglow (Baha'i Writings) (1972)
(chor and instr or acap)   2   C

Two Meditations (Baha'i Writings) (1972)
(chor and instr or acap)   2   C

Darkness Hath Fallen (Baha'i Writings) (1974)
(chor and instr or acap)   2   C

Love and Unity (Baha'i Writings) (1973)
(chor and instr or acap)   2   C

Many a Chilled Heart (Baha'i Writings) (1974)
(chor and instr or acap)   2   C

May the Words (1976)
(chor and instr or acap)   2   C

O Son of Man! Rejoice (Baha'i Writings)(1974)
(chor and instr or acap)   2   C

Three Prayers (Baha'i Writings) (1971)
(chor and instr or acap)   2   C

Two Biblical Settings (1972)
(chor and instr or acap)   2   C

BRITAIN

The Flute Song (Catherine Manore) (1965)
(SSAA chor, fl, pno)   8:00   C

† *Nisan* (Kate Hammond) (1961)
(SSAA chor, stgs, pno)   8:00   Hero

DIEMER

Alleluia! Christ is Risen (1964)
(mixed chor, tpt, pno or org)   2   HF

Awake My Glory (1976)
(mixed chor, pno or org, gtr opt)   1   AbP

A Babe is Born (1965)
(mixed chor, pno or org, brass qt, tamb)   2   SacM

Blessed Are You (1969)
(mixed chor, pno or org, gtr opt)   1   CF

The Call (1976)
(mixed chor, pno, stgs, perc opt)   2   GSch

Choruses on Freedom (1976) (mixed chor, pno, stgs, perc)	4:00 each	2	L-G
Come Hither, You That Love (1963) (SSA chor, fl, pno)		2	EBM
Dance, Dance My Heart (1967) (mixed chor, pno, perc)	4:00	2	CF
From This Hour, Freedom (1976) (mixed chor and pno, stgs, perc opt)		2	GSch
Hast Thou Not Known (1977) (mixed chor, org, brass, timp)	5:00	2	RgD
Jesus, Lover of My Soul (1974) (2-part chor, fl)		1	Tri
Praise To The Lord (1974) (mixed chor, org, brass qnt, timp)	5:00	2	CF
Proclaim The Day (1962) (mixed chor, pno or org, brass qt)		2	HF
The Shepherd To His Love (1959) (women's chor SSA or SA, fl, pno)		1	EBM
The Shepherd To His Love (1959) (SATB or SAB chor, fl, pno)		1	EBM
⊕ *Three Poems by Alice Meynell* (1976) (mixed chor, ww qnt, perc [4] , marmb, vibe, pno, org)	12:00	2	C

FRASIER

God is Love (2-part chor, cl, pno)	3:15	2	C
Joy, Peace and Singing (SSA chor, fl)	3:00	3	C

GARDNER

Did You Know That I Can Fly? (1975) (SA chor, hrp (or pno), Enghn, vln, vla, vcl)	4:00	3	Iris
⊕ *Mermaids* (1978) (SSAA chor, fl, al-fl, vcl, pno)	6:00	2+	Iris
When We Made the Music (1977) (SSAA chor, Enghn, stg qt and pno)	8:00	3	Iris

HOOVER

Four English Songs (1976)
(SATB chor, ob, Enghn, pno)   12:00   2   AMC

Songs of Joy (1974)
(SATB chor, 2 tpts, 2 tbns)   11:00   2   CF

Syllable Songs (1977)
(SSA chor, woodblock)   4:00   2   AMC

Three Carols (1972)
(SSA chor, fl)   9:00   2   CF

HSU

Praise the Lord (1980)
(mixed chor, tpt and ww)   5:00   W-Y

HYSON

An Island of Content (1974)
(SATB chor with S and fl solos, org)   15:00   2+ C

JANKOWSKI

Inside the Cube, Empty Air (1975)
(30 women's voice and var Renaissance instr) 13:00 3 C

Next To Of Course God (1976)
(SAB, 2 ten-tbns, pno)   4:00   2   C

LE BARON

† *Light Breaks Where No Sun Shines* (Dylan Thomas) (1977)
(soli SAT, chor SATB, 2 perc players: large battery
including xylo, timp, 2 b dm)   20:00   3   AMC

MAGEAU

A Chime of Windbells (1971)
(SSATB, fl, perc)   6:00   C

Faces of Time (1980)
(SSATB, perc)   C

Lacrimae (1972)
(SAT, perc)   3:00   3   C

MARCUS

Christmas Bells (Longfellow)
(SATB with brass qt or fl qt)   7:00   2   C

"God, Whom Shall I Compare to Thee!" (Halevy)
(SATB with brass qt)   8:00   2   C

MEACHEM

Chanson d'Automne (Verlaine) (1975)
(SATB chor, ob solo, xylo, freakas (whirling tubes))   3:00   2+ C

PARKER

All Creatures of Our God and King
(chor, cong, brass qt, org, opt timp)   1+ Hin

Away, Melancholy (S. Smith) (1972)
(SSA-SSAA, tamb)   8:00   2   ECS

Be Thou My Vision (1973)
(Mez solo, mixed chor, stgs, hrp)   5:00   1+ Hin

Children, Saints and Charming Sounds (1979)
(5 movements)
(mixed chor, children's chor, fl, ob, bsn, 2 tpts,
    tbn, tuba)   18:00 2   Hin

The Day-Spring (1978)
(mixed chor, children's chor, fl, org)   18:00 1+ Hin

An Easter Rejoicing (1968)
(13 movements)
(soli SATB, chor SATB, org, hrp, perc)   30:00 2   ECS

God, Be Merciful Unto Us (Psalms) (1980)
(SSA, 2 vlns, vla, vcl, contrabass)   7:00   3   Hin

Grace and Glory (Watts) (1967)
(SATB, bell in E, temp blks)   5:00   3   ECS

In Bethlehem (1969)
(SATB, org, perc)   2   ECS

I Saw a Stable (Coleridge) (1969)
(SATB, org, perc)   2   ECS

Melodius Accord (1974)
(13 movements)
(soli SATB, chor SATB, 2 tpt, tbn, tuba, hrp [or
    org or pno])   40:00 2   ECS

Now Thank We All Our God
(chor, congregation, brass qt, org, opt timp)   1+ CF

Phonophobia (tongue-twisters) (1976)
(4 movements)
(SATB, gtr (or pno), perc)   10:00   2   Hin

Praise to the Lord
(chor, congregation, brass qt, organ, opt timp)   1+   L-G

Praise with Understanding (Psalms) (1979)
(2 choirs SATB, 2 brass qts)   8:00   3   Hin

Psalms of Praise (1964)
(TB, perc)   2   L-G

A Sermon from the Mountain: Martin Luther King (1969)
(New Testament, Spirituals)
(soli SAT Bar, chor SATB, speaker, stgs, gtr, perc,
    opt improvisation)   40:00   2   ECS

Shrill Chanticleer (Austin) (1969)
(SATB, org, perc)   2   ECS

The Song of Simeon (1978)
(SATB, 2 tpts, 2 tbns)   6:00   2   Hin

Street-Corner Spirituals (1964)
(SATB, tpt, gtr, perc)   2   L-G

There and Back Again (Pyle) (1977)
(5 movements)
(SATB, fl, ob, cl, bsn)   20:00   2   Hin

Three Circles (Folk, Swift) (1972)
(SATB, perc)   8:00   2   CF

Universal Praise (Watts) (1974)
(SATB, brass qt)   4:00   2   ECS

PAULL

The Snow Moth (1974)
(SATB chor, 2 perc)   17:00   3   AMC

PIERCE

Hamaguchi (Milton Miller) (1973)
(chamber oratorio)
(2 Bar soli, A, T soli, chamber chor SATB,
    prepared pno, fl, vcl)   30:00   2+   C

Resurrection (Robert Stuart) (1979)
(SATB, fl, pno)   6:00   2   C

PIZER

Slow, Slow, Fresh Fount, Op. 44 (Ben Jonson) (1977)

(S solo, fl solo, SSAATTBB chor)   5:00   3   AMC

PROCACCINI

Tre Canti Popolari, Op. 77 (1979)
(treb chor [unis] , al-fl, gtr, perc)   6:00   1   C

RICHTER

Three Christmas Songs (1964)
(chor SA with 2 fl or pno)   7:00   1+   CF

ROGERS

Crabbed Age and Youth (Shakespeare)
(chor SATB, cl, bsn, hn, 2 tpts, 2 tbns, 4 perc, pno)   7:00   1+   C

Follow Thy Fair Sun (Thomas Campion)
(chor SATB, fl, cl, bsn, hn, 2 tpts, 2 tbns, 4 perc,
pno, stg qt)   5:00   2   C

Hymn (H. O. Rogers)
(chor SATB, org, 2 or 3 tpts, 4 or 3 tbns, tuba)   5:30   2   C

In Celebration: Elizabeth Blackwell (Eve Merriam)
(chor SAB, pno, 4 perc)   12:00   1+   C

VAN DE VATE

An American Essay (Walt Whitman) (1972)
(SATB, pno, perc - 2 players)   30:00   2+   AMC

WALKER

The Radiant Dawn (1978)
(chor SATB, org and vcl)   10:00   3   Walk

ZAIMONT

DEVILRY: Black Massing (1980-81)
(SSAATTBB, choral soloists, 8 tambs)   15:00   3   C

† *"They flee from me . . . "* (Sir Thomas Wyatt) (1966)
(SSATB, fl)   5:30   3   C

CHORAL MUSIC — CANTATAS, ORATORIOS, AND OTHER LARGE-SCALE WORKS WITH ORCHESTRA AND BAND

BARTHELSON

The First Palm Sunday (1968)
(sacred dramatic cantata)
(narr, 4 soli, senior and junior choirs, org,
   opt fl and ob)   30:00   2   C

BOLZ

Day and Dark (George Cabot Lodge) (1958)
(cantata: Bar solo, chor SATB, orch)   12:00   3   C

BRENNER

Cantata No. 1: The Choice   15:00   2   BW

The Trumpet Pen (Baha'i Writings) (1977)
(oratorio: narr, solo voices SAB, chor SATB,
   children's chor, orch)   30:00   2   C

BRITAIN

Brothers of the Clouds (1963)
(chor TTBB, orch: 2222 4331 timp, perc, stgs)   10:00   See

CECCONI-BATES

We Have a Dream (A. Cecconi-Bates, Dr. M. L. King, Jr.)
(1974)
(solo voices ST, chor SATB, orch)   18:00   2   C

DIEMER

Anniversary Choruses (1970)
(chor and orch)   15:00   2   CF

Cantata (1957)   C

Cantata (1967)   C

To Him All Glory Give (1960)
(chor and orch)   4:00   2   EV

FRASIER

An American Requiem (Walt Whitman)
(chor SATB and orch)   20:00   3   C

GARDNER

Night Chant (1979)
  (women's voices: S Mez A soli, chor SSAA; chamber
    orch: 1111 2000 2 perc, pno, stgs)   13:00   3   Iris

HEINRICH

The Nazarene, Op. 19
  (chor SATB, narr, vocal soli, 3 tpt in C, timp, org) 48:00   2+   C

LOMON

Requiem (1977)
  (S solo, chor SATB, 2 fl, 2 cl, bcl, bsn, tpts, tbns) 35:00   3   AMC

MARCUS

A Setting to Seasons (Robert Frost)
  "My November Guest"
  "A Winter Eden"
  "A Prayer in Spring"
  "Sitting by a Bush in Broad Sunlight"
  (SSA, stg orch, pno)   25:00   2   C

MEACHEM

In the Beginning (Dylan Thomas) (1973)
  (cantata: S and T soli, chor SATB, double wind qnt,
    stg qnt, brass qnt, 3 perc)   30:00   3   C

PARKER

Commentaries (Dickinson; Folk) (1978)
  (5 movements)
  (Mez solo, small chor SSA, large chor SSAA,
    orch: 2222 2221 timp, perc, hrp, stgs)   35:00   2   Hin

Gaudete: Six Latin Christmas Hymns (1973)
  (6 movements)
  (opt S solo, chor SATB, orch: 2222 4221 timp,
    perc, hrp, stgs)   23:00   2   ECS

Journeys: Pilgrims and Strangers (Folk) (1975)
  (6 movements)
  (S and Bar soli, chor SATB, orch: 32/Enghn/2/bcl/2/cbsn
    4221 timp, perc, hrp, stgs)   50:00   2   Hin

Seven Carols (1972)
  (S solo, chor SATB, orch: 2222 4221 timp,
    perc, hrp, stgs)   17:00   1+   CF

PROCACCINI

Il Giudizio di Salomone, Op. 15 (1958)
   (oratorio)
   (S Mez T B soli, chor SATB, orch: 322/bcl/2
     4331 timp, side dm, stgs)   16:00 2 Cari

La Peste di Atene, Op. 17 (1958)
   (cantata)
   (chor SATB, orch: 322/bcl/2 4331 timp, perc)   14:00 2 Cari

REED

Shir Kadosh
   (boy's choir and orch)   20:00 3 See

SILSBEE

Diffraction (1974)
   (S solo, chor SATB, fl, pno, 2 perc)   16:00 3 ACA

SMELTZER

The Bald Eagle March (1979)
   (chor SATB, narr, 3 tpt, 4 hn, 3 tbn, 2 tuba, dm,
     timp, cym)   15:00 2 C

The Brotherhood March (1977)
   (chor, 2 tpt, dm, cym, gong)   5:00 2 ISWP

Psalm 121 (1979)
   (chor, orch, brass choir)   25:00 2+ ISWP

SMITH

Our Heritage (Arthur M. Sampley) (1956)
   (S solo, chor SSAATB, orch: 2222 4331 timp, perc, stgs)   10:00   TPres

Our Heritage (1958-59)
   (S solo, chor SSAATB, small orch, symphonic band)   10:00   TPres

Remember the Alamo (with Cecile Vashaw) (1964-65)
   (chor SSAATB, opt narr, full band accompaniment,
     symphonic band accompaniment or orch accomp)   12:00 2 TPres

STANLEY

Night Piece (1949)
   (cantata: 4-part women's voices SSAA, and chamber
     orch: fl, ob, cl, bsn, 3 hn, timp, stgs)   10:30 2 C

VAN DE VATE

Cantata for Women's Voices (1979)
"Voices" (James Joyce)
"Nightsong, Daylong, as the Sweet" (anonymous
Provençal - 12th cent., trans Maurice Valency)
"Faces" (Walt Whitman)
"The Little Old Women" (Baudelaire, trans Barbara Gibbs)
"Tears" (Walt Whitman)
(SSAA, pic, fl, B-flat cl, timp, 2 perc, hrp, cel)   15:00   3   C

VELLÈRE

Ce Fut un Trouvère qui Chanta et une Dame qui en Mourut
(P. Gérardy) (1949)
(chor SATB and orch)   9:00   2   C

WARREN

⊕ *Abram in Egypt* (Bible, Dead Sea Scrolls)
(Bar solo, chor SATB, orch: 2(pic)222 4231 timp,
2 perc, hrp, stgs)   23:00   HWG

Good Morning, America! (Carl Sandburg)
(chor SATB, narr, orch: 2(pic)2(Enghn)22 4231
timp, 2 perc, pno, cel, stgs, [alternate orch with
brass: 2220])   17:00   CF

The Harp Weaver (Edna St. Vincent Millay)
(Bar solo, chor SSA, hrp solo, orch: 2(pic)2(Enghn)22
0231 timp, 2 perc, hrp, stgs)   15:00   HWG

The Legend of King Arthur (Tennyson) (revised 1974)
(Bar and T soli, chor SATB, orch: 3(pic)2(Enghn)2(bcl)2
2331 timp, 3 perc, cel, hrp, opt org, stgs)   60:00   HWG

Requiem (Latin and English)
(S [or Mez] and Bar soli, chor SATB, orch:
2(pic)2(Enghn)02 4231 timp, 2 perc, cel, hrp, stgs)   53:00   L-G

Transcontinental (A. M. Sullivan)
(Bar solo, chor SATB, orch: 2(pic)121 2220
timp, 2 perc, pno, stgs)

WEIGL

† *The People Yes!* (Carl Sandburg)
(cantata: chor, soli, narr, pno, tpt, tbn, timp,
stg qt or stg orch)   2+   ACA

WYLIE

† *Echo,* Op. 22 (Christina Rossetti)
(SA and stg orch)   8:00   1+   C

". . . in Just Spring," Op. 19 no. 1 (E. E. Cummings)
(SA and stg orch)   8:00   2   C

ZAIMONT

† *Man's Image and His Cry* (1968)
(Bar and A soli, chor SSATB, orch)   20:00   3   AMC

Sacred Service for the Sabbath Evening (1976)
(oratorio)
(Bar or A solo, chor SSATB, orch: 2(pic)2(Enghn)22
2220 timp, perc, pno, stgs)   70:00   2+   Gal

● CHORAL MUSIC — MIXED CHORUS WITH TAPE ●

HAYS

Dreams, Choral Scenes (from *Uni Suite*)
1. Chief of Police and Politicians   3:30
2. Park People (opt), tape solo   6:00
3. Uni's Dream   4:10
(chor SATB and tape)   3   ABI

Hands Full
(2-part chor, tape, opt dm)   3:00   1   ABI

Star Music
(2-part chor, tape, bells)   5:00   Q-H

Uni
(suite: stg qt, fl, tape, chor)   37:00   3   ABI

SILSBEE

Prometheus (1972-73)
(dramatic cantata)
(B solo, chor SATB, cl, vcl, pno, 2 perc, tape)   3   C

● STAGE WORKS — OPERA/MUSICAL THEATER, BALLET, MULTIMEDIA PIECES ●

ANDERSON, BETH

The Bridegroom is Here (originally called *The Messiah
is Come*) (collaboration with Paul Cotton)
(1974, revised 1976)
(fl, vln, db, perc, pno, tape, voices/speakers,
sculpture person, slides)   15:00   2+   C

Hallophone (1973)
(voice, 2 sax, steel gtr, tapes, slides, dancers)　　　　60:00　2+　C

He Said (1975)
(actor, 2 cl, tape, video)　　　　10:00 - 20:00　2+　BGCE

I Am uh Am I (1973)
(2 stgs, 2 lighting technicians)　　　　varies　2+　C

Joan (1974)
(oratorio: 2 S, T, Bar, dancer, orch, tape [live mix],
lights, scaffolding)　　　　18:00-30:00　2+　ACA

Morning View and Maiden Spring (1978)
(tape, speaker, slides, light)　　　　15:00-30:00　2+　C

Music for Myself (1973)
(voice, vibe, slides, elect.s)　　　　10:00　2+　C

Peachy Keen-O (1973)
(voices, org, elect. gtr, vibes, perc, dancers, light,
tape, Hysteresis)　　　　15:00　2+

Queen Christina (1973)
(opera: S Bar Mez soli, small orch, film, live
elect.s, audience participation)　　　　120:00　2+　C

Soap Tuning (1976)
(2 - 4 speakers)　　　　3:00 - 30:00　2+　Dram

Zen Piece (1976)
(2 speakers)　　　　5:00-7:00　2+　C

BARTHELSON

† *Chanticleer* (Adapted from Chaucer's "The Nun's
Priest's Tale")
(1967)
(a contemporary comic fantasy: narr, 5 soli, chor,
pno 4-hands, or orch)　　　　43:00　2　CF

The Devil's Disciple (based on the play by George
Bernard Shaw)
(1976)
(opera: 8 soli, chor, orch)　　　　135:00　2　CF

Feathertop (based on the satiric fantasy by Hawthorne)
(1965)
(overture and opera buffa: 5 soli, chor, orch)　　　　120:00　2　CF

Greenwich Village, 1910 (adapted from O. Henry's
"Gift of the Magi") (1969)
(one act opera buffa: 4 soli, pno)　　　　50:00　2　C

The King's Breakfast (adapted from Maurice Baring's
   "Catherine Parr") (1972)
   (a diminutive comic opera: S, Bar, page [speaking part] ,
      pno 4-hands, or chamber orch)   30:00   2   CF

Lysistrata (adapted from Aristophanes' play) (1979)
   (one act comic opera: 6 soli, chor, orch, or pno)   60:00   2   CF

BEATH

Abigail and the Mythical Beast (David Cox) (1980)
   (musical play)   20:00   C

Francis (David Cox) (1974)
   (music drama)   40:00   LR

Marco Polo (David Cox) (1977)
   (music drama for children)   30:00   JAS

The Raja Who Married an Angel (David Cox) (1979)
   (one act music drama)   35:00   Play

BRITAIN

Carillon (Rupert Hughes) (1952)
   (opera in 3 acts)   150:00   C

Happyland (Ada Greenfield) (1946)
   (operetta)   60:00   C

Kambu Ballet (1963)
   (orch: 2222 4331 timp, perc, stgs)   8:00   C

Kutharo (Lester Luther) (1960)
   (chamber opera in 1 act)   60:00   AMC

Lady in the Dark (from Shakespearean sonnets)
   (1962)   60:00   C

Red Clay (1950)
   (ballet)   15:00   C

Shepherd in the Distance (1929)
   (ballet: orch)   15:00   C

Ubiquity (Lester Luther) (1937)
   (musical drama)   60:00   C

Wheel of Life (1937)
   (ballet: orch)   15:00   C

BRUSH

The Street Singers of Market Street (1965)
   (one-act folk opera)   45:00   2+   C

CLARK

The Doll with the Blue Bonnet (1976)
(3 act children's musical)   75:00   2+   EldP

Jesus Lives (from the New Testament) (1977)
(collection of musical plays)   1:00-3:00   1   PP
                                                                each

Will Jack be Here for Christmas? (1973)
(3 act operetta for children)   75:00   2   EldP

COHEN

Double Play (1970)
(2 dancers and tape)   10:00   2   C

Stopgo (1970)
(dance troupe, sculpture, tape)   10:00   2   C

DEMBO

The Story of Beowulf
(narr, rec, crumhorns, rauschpfeife, lute,
    kortholt, baroque fl, vla da gamba, perc)   45:00   3   C

FORMAN

The Blind Men (based on painting by Breugel)
(opera: S, T, 2 Bar, cl, vcl, chimes)   45:00   2+   C

Love the Painter (based on play by Molière)
(opera: S, Mez, T, Bar, B, chor, 2 gtr)   15:00   2+   C

Polly Baker (based on a sketch by Benjamin Franklin)
(opera: 2 S, Mez, T, Bar, male speaking part, hpsd)   20:00   2+   C

GARDNER

Ladies Voices (Gertrude Stein) (1980)
(opera)   20:00   3   Iris

GILBERT

Mass for Dancers (1972)
(tape, dance)   17:00   C

Oenone (Mario Castillo) (1975)
(tape, visuals)   6:00   C

. . . out of the Looking Glass (1975)
(tape, dance, visuals)   16:00   C

Timelapse (choreography by Ruth Emerson) (1977)
(tape, dance) — 5:00 — C

Un Coup de Dés (Mallarmé) (1979)
(chant: chor, tape, visuals, readers) — 20:00 — 2 — C

HAYS

Hands and Lights
(pno, photocells, flashlights, flood lamps) — 13:00 — 3 — Q-H

In-de-pen-dance
(chanter-actor and nylon strings) — 10:00 — 2 — Q-H

Sensevents
(vln, vla, vcl, fl, hn, ob, programmed lights,
motorized sculpture, opt elect. music on
cassettes — 30:00 - 60:00 — 3 — Q-H

Water Music
(running fountain, 2-4 melodic instr, tapes,
opt film) — 60:00 — Q-H

HEINRICH

Alleluia, Alleluia!: A Choric Dance (1969)
(dbl chor [SSAA, SATB] , S solo, vln, pno or org,
dance) — 10:00 — 2+ — C

Chamber Suite: Shakespearean Women, Op. 11
(pic, 2 fl, vln, pno, 2 voices, dancers) — 22:00 — 2 — C

Duologue: Romeo and Juliet, Op. 16
(2 fl, vln, 2 dancers) — 10:00 — 1+ — C

Dramatic Banquet: Shakespearean Men, Op. 17
(pic, 2 fl, tpt, sn dm, pno, dancers) — 25:00 — 2 — C

LACKMAN

Lisa Stratos
(chamber opera in 1 Act, 2 Scenes)
(2S Mez T B soli, women's chor, chamber
orch [1 player per part]) — 45:00 — 2+ — C

MARCUS

Snow (Robert Frost)
(chamber opera: Mez T B soli, dancers, 2 pno) — 60:00 — C

MEACHEM

Alice in Wonderland (1980)
(1-Act opera: multi-media)   C

An African Folktale (1980)
(theater piece: music, mime, dance)   C

PARKER

The Family Reunion (Parker) (1975)
(opera in 1 Act)
(4S 4A 2T Bar B soli, 6 children, chor, children's chor,
fl, bsn, hn, tpt, tbn, tuba, gtr, banjo, vln, perc)   60:00   2   CF

The Martyrs' Mirror (Ruth) (1971)
(opera in 2 Acts)
(S A T 2B soli, 2 children, 2 male speakers, chors:
large, small, children's, 2 rec, ob, bsn, tpt, 3 tbn,
harmonium, perc, hand bells)   100:00   2   ECS

Singers Glen (Parker) (1977)
(opera in 2 Acts with prologue)
(2S A 3T 2Bar 2B soli, 4 children, chor SATB, fl, tpt,
tbn, gtr, harmonium, 4 stgs)   100:00   2   Hin

PAULL

Asylum (1974)
(theater piece)
(concrete/elect. tape with 35mm slide projections,
improvising performers, dancers, players)   11:00   AMC

Blues for Saeko (1971-78)
(dance theater work)   15:00   1   AMC

A Christmas Carol (based on Dickens tale) (1978)
(theater piece)
(chor SATB, narr, pno, opt instrs)   60:00   1   AMC

Earth Pulse (1971)
(concrete/elect. cantata for the dance)   8:00   AMC

In the Vast Space of World (1975)
(theater piece)
(Mez, narr, pno/electric pno, perc,
35mm slide projections)   15:00   2   AMC

A Land Called the Infinity of Love (1975)
(theater piece)
(narr, elect. tape, strobe lights)   9:00   1   AMC

The Land (1971-76)
(theater piece)
(Bar solo, org, pno, perc, lights, projections)   15:00   3   AMC

Requiem (1975)
(tape, perc, 35mm projections)   12:00   3   AMC

Requiem for Greece '67 (1973)
(tape with red light wheel)   5:00   2   AMC

The Snow Moth (1974)
(theater piece)
(chor SATB, 2 perc, 35mm projections)   17:00   AMC

A Song of Earth and of the Sky (1975)
(theater event)
(chor SATB, narrs, dancers, tape, lights,
    35mm slide projections)   120:00   3   AMC

Time (1971)
(ballet)
(concrete/elect. tape, 35mm slide projections)   16:00   AMC

Time Pulse (1973)
(ballet)
(tape with strobe lights)   12:00   AMC

PREOBRAJENSKA

Crime and Punishment (1956)
(ballet: dance drama)
(cl, stg qt or pno)   60:00   AMC

PROCACCINI

In Prima Notte, Op. 55 (1973)
(comic opera in 1 Act)
(solo voices, orch: 1121 2100 perc, stgs)   40:00   2   C

Questione di Fiducia, Op. 56 (1973)
(comic opera in 1 Act)
(solo voices, orch: 2222 2200 stgs)   28:00   2   C

La Vendetta di Luzbel, Op. 45 (1970)
(dramatic opera in 1 Act, 2 Scenes)
(Mez 2T Bar soli, orch: 2222 2220 timp, perc, pno, stgs)   32:00   3   C

RICHTER

Bird of Yearning (1967)
(ballet)
(orch: 2222 4220 timp, perc, cel, hrp, pno, stgs)   27:00   3   CF

ROBERTS

Alice in Wonderland
(incidental music; hpsd solo)   C

Thieves Carnival (Jean Anouilh)
(incidental music; hpsd solo)   C

Yerma (Lorca)
(incidental music; hpsd solo)   C

ROGERS

Crayons: A Ballet (fl, cl, ob/Enghn, vln, vla, vcl, electric pno, perc)	45:00	2	C
How the Elephant Got Its Trunk (ballet) (fl, ob/Enghn, cl, vln, vla, vcl, electric pno, perc)	45:00	2	C
"A Husband's Notes about Her" or "The Double Bed" (Eve Merriam) (T-actor, S-actress, fl/al-fl/pic, cl/bcl, ob, Enghn, vcl, db, electric pno/pno, 2 perc)	75:00	2+	C
A Woman Alive: Conversation Against Death (chamber opera or vocal drama) (S, actor, fl, cl, bsn, vln, 2 vla, vcl, db, pno, 2 perc)	40:00	2+	C

SAMSON

Montage: A Journey through Youth (1975) (theater piece) (3S, pno, dancer, lights)	12:00	2	C

SAMTER

Die Bettleroper (Gay-Pepusch)
(small orch)   C

Die Schule der Witwen (J. Cocteau)
(incidental music)   C

Die Nachtwache (Nelly Sachs)   C

Proteus (P. Claudel)   C

Der Falsche Graf (after G. Keller)
(school opera)   C

Das Zauberhorn
(puppet-play for young people)   C

Die Drei Spinnerinnen (Brothers Grimm)
(play)   C

SCHONTHAL

The Courtship of Camilla (original play by A. A. Milne)
  (1980)
  (opera in 1 Act)   110:00   C

The Transposed Heads (1963)
  (ballet; suite for orch)   28:00   C

SIMONS

Bell Witch of Tennessee (Joan Simon [based on
  American folk tale])
  (opera in 1 Act, 4 Scenes)
  (SS Mez T Bar B soli, chor SATB, orch:
  1(pic)02/bcl/1(cbsn) 0220 pno, vibes,
  5 timp, perc, stgs)   60:00   ACA

Buckeye has Wings
  (ballet; 1 to any number of players in combination)   varies   Mer

Circle of Attitudes
  (ballet; vln solo)   17:00   ACA

⊕ *Puddintame* (Limericks)
  (stage piece)
  (narrs: 1 to any number of players in combination)   varies   ACA

Too Late - The Bridge is Closed
  (ballet; 1 to any number of players in combination)   varies   Mer

SMELTZER

Music for "A Midsummer Night's Dream" (1976)
  (incidental music)
  (women's chor, orch: 2(pic12(bcl)0 3220 triangle,
  wood block, electric org/pno)   20:00   2 ISWP

SMITH

Cynthia Parker (Jan I. Fortune) (1935-38, revised 1945)
  (opera in 2 Acts with prologue)
  (SSAT 4B soli, chor SATTBB, ballet: male and female,
  10 supers)   90:00   TPres

Cockcrow (C. D. Mackay) (1953)
  (fairy tale opera in 1 Act)
  (SSS, A, TT, BB, orch: 1111 1100 timp, perc, pno, stgs)   25:00   TPres

⊕ *Daisy* (Bertita Harding) (1973)
  (opera in 2 Acts with dances)
  (4S 4A T Bar B soli, chor SSAATB, dancers, orch: 1121
  2211 timp, perc, xylo, cel, hrp, pno, stgs)   90:00   TPres

The Gooseherd and the Goblin (Josephine Fetter Royle)
(1946)
(opera in 1 Act with prologue)
(SSAT solo, chor SSA, orch: 1111 1100 perc, pno, stgs)   45:00   TPres

The Shepherdess and the Chimneysweep (C. D. Mackay)
(1963)
(christmas opera in 1 Act)
(STB solo, chor SSAA, orch: 2222 2220 timp, perc,
    xylo, vibes, cel, chimes, hrp, stgs)   30:00   TPres

The Stranger of Manzano (John W. Rogers) (1943)
(opera in 1 Act with prologue and ballet)
(SAT 5B soli, chor SSAATB, orch: 1121 2210 timp,
    perc, xylo, vibes, cel, hrp, stgs)   45:00   TPres

SWISHER

The Happy Hypocrite
(opera)
(S A T B soli, chor, full orch or chamber orch)   60:00   3   AMC

VELLÈRE

Puck, Compositeur: A Musical Story
(narrs, ww qt, pno)   30:00   2   C

WYLIE

Facades, Op. 18 no. 1 (Edith Sitwell) (1956)
(ballet)
(fl, cl, perc, pno)   2   C

Spring Madness (1951)
(ballet)   2   C

The Ragged Heart, Op. 21 (1961)
(ballet)   18:00   2   C

ZIFFRIN
"Drinking Song and Dance" (from the opera *Captain Kidd*)
(1970-71)
(Bar solo, men's chor, 2 gtrs, S rec, perc ensemble)   10:00   2+   C

MUSIC FOR YOUNG PEOPLE — VOCAL/CHORAL MUSIC, STAGE WORKS ●

BEATH

Abigail and the Bushranger (David Cox) (1976)
(musical story for children's voices and
    perc accompaniment)   20:00   JAS

Abigail and the Rainmaker (David Cox) (1976)
(musical story for children's voices and
perc accompaniment)   JAS

BRITAIN

The Spider and the Butterfly (Lena Priscella Hasselberg)
(1953)
(operetta in 3 Acts)   25:00   UCLA

BRUSH

Moses (1978)
(children's cantata; with kybd)   C

Sing a New Song
(musical)   30:00   1+ C

DIEMER

Geronimo (1970)
(chor)   C

A Little Song of Life (1970)
(chor)   C

Two Haiku (1970)
(chor)   C

Your Friends Shall Be the Tall Wind (1970)
(chor)   C

HAYS

Clementine
(tape and chor)   3:00   1   S-B

Look Out
(choral canon)   1:00   1   S-B

⊕ *Mouth Sounds*
(4-part chor)   2:00   1   S-B

O Susanna
(tape and chor)   3:00   1   S-B

⊕ *Walkin' Talkin' Blues*
(speaker(s), with or without db)   1   S-B

PARKER

A Sun, A Shield (Psalms) (1975)
(1 or 2 part chor, autoharp, electric bass,
perc, opt solo instr)   3:00   1+ ECS

A Prayer for Choirs (Bartlett) (1975)
(1 or 2 part choir, electric bass, opt solo instr)   1:15   1+   ECS

PAULL

I Got to Fly Free
(chor, pno)   1   CPic

Jesus, Closer to You
(chor and pno)   1   CPic

May the Fairies Kiss Your Nose
(chor and pno)   1   CPic

The Gumdrop Castle Adventure (1979)
(musical)   90:00   1   Hal

The Wind and the Willows
(2 act musical)   1   Hal

PROCACCINI

21 Canti Infantili on the Pentatonic Scale, Op. 73 (1979)
(one voice, a cappella)   16:00   1   C

22 Conte E Filastrocche for Childhood, Op. 74 (1979)
(one voice, a cappella)   18:00   1   C

Piazza Della Musica No. 1, Op. 54
(children's opera with dance)
(narr and 15 instr: fl, ob, cl, bsn, hrn, tpt, tbn, timp,
b dm, 2 vln, vla, vcl, db)   45:00   2   C

Piazza Della Musica, Op. 72 (same as above)
(chor of treb voices, narr, instr [as above], toy orch)   45:00   2   C

ROGERS

Anthem for Children's Choir (Patsy Rogers)
(unison chor, opt descant, org)   3:00   1   C

VELLÈRE

Chansonnettes (P. Coran, *Fr*) (1964)
(6 songs for children's choir and pno)   1   JM

Petites Histoires (various, *Fr*) (1948)
(5 songs for children's choir and pno)   1   C

ZAIMONT

Moses Supposes (1975)
(3 part canon for treb voices and perc)   1   Tetr

MUSIC FOR YOUNG PEOPLE — KEYBOARD MUSIC, ONE OR MORE PLAYERS

ANDERSON, BETH

Four Ephemera (1966)
(pno)   3:00   1   C

Recital Piece (1973)
(pno and tape)   10:00   1   C

Scherzo (1965)
(pno)   1:00   1   C

BEESON

Angels Are Coming
(pno)   1:00   1   C

The Bulgarian Valley Dance
(pno)   3:00   2   C

† *The Days in New England*
(pno)   3:30   2   C

The Midday Waltz
(pno)   2:00   2   C

Passing Thoughts
(pno)   2:30   2   C

Russian Madness
(pno)   1:30   2   C

Seven
(pno)   1:30   2   C

Sweet Little Angel Wings
(pno)   1:00   1   C

To Calvary
(pno).   2:00   2   C

Waiting for the Next Step
(pno)   3:00   2   C

BRITAIN

Dance of the Clown (1945)
(pno)   3:00   1   APS

Geppetto's Toy Shop (1940)
(pno)   3:00   1   APS

How to Play the Piano (1950)   WTF

Little Spaniard (1938) (pno)	3:00	1	APS

BRUSH

Playtime Piano Pieces	15:00	1	Dee

CECCONI-BATES

Early Grade Four-Hand Piano Pieces		1	C

DEMBO

Seven Pieces for the Beginning Student (pno)	6:00	1	C

DIEMER

Four Piano Teaching Pieces (1961)	3:00	1	B&H

GLAZIER

From a Poem (pno)		2	C

HAYS

Sound Symbol Structures		var.	Q-H

HSU

Little Soldier's March (1952) (2 pnos)	2:00	1	W-Y
Scenes in a Chinese Village (1956) (suite for pno)	6:00	2	W-Y

MAGEAU

Australia's Animals (1976) (pno)	4:00	2	GSch
Clouds (in *Piano Strategies*) (1980)			GSch
Forecasts (1974) (pno)	3:00	1	GSch
March (in *Duet Book III*) (pno 4-hands)		2	C

MARCUS

Melodies Near and Far - Suite for Piano	15:00	1	Temp
Three Dances for Children (pno)	10:00	1	Temp

PAULL

A Christmas Carol (pno)	1	CPic
Holidays (pno)	1	CPic
The Musical Calendar Song Book (1979) (pno)	1	CPic
The Musical Guide to Astrology (pno)	1	CPic

PROCACCINI

6 Pezzi Infantili, Op. 25 (1961) (pno)	12:00	1	C

RICHTER

Bits and Snatches (1971)	2	CF
Elephants and Violets (1971)	1+	CF
A Farewell (1961)	2	CF
For Something that Had Gone Before (1971)	2	CF
Hugh's Piece (1971)	1+	CF
The Lost People, The Dancers (1965)	2	CF
⊕ Two Short Suites for Young Pianists (1947) Suite No. 1 Suite No. 2	1	MCA

SCHONTHAL

Miniatures: Volumes I and II (pno)	1+	Gal
Minuscules (pno)	1	CF
Near and Far (pno)	1+	CF

Potpourri
(pno)   1+ CF

SEMEGEN

Five Early Pieces (1967)
(pno)   7:00 1   ACA

VELLÈRE

Préludes pour la Jeunesse (1950)
(12 preludes for pno)   25:00 1   JM

WEIGL

Piano Pieces
"Kitten Stories"
"Who is Afraid of the Big Black Keys", others
(2 and 4 hands)   1   ACA

WYLIE

Five Easy Pieces, Op. 4   7:00 1   Cor

Six Little Preludes, Op. 19 no. 2   9:00 1   Cor

ZAIMONT

Keyboard Cousins: Suite for Young Pianists (1979-81)
"The Harp"
"The Guitar"
"The Cymbalom"
"The Celeste"
"The Organ"
"The Harpsichord"   12:30 1+ C

Solitary Pipes (in *The Joy of Modern Piano Pieces*) (1977)   1:30 1   YMP

● MUSIC FOR YOUNG PEOPLE — CHAMBER INSTRUMENTAL MUSIC ●

CECCONI-BATES

Graded Solos for Various Instruments
(suitable for teaching pieces)   1   C

HAYS

For Four
(bongos, rec, autoharp, paper rip)   2:00 2   Q-H

⊕ *Juncture Dance*
(rec, harmca, triangle, autoharp, gtr [opt versions with vln, other melodic instr])   2:00   1   S-B

MARCUS

Blue Flute
(fl and pno)   5:00   2   HB

A Song for Flute
(fl and pno)   12:00 3   Temp

PROCACCINI

3 Pezzi Facili, Op. 26 (1961)
(bsn and pno)   5:00   1   C

MUSIC FOR YOUNG PEOPLE — INSTRUMENTAL ENSEMBLES (ORCHESTRA, BAND)

BRITAIN

Chicken in the Rough (1951)
(high school orch: 2121 2221 timp, perc, stgs)   4:00   C

Little Per Cent (1963)
(high school orch: 2212 2331 timp, perc, stgs)   8:00   C

DIEMER

Rondo Concertante (1960)
(youth/community orch)   5:00   2+ B&H

Symphonie Antique (1961)
(youth/community orch)   10:00   Bel-M

Youth Overture (1959)
(youth orch: 3222 4331 perc, stgs)   3:00   1   Bel-M

Suite, "Brass Menagerie" (1960)
(youth/college/community band)   8:00   Bel-M

FRASIER

Chorale/Canon
(band)   1:15   1   C

Minor Moods
(band)   3:00   1+   C

Trumpet March/Woodwind Tune
(band)   2:00   1   C

HYSON

Suite for Young Orchestra (1965)
(orch: 1010 0000 stgs)   15:00   2   E-V

MAGEAU

Indian Summer (1976)
(youth orch)   15:00   C

MARCUS

Jazz Prelude
(ww, brass, cbsn, perc)   8:00   2   C

RICHTER

Country Auction (1976)
(JHS/HS band)   3:30   2   CF

Ricercare (1958)
(JHS/HS band)   4:00   2   CF

SMITH

Work and Play String Method (with Cecile Vashaw)
Book I (1964)
Book II (1967)

ZIFFRIN

A Small Suite for String Orchestra (1963, revised 1975)
(JHS orch)   5:30   1   C

PUBLISHER/ARCHIVE/COMPOSER ADDRESS LIST

APR   APR Publishers, Inc. — Post Office Box 5075, Fresno, California 93755

AbP   Abingdon Press, United Methodist Publishing House — 201 Eighth Avenue South, Nashville, Tennessee 37202

Ag   Agape — c/o Hope Publishing Company, 380 South Main Place, Carol Stream, Illinois 60187

ABI   Alexander Broude, Inc. — 225 West 57th Street, New York, New York 10019

Alf   Alfred Publishing Company, Inc. — 15335 Morrison Street, Sherman Oaks, California 91403

Allen, Judith Shatin — 117-102 Mimosa Drive, Charlottesville, Virginia 22903

ACA   American Composers Alliance — 170 West 74th Street, New York, New York 10023

AMC   American Music Center (perusal copies only) — 250 West 54th Street, New York, New York 10019

AME   American Music Edition — c/o Ray Green, 263 East 77th Street, New York, New York

ASUC   American Society of University Composers, Journal of Music Scores — c/o European American Retail Music, Inc., Post Office Box 850, Valley Forge, Pennsylvania 19482

Anderson, Beth — 32 East 2nd Street, New York, New York 10003

Anderson, Jay — 389 Kailua Road, Apt. 201, Kailua, Hawaii 96734

Arm   Armstrong Publishing Company — 1000 Industrial Parkway, Elkhart, Indiana 46515

Ars   Arsis Press — 1719 Bay Street S.E., Washington D.C. 20003

APS   Arthur P. Schmidt — c/o Summy-Birchard Company

Arv   Arvon Publications — Post Office Box 93, Manketo, Minnesota 56001

Asm   Assembling Press — c/o Richard Kostelanetz, Post Office Box 1967, Brooklyn, New York 11202

APH   Augsburg Publishing House — 426 South 5th Street, Minneapolis, Minnesota 55415

BW   The Bahá'i World: An International Record — Bahá'i World Center, Haifa, Israel

Barnett, Carol — 2106 Elliot Avenue South, Minneapolis, Minnesota 55404

Barthelson, Joyce — Chateaux Apartments, Chateau Touraine 7Y, Scarsdale, New York 10583

Brt   Bartlesville Publishing Company — Box 265, Oklahoma, 74003

Beath, Betty — 8 St. James Street, Highgate Hill, Queensland, Australia 4101

Beeson, Elizabeth R. — 1370 Afton, Apt. 628, Houston, Texas 77055

Bel-M   Belwin-Mills Publishing Corporation — 25 Deshon Drive, Melville, New York 11746

BigD   Big Deal Magazine — c/o Barbara Baracks, 52 Bank Street, New York, New York 10014

BBx   Black Box 15 (Breathing Space/77) — Allen D. Austin, Post Office Box 4174, Washington D.C. 20015

Bolz, Harriett — 3097 Herrick Road, Columbus, Ohio 43221

Bng   Casa Musicale Francesco Bongiovanni — Via Rizzoli 28 E, Bologna, Italy

Boone, Clara Lyle [Lyle de Bohun] — 1719 Bay Street S.E., Washington D.C. 20003

B&H   Boosey and Hawkes, Inc. — 30 West 57th Street, New York, New York 10019

Bos	Boston Music Company — 116 Boylston Street, Boston, Massachusetts 02116
BGCE	Break Glass in Case of Emergency — Mills College, c/o Center For Contemporary Music, Oakland, California 94613
	Brenner, Rosamond — 726 North Park Boulevard, Glen Ellyn, Illinois 60137
	Britain, Radie — 1945 North Curson Avenue, Hollywood, California 90046
Brg	Brogneaux — 73 Avenue P. Janson, 1070 Brussels, Belgium
BrB	Broude Brothers, Inc. — 56 West 45th Street, New York, New York 10036
	Brush, Ruth J. — 3413 Wildwood Court, Bartlesville, Oklahoma 74003
Calv	Calvi Music Company — (see **Britain**)
Cari	Carisch S.p.A. — Via Generale Fara 39, 20124 Milano, Italy
CF	Carl Fischer, Inc. — 56-62 Cooper Square, New York, New York 10003
CFFE	Carl Fischer Facsimile Edition — 56-62 Cooper Square, New York, New York 10003
CBD	CeBeDem — Rue de l'Hôpital 31, 1000 Brussels, Belgium
	Cecconi-Bates, Augusta — Box 49-D, West Monroe, New York 13167
CFP	C. F. Peters Corporation — 373 Park Avenue South, New York, New York
	Chance, Nancy — 538 East 89th Street, Apt. 3E, New York, New York 10028
ChorAP	Choral Art Publications — c/o Sam Fox Publishing Company
ChorAS	Choral Art Series — c/o Sam Fox Publishing Company
CFSum	Clayton F. Summy Company — c/o Summy-Birchard Company
	Clark, Mary Margaret — 35 North Road, East Granby, Connecticut 06026
	Cohen, Marcia — 211 Sabine Drive, Pensacola Beach, Florida 32561
CPic	Columbia Pictures Publications — c/o Columbia Pictures Industries, Inc., 711 Fifth Avenue, New York, New York, 10022
ColU	Columbia University Press — c/o E. C. Schirmer Music Company
ComP	Composers Press — c/o Opus Music Publishers, Inc., Post Office Box 111, Northfield, Illinois
CMP	Continuo Music Press Limited — c/o Alexander Broude Inc.
Cor	Cor Publishing Company — 67 Bell Place, Massapequa, New York 11758
	Danforth, Frances — 1411 Granger Avenue, Ann Arbor, Michigan 48104
Dee	Dee Publishing Company — Weston, Ontario, Canada
	Dembo, Royce — 5 Beach Street, Madison, Wisconsin 53705
	Diemer, Emma Lou — 77A North San Marcos Road, Santa Barbara, California 93111
Dram	Dramatika Magazine — c/o John Pyros, 390 Riverside Drive, Apt. 10B, New York, New York 10025
Ear	Ear Magazine — 99 Prince Street, New York, New York 10012
EBM	E. B. Marks Music Corporation — 1790 Broadway, New York, New York 10019
ECS	E. C. Schirmer Music Company — 112 South Street, Boston, Massachusetts 02111
EdC	Edition Corona — 54A Hohenzollerndam, 1000 Berlin 33, German Democratic Republic

ECG   Edition Cranz Gmbtt. — 68 Adelheidstrasse, 6200 Wiesbaden, German Democratic Republic

EldP   Eldridge Publishing Company — Franklin, Ohio 45005

E-V   Elkan-Vogel Inc. — Presser Place, Bryn Mawr, Pennsylvania 19010

Fem   Fema — c/o Crescendo, Box 395, Naperville, Illinois 60540

Fern   Fernwood Publications — 383 East 1980 North, Provo, Utah 84601

Flash   Flash Art — Giancarlo Politi Editore, 36 Via Donatello, 20131 Milano, Italy

FC   Fleisher Library Collection (perusal copies only) — Free Library of Philadelphia, Logan Square, Philadelphia, Pennsylvania 19103

   Forman, Joanne — Post Office Box 3181, Taos, New Mexico 87571

   Frasier, Jane — 140 23rd Avenue, Apt. 48, Greeley, Colorado 80631

   Fuller-Hall, Sarah — 307 Hardin Street, Boone, North Carolina 28607

Gem   Gemini Press — c/o Alexander Broude, Inc.

GKH   G. K. Hall — 70 Lincoln Street, Boston, Massachusetts 02111

GSch   G. Schirmer Inc. — 866 3rd Avenue, New York, New York 10022

Gal   Galaxy Music Company — 2121 Broadway, New York, New York 10023

   Gardner, Kay — Post Office Box 33, Stonington, Maine 04681

   Gilbert, Janet — 216 College Street, Northfield, Minnesota 55057

GSC   Girl Scout Council of Tropical Florida — 11347 S. W. 160 Street, Miami, Florida 33157

   Glazier, Beverly — 5212 Winterton Drive, Fayetteville, New York 13066

GoC   The Guild of Carillonneurs in North America — c/o B. Buchanan, Christ Church Cranbrook, 470 Church Road, Bloomfield Hills, Michigan 48013

HWG   H. W. Gray Company — c/o Belwin-Mills Publishing Corporation

Hal   Hal Lenard Publications — 960 East Mark Street, Winona, Minnesota 55987

HML   Hans Moldenhauer Library/Collection — 1011 Comstock Court, Spokane, Washington 99203

HB   Harold Branch Publishing, Inc. — 42 Cornell Drive, Plainview, Long Island, New York 11803

HF   Harold Flammer Inc. — c/o Shawnee Press Inc., Delaware Water Gap, Pennsylvania 18327

   Hays, Doris — 697 West End Avenue, Penthouse B, New York, New York 10025

   Heinrich, Adel — 1 Highland Avenue, Waterville, Maine 04901

Hen   Hendon Music Company — Post Office Box 66, Ansonia Station, New York, New York 10023

HerM   The Heritage Music Press — c/o Lorenz Publishing Company

Hero   Heroico Music Publishers — 1945 North Curson Avenue, Hollywood, California 90046

HtK   Heute Kunst — Gianocarlo Politi Editore, Via Donatello 36, 20131 Milano, Italy

Hin   Hinshaw Music Inc. — Post Office Box 470, Chapel Hill, North Carolina 27514

HoE   Ho'okani Enterprises — 4723 Moa Street, Honolulu, Hawaii 96816

   Hoover, Katherine — 160 West 95th Street, New York, New York 10025

   Hsu, Wen-ying — Pilgrim Tower East, 440 North Madison Avenue, Apt. 117, Pasadena, California 91101

Hyson, Winifred P. — 7407 Honeywell Lane, Bethesda, Maryland 20014

Intr   Intermedia — Post Office Box 31-464, San Francisco, California 94131

ISWP   The International Symphony for World Peace, Inc. — 866 United Nations Plaza, Suite 570, New York, New York 10017

Iris   Iris Publications — Box 33, Stonington, Maine 04681

IsH   Island Heritage — 4723 Moa Street, Honolulu, Hawaii 96816

JAS   J. Albert and Son, Pty. Limited — 139 King Street, Sydney NSW 2000, Australia

JF   J. Fischer and Brothers — c/o Boston Music Company, 116 Boylston Street, Boston, Massachusetts 02116

JM   J. Maurer — 9 Avenue du Verseau, 1150 Brussels, Belgium

Jankowski, Loretta — 3643 Lewis Avenue, Long Beach, California 90807

Jel   Jelsor Music Company — 42 Cornell Drive, Plainview, New York 11802

Jsh   Joshua Corporation — 145 Palisade Street, Dobbs Ferry, New York 10522

Kendrick, Virginia — 5800 Echo Road, Shorewood, Minnesota 55331

Lackman, Susan Cohn — 7 Sherman Circle, Somerset, New Jersey 08873

L-G   Lawson-Gould Music Publishers — 866 3rd Avenue, New York, New York 10022

Le Baron, Anne — Instructional Services Center, 408 Bank Street N. E., Decatur, Alabama 35601

Ledc   Editions Alphonse Leduc — 175 Rue St. Honoré, Paris, France

LR   Leichhardt Reprographics — 24 Little Edward Street, Spring Hill, Queensland 4000, Australia

LPI   Leonarda Productions, Inc. — Post Office Box 124, Radio City Station, New York, New York 10101

LC   Library of Congress — Washington D. C. 20559

Lomon, Ruth — 18 Stratham Road, Lexington, Massachusetts 02173

LorP   Lorenz Publishing Company — c/o Lorenz Industries, 501 East 3rd Street, Dayton, Ohio 45401

Mageau, Mary — 57 Ironside Street, St. Lucia, Queensland, Australia 4067

Marcus, Adabelle — 9374 Landings Lane, Apt. 502, Des Plaines, Illinois 60016

Mrg   Margun Music, Inc. — 167 Dudley Road, Newton Centre, Massachusetts 02159

Meachem, Margaret — Petersburg Road, Williamstown, Massachusetts 01267

Mer   Merion Music, Inc. — c/o Theodore Presser Company

MK   Michael Kysar — c/o Hinshaw Music, Inc., Post Office Box 470, Chapel Hill, North Carolina 27514

Mowb   Mowbray Music Publishers — Post Office Box 471, Cathedral Station, New York, New York, 10025

Mont   Montgomery Music, Inc. — 1402 Liberty Bank Building, Post Office Box 157, Niagara Square Station, Buffalo, New York 14202

MCA   Music Corporation of America — c/o Belwin-Mills

MfP   Music for Percussion — 17 West 60th Street, New York, New York 10023

Msg   Musicgraphics, Inc. — San Diego, California

NK   Neil Kjos Music Company — 4382 Jutland Drive, San Diego, California 92117

NSM   New Scribner Music Library — 597 Fifth Avenue, New York, New York, 10020

         Orenstein, Joyce — 322 Harper Place, Highland Park, New Jersey 08904

OPP   Orthodox Press Publications — c/o Very Reverend Nikolaijs Vieglais, St. John Russian Orthodox Church, 1908 Essex Street, Berkeley, California 94703

Oss   Ossian — c/o 1945 North Curson Avenue, Hollywood, California

OH   Otto Halbreiter — Munich, Germany (see **Britain**)

OUP   Oxford University Press, Inc. — 200 Madison Avenue, New York, New York, 10016

         Parker, Alice — 801 West End Avenue, Apt. 9D, New York, New York 10025

PP   Paulist Press — 1865 Broadway, New York, New York 10023

         Paull, Barberi — 15 West 72nd Street, New York, New York 10023

P-S   Peer-Southern Music Inc. — 1740 Broadway, New York, New York

         Pierce, Alexandra — School of Music, University of Redlands, Redlands, California 92373

         Pizer, Elizabeth — 555 Penitencia Street, Apt. 1, Milpitas, California 95035

Play   Playlab Press — Ashgrove, Queensland, Australia

Poet   Poetry Mailing List — c/o Stephen Paul Miller, 18 Cheshire Place, Staten Island, New York 10301

         Preobrajenska, Vera — 935 High Street, Santa Cruz, California 95060

         Procaccini, Teresa — Via Lorenzo di Magnifico, 40, 00162 Rome, Italy

Q-H   Quinska-Hays Music — 697 West End Avenue, Penthouse B, New York, New York 10025

RG   Ray Green — 263 East 77th Street, New York, New York 10021

         Reed, Marlyce P. — 1717 Peabody Street, Appleton, Wisconsin 54911

         Reid, Sally Johnston — Box 8205, Station ACU, Abilene, Texas 79601

Rem   Remick Music Corporation — c/o Warner Bros. Music Publications, 14th Floor, 75 Rockefeller Plaza, New York, New York 10019

         Richter, Marga — 3 Bayview Lane, Huntington, New York 11743

Ric   Ricordi and Sons — c/o Associated Music Publishers, Inc., 866 3rd Avenue, New York, New York 10022

Rga   Riga Publications — 6192 Oxon Hill Road, Washington D. C. 20021

         Robert B. Brown Music Company — c/o Heroico Music Publishers

         Roberts, Gertrud — 4723 Moa Street, Honolulu, Hawaii 96816

RgD   Roger Deane Publishing Company — 324 West Jackson, Macomb, Illinois 61455

         Rogers, Patsy — 61 Jane Street, Apt. 19A, New York, New York 10014

SacM   The Sacred Music Press — c/o Lorenz Publishing Company

SF   Sam Fox Publishing Company — 73-941 Highway 111, Suite 11, Palm Desert, California 92260

         Samson, Valerie — 1373 Clay Street, San Francisco, California 94109

         Samter, Alice — 14 Friedbergstrasse, 1000 Berlin 19, West Germany

SHMC   Schmitt, Hall and McCreary — c/o Belwin-Mills Publishing Corporation

SMC	Schmitt Music Center, Inc. — 110 North Fifth Street, Minneapolis, Minnesota 55403
SMus	Schmitt Music Company — 88 South 10th Street, Minneapolis, Minnesota 55403
	Schonthal, Ruth — 12 Van Etten Boulevard, New Rochelle, New York 10804
	Scores — editor Roger Johnson, Shirmer Books
See	Seesaw Music Corporation — 1966 Broadway, New York, New York 10023
	Semegen, Daria — Electronic Music Studio, Department of Music, State University of New York, Stony Brook, New York 11794
Shaw	Shawnee Press Inc. — Delaware Water Gap, Pennsylvania 18327
	Silsbee, Ann — 915 Coddington Road, Ithaca, New York 14850
S-B	Silver-Burdett Music Company — 250 James Street, Morristown, New Jersey 07960
	Simons, Netty — 303 East 57th Street, Apt. 47E, New York, New York 10022
	Singer, Jeanne — 64 Stuart Place, Manhasset, Long Island, New York 11030
Sis	Sisra Publications — 1719 Bay Street S. E., Washington D. C. 20003
	Smeltzer, Susan — 8102 Tavenor, Houston, Texas 77075
	Smith, Julia — 417 Riverside Drive, New York, New York 10025
Sonz	Casa Musicale Sonzogno — c/o Belwin-Mills
SMP	Southern Music Publishing Company, Inc. — 1740 Broadway, New York, New York 10019
	Stanley, Helen — 1768 Emory Circle South, Jacksonville, Florida 32207
SumB	Summy-Birchard — 1834 Ridge Avenue, Evanston, Illinois 60204
	Swisher, Gloria — 7228 Sixth N.W., Seattle, Washington 98117
Temp	Tempo Music Publishers, Inc. — Box 392, Chicago, Illinois 60690
Teto	Teton Music Corporation — c/o Alexander Broude Inc.
Tetr	Tetra Music Corporation — c/o Alexander Broude Inc.
T-St	Text-Sound Texts — William Morrow and Company, Inc., 105 Madison Avenue, New York, New York 10016
TPres	Theodore Presser Company — Presser Place, Bryn Mawr, Pennsylvania 19010
Tri	Triune Music Inc. — 824 19th Avenue South, Nashville, Tennessee 37203
UCLA	University of California at Los Angeles Music Library (perusal copies only) — 405 Hilgarde Avenue, West Los Angeles, California 90024
UW	University of Wyoming Music Department Library (perusal copies only) — Laramie, Wyoming
	Van de Vate, Nancy — Post Office Box 23152, Honolulu, Hawaii 96822
	Vellère, Lucie — c/o Micheline Von Steenberghe, 121 Avenue G. E. Lebon, Bte. 7, 1160 Bruxelles, Belgique
	Vercoe, Elizabeth — 381 Garfield Road, Concord, Massachusetts 01742
	Walker, Dr. Gwyneth — 643 Oenoke Ridge, New Canaan, Connecticut 06840
Walk	Walker Publications — 643 Oenoke Ridge, New Canaan, Connecticut 06840
	Wallach, Joelle — 8 Jones Street, New York, New York 10014
WTF	Walter T. Foster — 2190 Temple Hills Drive, Laguna Beach, California 92651

Walt   Walton Music Corporation — c/o Lorenz, Box 802, 501 East Third Street, Dayton, Ohio 45401

Warren, Elinor Remick — 154 South Hudson Avenue, Los Angeles, California 90004

WMC   Waterloo Music Company Limited — 3 Regine Street North, Waterloo, Ontario, Canada N2J2Z7

Weigl, Vally — 55 West 95th Street, New York, New York 10025

W-Y   Wen-Ying Studio — Pilgrim Tower East, 440 North Madison Avenue, Apt. 117, Pasadena, California 91101

WilM   Willis Music Company — 7380 Industrial Road, Florence, Kentucky 41042

Wit   Witmark and Son — c/o Warner Bros. Music, 75 Rockefeller Plaza, New York, New York 10019

WLSM   The World Library of Sacred Music, Inc. — 2145 Central Parkway, Cincinnati, Ohio 45214

Wylie, Ruth Shaw — 1251 Country Club Drive, Long's Peak Route, Estes Park, Colorado 80517

YMP   Yorktown Music Press — 33 West 60th Street, New York, New York 10023

Zaimont, Judith Lang — c/o Allied Artists Bureau, Michael Leavitt, 195 Steamboat Road, Great Neck, New York 11024

Zan   Edizioni Zanibon — G. Zanibon Editions, c/o C. F. Peters

Ziffrin, Marilyn J. — Post Office Box 179, Bradford, New Hampshire 03221

Zwilich, Ellen Taaffe — 600 West 246th Street, Riverdale, New York 10471

Discography

DISCOGRAPHY

All recordings listed are currently in print, except as noted. Additional information, such as the duration of works and abbreviations used for instruments and voice categories, can be found in the preceding section devoted to a classified list of music.

ANDERSON, BETH

Torero Piece
> Beth Anderson, voice
>> **"10+2+12 American Text-Sound Pieces"**
>> **— 1759 Arch Records No. 1752**

BEESON, ELIZABETH R.

Faraway Love
> Kay Weaver, S
>> **"Now Sounds of Today" — Columbine Records CHR-218**

CHANCE, NANCY

Daysongs
> Katherine Hoover, fl; Glen Velez, perc; James Priess, perc
>> **Opus One Records**

Ritual Sounds, for Brass Quintet and Percussion
> Arthur Weisberg, cond; Apple Brass Quintet; Glen Velez, perc;
> Jeff Kraus, perc
>> **Opus One Records**

CLARKE, MARY MARGARET

Includes all songs in *Classical Melodies for Children to Sing*
> St. Matthew's Children Choir
>> **"Classical Melodies for Children — Paulist Press**

DIEMER, EMMA LOU

Three Poems of Alice Meynell
Madrigals Three
Fragments from the *Mass*
  "Psalm 134"
  "Hast Thou Not Known"
  "O Come Let Us Sing Unto the Lord"
  "Laughing Song"
  "Wild Nights! Wild Nights!"
> West Texas State University Chorale, High Sanders, cond;
> Collegiate Choir and Chorale; Schola Madrigalis
>> **The Compositions of Emma Lou Diemer" — Golden Crest 5063**

Toccata for Flute Chorus
> The Armstrong Flute Ensemble: Britton Johnson, Walfrid Jujala,
> Harry Moskovitz, Mark Thomas
>> **"Quartet Music for Flute" with the Armstrong Flute Ensemble**
>> **— Golden Crest CR4088**

Toccata for Piano
> Rosemary Platt, pno
>> **"Music by Women Composers" — Coronet Records LPS 3105**

FORMAN, JOANNE

E.E. Cummings Songs
> Kristen Woolf, S; Carla Scaletti, hrp; Geoffrey Butcher, org
>> **Opus One Records — No. 34**

Lorca Songs
> Sally Bissell, S; Glenn McFarland, gtr
>> **Opus One Records — No. 44**

GARDNER, KAY

Prayer to Aphrodite - al-fl and stgs
Changing - Mez and stgs
Beautiful Friend - Mez, vln, gtr, pno
Moonflow: a vocalise - al-fl and pno
Wise Woman - Mez, autohrp, vcl, small perc
Innermood I - al-fl
Touching Souls - al-fl, gtr, small perc
Innermood II - fl and gtr
Lunamuse - fl, gtr, vcl, small perc, tape loop
> Kay Gardner: fl, voice, gtr, autohrp; Dora Short, vln; Olga
> Gussow, vln; Nancy Uscher, vla; Martha Siegel, vcl;
> Juliana Smith, voice; Meg Christian, gtr; Bethel Jackson,
> handdrums and small perc; Angela Walls, small perc;
> Jenny Smith, small perc; Althea Waites, pno
>> **"Mooncircles" — WWE/Urana Records WWE ST-80**

The Cauldron of Cerridwyn - al-rec, lute, Mez, vlas da gamba, Baroque
vln, elect. effects
Romance - al-fl, vcl, gtr
Crystal Bells - fl, vln, vcl, gtr
Rhapsody - pno
Pisces - two fl, elect. tape
Mermaids - fl, al-fl, vcl, pno, small perc, women's voices, elect. tape
Atlantis Rising - fl, vln, vcl, prepared pno, small perc, elect. tape
> Kay Gardner: fl, voice, small perc; Susan Hansen, vln;
> Martha Siegel, vcl; Janice D'Amico: gtr, lute; Root,
> Baroque vln; Sarah Cunningham, vla da gamba; Althea
> Waites, pno; Mojo, fl; Marilyn Ries, elect. effects and
> tape preparation
>> **"Emerging" — WWE/Urana Records WWE ST-83**

New Chamber Music
>> **"A Rainbow Path" — Even Keel Records EKR ST-101**

HAYS, DORIS

Sunday Nights
> Doris Hays, pno
>> **"Adoration of the Clash" — Finnadar/Atlantic Records SR 2-720**

Juncture Dance
Walkin' Talkin' Blues
Mouth Sounds and ten other pieces for children
>> **Silver Burdett Co. — 74-183-04, 74-185-02 . . .186-02 . . .
>> 184-05 . . . 183-08 . . . 184-01 . . . 184-03**

13th Street Beat
Arabella Rag
Syn-Rock

Southern Library of Recorded Sound MQLP 38

HOOVER, KATHERINE

On the Betrothal of Princess Isabelle of France, Aged 6
Katherine Hoover, fl; Virginia Eskin, pno
"For the Flute" — Leonarda Productions LPI 104

Divertimento
Diane Gold, fl; Joanne Zagst, vln; Raymond Page, vla;
Leonard Feldman, vcl
**"Music for Flute and Strings by Three Americans"
— Leonarda Productions LPI 105**

Sinfonia
New York Bassoon Quartet: Bernadette Zirkuli, Lauren
Goldstein, Jane Taylor, Julia Feves
**"The New York Bassoon Quartet"
— Leonarda Productions LPI 102**

Trio
The Rogeri Trio: Karen Clarke, vln; Carter Brey, vcl;
Barbara Weintraub, pno
"Piano Trios" — Leonarda Productions LPI 103

LEBARON, ANNE

Concerto for Active Frogs
Anne LeBaron, perc and tape; Adrian Dye, vocal soloist;
Davey Williams, al-sax; Roger Hagerty, ob and musette;
Frog Chorus: Janice Hathaway, Nolan Hatcher, Craig
Nutt, LaDonna Smith, Theodore Bown, Johnny Williams,
Mitchell Cashion
"Raudelunas Pataphysical Revue" — Say Day-Bew No. 1

Butterfly Collection
Siesta
Jewels
Transparent Zebra
Rare Seal Wolves
Ukranian Ice Eggs
Drunk Underwater Koto
Sudden Noticing of Trees
Anne LeBaron; hrp, metal rack, gong; LaDonna Smith: pno,
hrp, vla; Davey Williams: acoustic and elect. gtrs, mand
"Jewels" — Trans Museq No. III

RICHTER, MARGA

Sonata for Piano
Peter Basquin, pno
Grenadilla GS 1010

Sonata for Piano
Menahem Pressler, pno
MGM E3244

Concerto for Piano and Violas, Cellos and Basses
William Masselos, pno; Carlos Surinach, cond
MGM E3547

Lament
        Izler Solomon, cond

                                                                MGM E3422

Aria and Toccata for Viola and Strings
        Walter Trampler, vla; Carlos Surinach, cond

                                                                MGM E3559

Transmutation
Two Chinese Songs
        Dorothy Renzi, S; Maro Ajemian, pno

                                                                MGM E3546

Two Short Suites for Young Pianists
        Marga Richter, pno

                                                                MGM E3417

ROBERTS, GERTRUD

Chaconne
Charlot Suite
Triptych
Rondo: Hommage to Couperin
Twelve Time-Gardens (Piano)
        Gertrud Roberts: hpsd, pno
                        "Gertrud Roberts, Composer, Harpsichordist, Pianist"
                        — Ho'okani Enterprises No. 78129

SAMTER, ALICE

Dialog for Violin and Piano
Eskapaden for Piano
Kontrapost for Flute, Alto Recorder and Piano
        Marianne Boettcher, vln; Philip Moll, pno; Irma
        Hofmeister, pno
                        Mixtur-Schallplatten GMBH   MXT 1002

SCHONTHAL, RUTH

Totengesange
        Berenice Bramson, S; Ruth Schonthal, pno
                "Songs for Soprano Plus" — Leonarda Productions LPI 106

Sonata Breve
Sonatensatz
Variations in Search of a Theme
Reverberations
        Gary Steigerwalt, pno

                                                                Capriccio Records

SEMEGEN, DARIA

Electronic Composition No. 1
                "Electronic Music Winners" — Columbia/Odyssey Y34139

Arc: Music for Dancers
                "Electronic Music for Dance" — Finnadar SR9020

Electronic Composition No. 2: Spectra
                                "Electronic Music" — CRI

Jeux des Quatres
> Cheryl Hill, cl; David Schecher, tbn; Martha Calhoun, vcl;
> George Fisher, pno

Music for Violin Solo
> Carol Sadowski, vln

Opus One Records No. 59

SILSBEE, ANN

Doors for Piano
> David Burge, pno

CRI

SIMONS, NETTY

Silver Thaw
Design Groups No. 1
Design Groups No. 2
> Bertram Turetzky, db

Desto 7128

The Pied Piper of Hamelin
Set of Poems for Children
Puddintame
> Lou Gilbert, Barbara Britton, narr; Paul Dunkel, fl; Netty
> Simons, pno; Richard Dufallo, cond; Edwin London, cond;
> Jean-Charles Francois, Ron George, perc

CRI SD309

SMITH, JULIA

Quartet for Strings
> Kohon Quartet

"Four American Composers" — Desto Records DC7117

Excerpts from the Opera in Two Acts: Daisy
> The Charlotte Opera Association; Charles Rosenkrans, cond;
> Charles Starnes, chor master; Elizabeth Volkman, S;
> David Rae Smith, B; Linda Smalley, contr; Larry Gerber, T

"Highlights from Daisy" — Orion Master Recordings ORS 76248

VAN DE VATE, NANCY

Sonata for Piano
> Rosemary Platt, pno

"Music by Women Composers" — Coronet Records LPS 3105

Music for Viola, Percussion and Piano

Orion Master Recordings

VERCOE, ELIZABETH

Fantasy
> Rosemary Platt, pno

"Music by Women Composers" — Coronet Records LPS 3105

WARREN, ELINOR REMICK

Suite for Orchestra
    Oslo Symphony Orchestra, Norway; William Strickland, cond

Abram in Egypt
    Roger Wagner Chorale; Ronald Lewis, Bar; London Philharmonic
      Orchestra; Roger Wagner, cond

          CRI 172

WEIGL, VALLY

Nature Moods
    George Shirley, Stanley Drucker, Kenneth Gordon

New England Suite
    Stanley Drucker, Ilse Sass, Kermit Moore

          CRI 326

Lyrical Suite
Echoes from Poems
Songs from "No Boundary"
Songs from "Do Not Awake Me"

          Musical Heritage Society 3880

Songs of Love and Leaving
    Shirley Love, David Holloway, Richard Woitach, Lawrence Sobol

Brief Encounters
    The City Winds

Dear Earth
    Robert Shiesley, Peter Gordon, Marilyn Dubov, David Moore,
    Ilse Sass

          Orion Master Recordings

Songs of Remembrance
Songs Newly Seen in the Dusk
Requiem for Allison
    NYU Contemporary Chamber Players

          Orion Master Recordings

WYLIE, RUTH SHAW

Psychogram for Piano
    Rosemary Catanese, pno

          CRI 353

ZAIMONT, JUDITH LANG

Sunny Airs and Sober
    "A Question Answered"
    "A Winter Mourning"
    "Sigh No More, Ladies"
    "Come Away, Death"
    "Life is a Jest"

Three Ayres
    "O Mistress Mine"
    "Slow, Slow, Fresh Fount"
    "How Sweet I Roam'd"

Greyed Sonnets
    "Soliloquy"
    "Let It Be Forgotten"
    "Love's Autumn"
    "Entreaty"

Songs of Innocence
"Piping Down the Valley Wild"
"The Garden of Love"
"I Asked a Thief to Steal Me a Peach"
"How Sweet I Roam'd"

Rosalind Rees, S; Priscilla Magdamo, A; The Gregg Smith Singers;
Gregg Smith, cond; Elaine Olbrycht, S; Judith Lang Zaimont, pno;
Price Browne, T; Patricia Spencer, fl; Barbara Bogatin, vcl; Nancy
Allen, hrp; Roger Nierenberg, cond

**"The Compositions of Judith Lang Zaimont"
— Golden Crest 5051**

A Calendar Set — 12 Preludes for Solo Piano
Chansons Nobles et Sentimentales for Tenor and Piano
Nocturne: La Fin de Siècle for Piano

Gary Steigerwalt, pno; Charles Bressler, T; Judith
Lang Zaimont, pno

**"Music by Judith Lang Zaimont"
— Leonarda Productions LPI 101**

Two Songs for Soprano and Harp
"At Dusk in Summer"
"The Ruined Maid"

Berenice Bramson, S; Sara Cutler, hrp

"Songs for Soprano Plus" — Leonarda Productions LPI 106

ZIFFRIN, MARILYN

Four Pieces for Tuba
Barton Cummings, tuba

"On Tuba" — Crystal Records No. S391

Trio for Xylophone, Soprano, and Tuba
Dean Anderson, xylo; Neva Pilgrim, S; Barton
Cummings, tuba

Capra Records

ZWILICH, ELLEN TAAFE

Chamber Symphony
Boston Musica Viva; Richard Pittman, cond
Sonata in Three Movements
Joseph Zwilich, vln; James Gemmell, pno
String Quartet 1974
New York String Quartet

Delos Records DEL-25444

EXPRESSIONS: The Radio Series of the International League of Women Composers

These eleven one-hour programs with commentary by Joelle Wallach were compiled by Doris Hays. They are available for airing, with payment of a handling fee and return postage. Contact Doris Hays, 697 West End Ave., New York, N.Y. 10025.

I. **"String Quartets"**
   Ellen Zwilich, *String Quartet*
   Gloria Coates, *String Quartet 3 and 4*
   Ann Silsbee, *Quest*

II. **"String Quartets and String Quintet"**
   Ruth Schonthal, *String Quartet*
   Marga Richter, *String Quartet 2*
   Joyce Orenstein, *String Quintet*
   Tui St. George Tucker, *String Quartet*

III. **"Text-sound and Electronics Using Voices"**
   Barberi Paull, *Time,* tape for ballet
   Beth Anderson, *Seven pieces of text-sound*
   Doris Hays, *Dream of Happiness Dream,* tape music
   Doris Hays, *Awakening,* tapeized poem
   Annea Lockwood, *Spirit Songs Unfolding,* tape music

IV. **"Vocal Music and Choral Music"**
   Beth Anderson, *Beauty Runs Faster*
   Judith Lang Zaimont, *Songs of Innocence*
   Judith Lang Zaimont, *Sunny Airs and Sober*
   Jeanne Singer, *A Cycle of Love*

V. **"Music for Piano, and Music for Piano and Tape"**
   Judith Lang Zaimont, *Nocturne: La Fin de Siècle*
   Doris Hays, *PAMP,* for piano, tape, and bird whistles
   Barberi Paull, *Antifon,* for piano and tape
   Joelle Wallach, *Wisps*
   Mary Baugh Watson, *Dish Rag*
   Doris Hays, *Four Wildflowers,* for Buchla Box and piano

VI. **"Music for Woodwinds"**
   Teresa Procaccini, *Clown Music,* four pieces for woodwind quintet
   Katherine Hoover, *Sinfonia,* bassoon quartet
   Nancy Van de Vate, *Woodwind Quartet*
   Katherine Hoover, *Woodwind Quintet*
   Vally Weigl, *Brief Encounters,* woodwind quartet

VII. "Vocal Chamber Music"

    Teresa Procaccini, *Canciones,* for soprano, clarinet, bassoon, and piano

    Vally Weigl, *Dear Earth,* for baritone, horn, violin, cello, and piano

    Judith Lang Zaimont, *Chansons Nobles et Sentimentales,* for tenor and piano

    Nancy Van de Vate, *Letter to a Friend's Loneliness,* for soprano and string quartet

VIII. "Music for Solo Instruments"

    Joelle Wallach, *Moment,* for oboe

    Ann Silsbee, *Three Chants,* for flute and alto flute

    Nancy Van de Vate, *Six Etudes for Solo Viola*

    Joelle Wallach, *Contemplation,* for bass clarinet

    Joyce Orenstein, *Piece 1 for Solo Clarinet*

IX. "Chamber Music With Voice"

    Kay Gardner, *Lunamuse,* for flute, guitar, drums, cello, bells, and vocal drone

    Elizabeth Pizer, *Five Haiku,* for soprano and chamber ensemble

    Winifred Hyson, *Winter Triptych,* for soprano, flute, violin, and piano

    Beth and Marjorie Anderson, *Torero Piece,* for speaker and chanter

    Jeanne Singer, *Art Songs—Selection,* for soprano, baritone, and piano

X. "Electronic Music, and Electronic Music With Voices and Orchestra"

    Doris Hays, *Southern Voices,* for speech and synthesizer

    Elizabeth Pizer, *Sunken Flutes,* electronic tape

    Beth Anderson, *Joan,* oratorio with orchestra and live electronics

XI. "Orchestral Music and Chamber Music"

    Teresa Procaccini, *Three Dances for Two Trumpets and String Orchestra*

    Nancy Van de Vate, *Two Sound Pieces for Brass and Percussion*

    Nancy Van de Vate, *Adagio for Orchestra*

    Marga Richter, *Landscapes of the Mind,* for piano, violin, and cello

    Kay Gardner, *Prayer to Aphrodite,* for alto flute, violins, clarinet, and cello

RECORD COMPANY ADDRESS LIST

Columbia/Odyssey	CBS Records 51 West 52nd Street New York, New York
Capra Records	317 Nobel Drive Santa Cruz, California 95060
Capriccio Records	6192 Oxon Hill Road Washington, DC 20021
Columbine Records Corp.	6430 Sunset Boulevard Suite 1221 Hollywood, California 90028
Composers Recording, Inc. (CRI)	170 West 74th Street New York, New York 10023
Coronet Records	4971 North High Street Columbus, Ohio 43214
Crystal Records	Post Office Box 65661 Los Angeles, California 90065
Delos	855 Via de la Paz Pacific Palisades, California 90272
Desto Records	c/o CMS 12 Warren Street New York, New York 10007
Even Keel Records	Box 33 Stonington, Maine 04681
Finnadar/Atlantic Records	75 Rockefeller Plaza New York, New York 10019
Golden Crest	220 Broadway Huntington Station, New York 11746
Grenadilla Enterprises, Inc.	345 Park Avenue South Seventh Floor New York, New York 10010
Ho'okani Enterprises	4723 Moa Street Honolulu, Hawaii 96816
Leonarda Productions, Inc.	Post Office Box 124 Radio City Station New York, New York 10101
MGM	c/o Marga Richter 3 Bayview Lane Huntington, New York 11743
Mixtur-Schallplatten GMBH	c/o Samter Friedbergstrasse 14 D-1000 Berlin 19
Musical Heritage Society	14 Park Road Tinton Falls, New Jersey 07724
Opus One Records	Post Office Box 604 Greenville, Maine 04441
Orion Master Recordings	5840 Busch Drive Malibu, California 90265

Paulist Press	1865 Broadway New York, New York 10023
Say Day-Bew	c/o Craig Nutt 2816 7th Street Tuscaloosa, Alabama 35401
1750 Arch Records	1750 Arch Street Berkeley, California 94709
Silver Burdett Co.	Music Series 250 James Street Morristown, New Jersey 07960
Southern Library of Recorded Sound	1740 Broadway New York, New York
Trans-Museq	6 Glen Iris Park Birmingham, Alabama 35205
WWE/Urana Records	20 West 22nd Street Room 612 New York, New York 10010

INDEX

Allen, Judith Shatin: biography, 2-3; address, 332. compositions: solo vocal, 161; chamber vocal, 177, 186; solo instrumental, 194, 208, 216, 219, 224; chamber instrumental, 233, 237, 240-41, 251; orchestral, 265, 272; choral, 294

Anderson, Beth: biography, 4-5; address, 332. compositions: solo vocal, 160, 161, 177; chamber vocal, 177, 186, 190, 193; solo instrumental, 197, 211, 226; chamber instrumental, 231, 237, 241, 251, 257; electronic, 259; choral, 280, 283, 289; opera/multi-media/stage works, 314-15; music for young people, 326; discography, 341, 348, 349

Anderson, Jay: biography, 6-7; address, 332. compositions: solo vocal, 161-62; choral, 280, 284

Barnett, Carol: biography, 8-9; address, 332. compositions: solo instrumental, 211, 219, 223, 226; chamber instrumental, 241; orchestral, 262, 266; band, 278; choral, 284, 303

Barthelson, Joyce: biography, 10-11; address, 332. compositions: orchestral, 266; choral, 281, 284, 310; opera/multi-media/stage works, 315-16

Beath, Betty: biography, 12-13; address, 332. compositions: solo vocal, 160, 162; chamber vocal, 178; orchestral, 273; opera/multi-media/stage works, 316; music for young people, 323-24

Beeson, Elizabeth R.: biography, 14-15; address, 332. compositions: solo vocal, 163; chamber vocal, 178; solo instrumental, 197, 219; choral, 294; music for young people, 326; discography, 341

Bolz, Harriett: biography, 16-17; address, 332. compositions: solo vocal, 163; chamber vocal, 178; solo instrumental, 195, 197, 211, 219, 224; chamber instrumental, 228, 233, 241, 251, 257; choral, 281, 290, 295, 303, 310

Boone, Clara Lyle [pseud. Lyle de Bohun]: biography, 18-19; address, 332. compositions: solo vocal, 163; chamber vocal, 178; solo instrumental, 197; chamber instrumental, 241; orchestral, 266; choral, 284

Brenner, Rosamond: biography, 20-21; address, 333. compositions: solo vocal, 163-64; orchestral, 273; choral, 304, 310

Britain, Radie: biography, 22-23; address, 333. compositions: solo vocal, 164; chamber vocal, 178, 186; solo instrumental, 195, 198-99, 212, 216-17, 219, 225; chamber instrumental, 228, 233, 237, 241-42; orchestral, 262, 265, 266-67, 273; band, 278; choral, 281, 284, 290-91, 295-96, 304, 310; opera/multi-media/stage works, 316; music for young people, 324, 326-27, 330

Brush, Ruth J.: biography, 24-25; address, 333. compositions: solo vocal, 165-66; solo instrumental, 195, 199, 212, 219; chamber instrumental, 228, 242; orchestral, 265, 267; choral, 281, 285, 291; opera/multi-media/stage works, 316; music for young people, 324, 327

Cecconi-Bates, Augusta: biography, 26-27; address, 333. compositions: solo vocal, 166; chamber vocal, 178, 190; solo instrumental, 199, 212, 219; chamber instrumental, 237, 242; band, 278; choral, 296, 310; music for young people, 327, 329

Chance, Nancy Laird: biography, 28-29; address, 333. compositions: chamber vocal, 178, 186, 193; chamber instrumental, 242, 251, 256; orchestral, 268; choral, 285; discography, 341

Clark, Mary Margaret: biography, 30-31; address, 333. compositions: opera/multi-media/stage works, 317; discography, 341

Cohen, Marcia: biography, 32-33; address, 333. compositions: solo vocal, 166, 177; chamber vocal, 186, 193; solo instrumental, 219, 223, 226-27; chamber instrumental, 242, 258; electronic, 259; orchestral, 262; opera/multi-media/stage works, 317

Danforth, Frances: biography, 34-35; address, 333. compositions: solo instrumental, 199, 227; chamber instrumental, 233, 237, 242-43

Dembo, Royce: biography, 36-37; address, 333. compositions: solo vocal, 166; chamber vocal, 179; solo instrumental, 199, 209, 212; chamber instrumental, 228, 231, 233, 243, 251; choral, 285, 291, 297; opera/multi-media/stage works, 317; music for young people, 327

Diemer, Emma Lou: biography, 38-39; address, 333. compositions: solo vocal, 167; chamber vocal, 179, 186, 190; solo instrumental, 195, 200, 212, 220, 223; chamber instrumental, 229, 232, 233, 243, 251, 257, 258; electronic, 259-60; orchestral, 268; choral, 281, 285, 291, 297-98, 304-5, 310; music for young people, 324, 327, 330; discography, 341-42

Famera, Karen McNerney: biography, 148; address, 148

Forman, Joanne: biography, 40-41; address, 334. compositions: solo vocal, 167; chamber vocal, 179, 187; chamber instrumental, 251; choral, 282, 298; opera/multi-media/stage works, 317; discography, 342

Frasier, Jane: biography, 42-43; address, 334. compositions: solo instrumental, 200, 209; chamber instrumental, 233, 243; choral, 292, 298, 305, 310; music for young people, 331

About the Compilers and Editors

JUDITH LANG ZAIMONT is an award-winning composer and a member of the faculty of the Peabody Conservatory of Music in Baltimore, Maryland. She has received both Woodrow Wilson and Debussy fellowships in composition. Many of her works are recorded and published, and have been performed in England, France, Germany, and Australia, as well as in the United States.

KAREN FAMERA is a music librarian, currently on the staff of the New York Public Library. She is the author of "Mutes, Flutters and Trills: A Guide to Composing for the Horn," among other works.